# Applied and Theoretical Econometrics and Financial Crises

*Edited by Brian William Sloboda and Chee-Heong Quah*

Published in London, United Kingdom

Applied and Theoretical Econometrics and Financial Crises
http://dx.doi.org/10.5772/intechopen.1003364
Edited by Brian William Sloboda and Chee-Heong Quah

Contributors
Brian William Sloboda, Chee-Heong Quah, Damilola S. Adebayo, Hector O. Zapata, Helga Kristjánsdóttir, Ignacio Urrutia Hoyos, Jacques Bughin, Jaime Marquez, Jón Jónsson, Kelu Ren, Kjartan Sigurðsson, Linda Pettersson, Pankaj Das, Raquel Ayestarán Crespo, Sabiou M. Inoua, Samir Barman, Taylan Mavruk, Vernon L. Smith, Xinyuan Zhang, Yahuza Abdul Rahman



First published in London, United Kingdom, 2025 by IntechOpen
IntechOpen is the global imprint of INTECHOPEN LIMITED, registered in England and Wales, registration number: 11086078, 167-169 Great Portland Street, London, W1W 5PF, United Kingdom

For EU product safety concerns: IN TECH d.o.o., Prolaz Marije Krucifikse Kozulić 3, 51000 Rijeka, Croatia, info@intechopen.com or visit our website at intechopen.com.

British Library Cataloguing-in-Publication Data
A catalogue record for this book is available from the British Library

Applied and Theoretical Econometrics and Financial Crises
Edited by Brian William Sloboda and Chee-Heong Quah
p. cm.

This title is part of the Business, Management and Economics Book Series, Volume 35
Topic: Economics
Series Editor: Taufiq Choudhry
Topic Editor: Jaime Ortiz

Print ISBN 978-1-83634-398-1
Online ISBN 978-1-83634-397-4
eBook (PDF) ISBN 978-1-83634-399-8
ISSN 2753-894X

IntechOpen Book Series

# Business, Management and Economics

Volume 35

## Aims and Scope of the Series

This series will provide a comprehensive overview of recent research trends in business and management, economics, and marketing. Topics will include asset liability management, financial consequences of the financial crisis and covid-19, financial accounting, mergers and acquisitions, management accounting, SMEs, financial markets, corporate finance and governance, managerial technology and innovation, resource management and sustainable development, social entrepreneurship, corporate responsibility, ethics and accountability, microeconomics, labour economics, macroeconomics, public economics, financial economics, econometrics, direct marketing, creative marketing, internet marketing, market planning and forecasting, brand management, market segmentation and targeting and other topics under business and management. This book series will focus on various aspects of business and management whose in-depth understanding is critical for business and company management to function effectively during this uncertain time of financial crisis, Covid-19 pandemic, and military activity in Europe.

# Meet the Series Editor

Prof. Choudhry holds a BSc degree in Economics from the University of Iowa, as well as a Masters and Ph.D. in Applied Economics from Clemson University, USA. In January 2006, he became a Professor of Finance at the University of Southampton Business School. He was previously a Professor of Finance at the University of Bradford Management School. He has over 80 articles published in international finance and economics journals. His research interests and specialties include financial econometrics, financial economics, international economics and finance, housing markets, financial markets, among others.

# Meet the Volume Editors

Brian W. Sloboda is an economist at the U.S. Department of Labor and a faculty member at the University of Maryland, Global Campus, where he teaches economics and finance. He also teaches at Johns Hopkins University in Washington, D.C. His research focuses on regional economics, economic growth, and labor economics, with avocational research interests in finance and presidential election forecasting models. He serves as a committee member of the Federal Forecasters Consortium (FFC), a board member of the Pennsylvania Economics Association, and a member of the editorial board of the *Pennsylvania Economic Review*. Dr. Sloboda is the former president of the Society of Government Economists (SGE) and is now its executive director. He is currently an assistant editor for the *Journal of Economics* and a senior social science editor for the *European Scientific Journal*. Additionally, he serves as a book review editor for the *Review of Regional Studies.*

Chee-Heong Quah, Ph.D., is an academic at the Faculty of Business and Economics, University of Malaya. His research interests encompass international economics, monetary integration, financial crisis, optimum currency areas, and Austrian economics. His works have been published in scientific journals such as *Asia Pacific Business Review, International Finance, Journal of Business, Economics, and Management, Journal of the Asia Pacific Economy, Actual Economic Problems, African Journal of Business and Management, South Asian Journal of Management,* and *International Journal of Asia Pacific Studies.*

# Contents

**Preface** **XIII**

**Chapter 1** **1**
Introductory Chapter: Boom-Bust Cycles, the Chronic Disease that Plagues World Economy
*by Chee-Heong Quah and Brian William Sloboda*

**Chapter 2** **7**
The Credit Boom as a Predictor of Financial Crisis
*by Jón Jónsson, Kjartan Sigurðsson and Helga Kristjánsdóttir*

**Chapter 3** **21**
Predicting Financial Crises: The Role of Shocks to Real Interest Rates and Credit on Aggregate Economic Activity, Lessons from the Austrian Business Cycle Theory
*by Yahuza Abdul Rahman*

**Chapter 4** **59**
Perspective Chapter: An Overview of Time Series Decomposition and Its Applications
*by Pankaj Das and Samir Barman*

**Chapter 5** **75**
A Decade of Machine Learning Applied to Management and Economics: Learning through a Case Study of Corporate Resilience
*by Jacques Bughin*

**Chapter 6** **107**
Economic Interdependence and Its Role in the Propagation of Financial Crises: A Theoretical Synthesis
*by Raquel Ayestarán Crespo and Ignacio Urrutia Hoyos*

**Chapter 7** **119**
Modeling the Relation between the Price of Oil and the Value of the U.S. Dollar: The Frequency of Observations Matters
*by Jaime Marquez and Kelu Ren*

**Chapter 8** 139
Flexible Error Specification in CAPM
*by Hector O. Zapata and Damilola S. Adebayo*

**Chapter 9** 155
Does Local Media Convey a Different Impression in Stock Markets?
*by Linda Pettersson and Taylan Mavruk*

**Chapter 10** 171
Strategic Flexibility, Firm Performance, and Firm Value
*by Xinyuan Zhang and Chee-Heong Quah*

**Chapter 11** 189
Adam Smith's Modeling of Agents: Roots versus Consequences of Action
*by Vernon L. Smith and Sabiou M. Inoua*

# Preface

The financial landscape has undergone a dramatic transformation over the past few decades, as evidenced by periods of intense volatility, systemic failures, and subsequent recoveries. From the collapse of major financial institutions to sovereign debt crises and unprecedented central bank interventions, these events have tested the resilience of economic models and the effectiveness of public policy approaches.

This book emerges from the recognition that financial crises are not merely the outcomes of isolated shocks, but rather complex phenomena driven by deep structural forces, behavioral responses, and institutional frameworks. Econometrics provides the foundation, enabling researchers and practitioners to distinguish between signal and noise and evaluate the effectiveness of policy interventions.

*Applied and Theoretical Econometrics and Financial Crises* bridges the gap between abstract modeling and real-world application. It comprehensively explores econometric tools and techniques, including machine learning methods and regime-switching models. These techniques, paired with case studies and empirical investigations of past crises, could be used to examine events such as the 2008 global financial meltdown, the Eurozone debt crisis, and the economic disruptions caused by the COVID-19 pandemic.

This book is intended for graduate economics and finance students, academic researchers, and policy analysts in nonprofit and government organizations. The latter would benefit from this book as they seek to deepen their understanding of how these methods can be applied and develop ideas for future research.

The editors hope that this book contributes to a more robust understanding of financial crises and supports the development of more resilient economic systems, utilizing sound methods.

**Brian William Sloboda**
University of Maryland,
Global Campus, Baltimore, Maryland, USA

**Chee-Heong Quah**
Faculty of Business and Economics,
University of Malaya,
Kuala Lumpur, Malaysia

Chapter 1

# Introductory Chapter: Boom-Bust Cycles, the Chronic Disease that Plagues World Economy

*Chee-Heong Quah and Brian William Sloboda*

## 1. Introduction

There is a consensus in the mainstream that a strong role for the government is necessary to tame the business cycle, because the free market, being unrestrained, will persistently veer into either unemployment or inflation [1]. In stark contrast, the Austrian School of Economics believes that meddling of the government in the credit market is ironically the true cause to the ups and downs in the market economy [2, 3].

According to the Austrian theory of business cycle (see, e.g., [4]), an economic boom begins with excessive investments in physical capital that need long-term financing. Capital, in this sense, refers to real capital such as machinery, technology, factories, premises, land, and plants. Facilitated by fractional reserve banking that the central bank backs, this long-term financing is made possible by credit expansion by commercial banks and the resulting low interest rates. Nonetheless, until a certain point in the expansion, when the backing of bank reserves over bank liabilities depletes, interest rates must be raised, and credit must be tightened or contracted.

The unnaturally low interest rate created by the banking system sends wrong signals to businesses, indicating that the factor, the intermediate, the upstream, and the downstream markets are ready to accommodate their expansions with adequate and affordable supplies of needed resources to complete their investment projects [5]. In reality, however, the supplies of land, capital, labor, and other inputs of production have not increased or been liberated by real savings.

Despite that, more businesses would start competing for the same amount of physical capital, labor, and other inputs. Sooner or later, the market of these inputs will inevitably tighten until it becomes unbearably costly to employ these input goods and labor. As a result, real investments that earlier appeared lucrative will now turn out to be unprofitable or loss-making. Whether by tightening bank credit or not, eventually, uncompleted investment projects must be called off.

Besides the primary- and intermediate-good sectors, the price of labor and other resources for the consumer-goods sector will also increase [6]. This is because consumers have not traded off present consumption for future consumption. There is no increase in real savings nor increase or liberation in the resources for the production of consumption goods. Not only prices of inputs, when newly created bank money gets into the hands of consumers, but also prices of consumer goods will rise as consumption increases without corresponding to offsetting savings.

In other words, the public preference for present consumption has not changed.

Hence, the demand for factors in this consumption-good sector will not change either. Despite the absence of an increased preference for future consumption, newly created credits and low interest rates by fractional-reserve banks will induce firms at different stages of production to embark on investments intended to increase the production of consumption goods in the future.

Ironically, these capital investments would not have been promising and hence undertaken, had it not been for the created credit. Recall that consumers have not refrained from present consumption, or decided to save more for the future, and hence have not saved as much for the future in the first place.

Since there has been no increased demand for future consumption, firms in phases of production further from present consumption will soon learn of the lack of prospects or demand for their malinvestments. And, at the same time, these firms have to confront the rising costs of inputs and resources as competition in those markets rises.

Ultimately, the investment projects must be terminated or paralyzed due to a lack of demand and rising investment costs. Crisis unveils when economic agents find out that the actual value of the loan assets held by the banks since the boom period is in fact very much smaller. Since the value of liabilities and other payables of the banks has virtually not reduced, the fractional-reserve banks are essentially bankrupt when the market realizes the diminished value of the loan assets of the banks.

## 2. Allocative effects of money creation

Monetary expansion directly affects business cycles by altering income distribution within the population and the corresponding pattern of spending [7]. When credit expansion is generated by central banks and commercial banks, those who receive the newly created money first will obtain greater purchasing power than those who receive the money later. These groups of people can include cronies of government officials who enjoy special privileges from banks that depend on the officials, as well as any individual or businessperson with legitimate reasons and collateral to borrow money from the banks. Since those who get the money first will spend on items according to their preferences, the pattern of prices in the economy will change. The spending of the new money on certain groups of products will bid up their prices.

If newly created money is spent on materials and equipment for the construction of real estate, those prices will be bid up, and resources and labor will be shifted to the activities related to construction. In other words, resources, including manpower in the economy, are reallocated to the real estate sector than otherwise would have been without the monetary expansion by the banking system.

Misallocation of resources and labor created by government intervention can be temporary or permanent, depending on whether the intervention is temporary or permanent. Permanent government subsidies in certain sectors, such as agriculture, fishing, healthcare, and energy, persistently incentivize the movement of resources into those sectors. Similarly, protectionist barriers against foreign competition, such as antidumping laws and tariffs in the steel and automobile industries, retain the capital and labor in those sectors that otherwise would have been utilized more efficiently and effectively in other activities. On the other hand, since monetary stimulus is always temporary, the reallocation of resources into stimulated sectors and the subsequent price increases in these sectors by the injection of money are temporary. As prices of other sectors are eventually bid up, the movement of resources into the initially stimulated sectors will slow down, stop, or even reverse.

This assertion of Austrian business cycle theory, however, receives many objections. According to critics such as the New Classicists, since market players anticipate the subsequent stoppage or reversal in the movement of resources, the initial reallocation of resources into the stimulated sectors would not take place. In other words, the self-reversing process of movement of resources becomes a self-preventing process. Hence, a business cycle can be prevented because the public possesses rational expectations.

This rebuttal against the Austrian business cycle theory that the public are rational and hence will not start the business cycle by investing or bidding up prices in certain groups of goods or assets is weak. Firstly, even if those who receive the newly created money first know exactly that prices will reverse later, there is every incentive for them to invest or speculate in those markets because the money that they receive from the banks in the first rounds of credit expansion has much larger spending power than received later by the rest of the population. If the public is indeed rational and knows that prices will soon rise and, hence, the purchasing power of their money will soon fall, they will invest and hedge against the fall in purchasing power by buying assets whose prices will rise faster than the general price. These assets include gold, silver, real estate, and foreign currencies and assets. Even if the early receivers of credit from banks do not know that they are early receivers of any particular monetary stimulus by the central bank, given the general tendency of rising prices and declining purchasing power of fiat money, these individuals will anyway invest in assets or any productive activities that are expected to yield returns significantly greater than their costs of borrowing and the rate of price inflation.

Secondly, speculative individuals will move into the market and move out in time, reaping lucrative profits before the bubble expansion reverses even if they know that the price bubble of that particular asset will burst one day and that the price will plunge. While long-term-oriented individuals may not be tempted by the possible short-term gains, there are always short-term-oriented individuals who are incentivized by highly risky short-term gains. Individuals who obtain the credit from banks can play the market, for instance, in housing and securities, buying low and selling high before the price increase reverses.

In conclusion, it is now clear to readers that monetary stimulus by the central bank, accompanied by fractional reserve banking, is the real cause of the boom-bust economic cycle. Other so-called explanations for business cycle, such as those that depend on the overproduction and underconsumption theories, psychology shocks, and irregular supply and demand shocks, are descriptions, not explanations, of the business cycle phenomenon. These supposed explanations do not explain why business cycles occur repeatedly. They merely describe the symptoms of the disease. They fail to address the root cause of the problem.

## 3. The role of econometric analysis

From an applied econometrics perspective, understanding and analyzing boom-bust cycles is essential for policymakers and financial institutions. Techniques such as time series analysis, regression models, machine learning methods, and vector autoregression (VAR) are commonly applied to study boom-bust dynamics. These methods help economists identify the key variables influencing the cycles, for example, interest rates, credit availability, consumer spending, and firm investment. Econometric models can also estimate the effects of policy interventions, like monetary stimulus or fiscal expansion, to reduce the adverse effects of these cycles.

Using econometric analysis to study boom-bust cycles also extends to identifying early warning signs of impending recessions or bubbles. By analyzing historical data and establishing patterns, econometric models can provide forecasts that help policymakers anticipate the onset of downturns or asset price corrections. The latter is important because early intervention can potentially reduce the severity of a bust or even avoid a full-blown economic recession or crisis. However, a challenge often encountered is that the precise timing of these cycles is difficult to predict. Also, external shocks, for example, geopolitical events, global pandemics, or sudden shifts in investor sentiment, often come as a surprise and are not predictable. These latter events can disrupt even the well-calibrated econometric models. Moreover, the complexity of international financial systems, where interconnected markets can amplify shocks, makes disentangling the causes of boom-bust phenomena challenging. Despite these challenges, econometrics remains vital in understanding the boom-bust cycles by providing valuable insights that can help stabilize economies in these tumultuous times.

## Author details

Chee-Heong Quah[1]* and Brian William Sloboda[2]

1 University of Malaya, Malaysia

2 University of Maryland, Global Campus, United States of America

*Address all correspondence to: quahch@um.edu.my

## References

[1] Frey BS, Pommerehne WW, Schneider F, Gilbert G. Consensus and dissension among economists: An empirical inquiry. American Economic Review. 1984;**74**(5):986-994

[2] Quah CH. Austrian Economics In One Lesson. Manipal: Manipal Universal Press; 2021

[3] Quah CH. The Case against Intervention. Johannesburg: UJ Press; 2023

[4] Mises LV. On the Manipulation of Money and Credit. New York: Free Market Books; 1978

[5] Quah CH. Eccentric Views on Money and Banking. Kuala Lumpur: UM Press; 2016

[6] Huerta de Soto J. Economic recessions, banking reform and the future of capitalism. Economic Affairs. 2011;**31**(2):76-84

[7] Garrison RW. The Austrian theory of the business cycle in the light of modern macroeconomics. Review of Austrian Economics. 1989;**3**:3-29

Chapter 2

# The Credit Boom as a Predictor of Financial Crisis

*Jón Jónsson, Kjartan Sigurðsson and Helga Kristjánsdóttir*

## Abstract

A developed nation's rate of economic growth relies on sustaining a modern and stable financial market to facilitate consistent capital investment over the long run. Starting from the last half of the twentieth century, sustained growth in total credit availability across developed nations has been linked to increased financial market volatility and subsequent interruptions in economic growth. This study examines empirical research aimed at determining the viability of using credit availability metrics to predict financial market volatility and economic recessions. Empirical research used a macro-prudential perspective to develop a model that examines whether metrics reflecting credit booms, like the credit gap, can be reliably used to predict increased future financial market variability and reductions in economic growth. The empirical research analysis employs a receiver operating characteristic methodology that reveals how metrics of credit leveraging have become useful predictive tools as total credit has increased over time.

**Keywords:** economic growth, credit boom, financial market bubble, fiscal and monetary policy, financial crisis

## 1. Introduction

The quantity of a nation's credit, as measured in the form of commercial bank loans, plays a paramount role in any central bank's economic stimulus strategy. A nation's central bank achieves optimal monetary policy by maintaining investor confidence, which requires promoting clear strategic direction in the long run, which is necessary for promoting effective policy design. Maintaining such goals can help mitigate excessive procyclical behavior and promote consistent economic growth over the long run [1]. In contrast, poorly designed monetary policy can produce financial market bubbles that exacerbate macroeconomic conditions of high leverage, deteriorating lending standards, and weak macroeconomic policies [2]. Such undesirable macro-financial conditions include maintaining artificially low interest rates relative to competitive financial market signals or lax rules on the securitization of loans, allowing for the bundling of high-risk loans with low-risk loans that effectively mask a true assessment of relative risk. This often results in a credit boom that creates a financial market bubble, endangering the sustainability of long-run growth or even promoting a recession [3].

Furthermore, the complex relationship between fiscal and monetary policy complicates a central bank's attempt at designing an optimal policy. Typically, this occurs when credit expansion outpaces economic growth, leading to unsustainable levels of debt [4].

Further, aggressive government fiscal policy that pursues too much deficit spending relative to the state of the economy will increase government borrowing costs, and place upward pressure on financial market interest rates. This in turn creates pressure on the central bank to lower market interest rates to maintain private sector lending and capital investment to sustain economic growth [5]. Even government tax breaks and direct mortgage subsidies for new homeowners can achieve the same result, creating a financial market bubble that endangers long-run economic growth [6].

This raises the following questions: Can the emergence of credit booms during the last half of the twentieth century produce sufficient evidence of future financial market volatility and resulting economic downturns? Could a leading indicator be developed from this information, perhaps leading to a metric that can reveal a link between the size of the credit markets and future financial market instability, along with the concomitant declines in a nation's economic performance? This paper explores this relationship, starting with insights gained from the empirical analysis that has been performed by Schularick and Taylor [4]. The goal is to apply theoretical focus supported by empirical support to attain applicable knowledge that can answer these intriguing questions.

## 2. Literature review

### 2.1 Competing credit boom paradigms in the finance literature

Various theoretical paradigms in the finance literature have been developed to explain the relationship between financial market performance, credit booms, and the economic growth of a nation's economy. Some paradigms, such as Austrian Business Cycle (ABC) Theory or Institutional theory models, identify the imposition of external factors that disrupt the efficient operations of finance markets and exacerbate business cycles. Other paradigms, such as Minsky's Instability theory and Behavioral Finance theory, posit that financial business cycles result from extreme, or even irrational, investor behavior in the face of actual or perceived market shocks.

ABC theory posits that credit booms are exogenous market-distorting interventions caused by the interest rate manipulations of a nation's central banks [7]. Indeed Hayek [8] and von Mises [9] first developed the broader ABC theory, which in part explained how such market distortions lead to malinvestment decisions and distorted capital allocations. When studying the 2008 financial crisis, Salerno [10] found much empirical support for the ABC perspective in explaining the onset of this global financial crisis.

Further, Institutional theory focuses on the quality of legal institutions that govern financial markets to explain financial booms and busts. La Porta et al. [11] find empirical evidence that higher-quality legal systems promote the development of sound financial markets and enhance investment efficiency. Acemoglu et al. [12] find evidence that specific political and economic institutions shape the performance of a nation's financial markets and facilitate higher rates of economic growth. Interestingly, Boettke and Coyne [13] incorporate ABC theory and institutional finance theory to show that each paradigm contains reinforcing influences for the other's perspective. They find that integrating the two paradigms provides a more robust explanation of global financial crises.

Minsky [14] argues that financial markets are inherently unstable due to the irrationally cyclical behavior of investors. He posits that such investors historically transition from rational hedge financing to more speculative financial behaviors, and finally succumb to Ponzi scheme financial commitments that create unsustainable leverage positions. Kindleberger [15] finds much empirical evidence to support this paradigm. Behavioral Finance theory suggests that psychological biases and false heuristics cause investors to persistently fail to make efficient decisions in the financial markets. Barberis and Thaler [16] and Shiller [17] both illustrate how overconfidence, excessive loss aversion, and herding behavior among investors lead investors to make persistent, irrational financial decisions.

Regardless of which paradigm appears to best explain the observed financial booms and busts of a nation's economy, a growing number of empirical studies have appeared in the literature that reveal how periods of loosened credit tend to foretell unsustainable credit booms that eventually result in economic busts [18]. For example, Laeven and Valencia [19] finds that rapid credit growth increases the likelihood of an economy experiencing a banking crisis and subsequent declines in economic growth. Taylor [20] examines the impact of credit booms and the resulting increase in leveraging on the financial stability and economic growth of a nation. Rajan and Zingales [21] show that, while economies with better-developed financial systems enjoy higher rates of higher growth, they are relatively more vulnerable to financial crises caused by credit booms. These and other studies have focused on using empirical information gained from examining the relationship that is revealed between the financial markets and the nation's economy. However, they each find separate, unique applications of this information to produce indicators with reliable predictive capacity to foresee changes in financial markets and rates of economic growth. This paper seeks to determine if these unique applications can potentially be collated to support the development of an innovative metric that yields meaningful insights into creating more effective macroprudential policy characteristics.

Additionally, Borio [22] has shown that more extensive periods of intense financial cycles have often resulted in the onset of subsequent business cycles that had a significant impact on financial market efficiency and national economic growth. Specifically, he focused on the existence of a credit gap, defined as an increase in the credit-to-GDP ratio from its long-term trend. This perspective viewed a large credit gap as a sign of potential financial turmoil that increases the risk of experiencing a banking system crisis, resulting in increased volatility in the growth path of a nation's economy [23].

This perspective motivates policymakers to carefully monitor the magnitude of the credit gap over time, acting as an early warning indicator of an upcoming economic recession. Indeed, empirical studies by Schularick and Taylor [4] and Borio [22] revealed that most banking crises happen near the financial cycle's peak after a rapid expansion of credit. Both studies indicate that credit variables alone could provide useful information about the plausibility of a future financial crisis leading to instability in long-run economic growth.

Further, studies such as Kaminsky and Reinhart [23] document the interconnected influence of financial institutions, illustrating how such relationships must be addressed to better understand the causal factors and mitigation needs for avoiding future financial crises. Gourinchas and Obstfeld [24] examine key historical events, including the Great Depression, the adoption of the Bretton Woods system, and the rise of financial globalization. They illustrate how such interconnected economic and political forces have impacted global financial stability. The authors highlight the importance of international financial cooperation and the role of institutions like the International Monetary Fund (IMF) in managing global economic stability. They discuss how the global economy's increasing interconnectedness has heightened the risks of financial contagion, making it imperative for countries to adopt coordinated policy responses. This perspective realizes the potential financial epidemic that a single financial institution can exert over the entire financial market.

Consequently, studies such as these illuminate the capacity for evidence from credit booms in a nation's economy to provide relevant information for assessing the impact of financial risks on finance market efficiency and national economic growth. This larger effort has led to two separate paradigms of analysis. On the one hand, the micro-prudential approaches assume that the primary drivers of financial market instability are those market risks that are generated by individual creditors in the various financial markets. On the other hand, the macro-risk precautionary approach considers financial risks as endogenous to the characteristics of the market structure, rather than to the individual financial institutions. Understanding the potential for each perspective to provide useful insights is considered in the following analysis.

On the one hand, effective micro-prudential policy design can facilitate stability in the financial markets by creating optimal capital and liquidity requirements that are placed on individual firms in the market. Empirical analysis to support this perspective requires collecting data on market and operational risks of the individual financial institutions, rather than over the entire financial markets. For example, Bernanke et al. [25] attempts to integrate the micro-prudential perspective into inform macroeconomic models to reflect how the financial health of individual financial institutions can impact the economic cycles of a nation's economy. The authors use a nation's balance sheet information to show how credit booms can lead to financial instability and economic downturns when institutions face financial distress. Likewise, analysis by Adrian and Shin [26] reveals that banks often increase both their leverage and their risk-taking during stable economic times, negatively affecting their ability to withstand even minor shocks. They find that the interconnectedness of financial institutions and the spread of financial risks require greater banking oversights and controls.

On the other hand, the macro-risk precautionary approach can be employed to inform effective macroprudential policy. This perspective considers financial risks as endogenous to the characteristics of the market structure, rather than to the individual financial institutions. Systemic risks to the financial markets can be identified that are caused by the interconnectedness of the many individual financial firms. This approach relies on market-wide risk indicators, such as the credit gap, to indicate potential financial market bubbles and subsequent financial market volatility [2]. Generalized policy changes, such as changing the capital requirements or loan-to-value rations of all financial institutions, can all be used to influence the behavior of all firms across the entire market [27]. The following empirical analysis will focus on a study that employs a macro-prudential model developed by Schularick and Taylor [4] to examine whether measures of credit trends in the financial markets can be used to predict a nation's future economic performance.

Regardless of the competing perspectives of how financial risk is experienced by firms, and how market risks can be effectively controlled by regulators, the key elements of an artificially created credit boom are the same. Financial markets experience sharply increasing leverage ratios, growing domestic credit, and rising real exchange rates. The concern is that a sharp expansion of credit is an unsustainable boom in a nation's economic activity, creating an overly optimistic expectation about the true value of financial assets and their prices. This can lead to ever higher levels of unjustified financial leverage, exacerbating financial market risk. This scenario often results in a credit market bubble, endangering a sustained rate of national economic growth in the long run.

### 2.2 A macro-prudential perspective on credit gap analysis

There are many models combining the effects of a credit gap with those of an asset price gap to analyze the impact of financial market volatility on national economic growth.

These studies effectively increased the power of financial models to predict short-run financial market instability and long-run rates of economic growth. Such models often examine the years of financial market and economic growth rates spanning a financial crisis or a period when credit payments had effectively peaked. Many of these empirical analyses have been conducted by examining various levels of inflation behaviors across various nations. Such studies indicate that the formation of financial crises can occur even during periods of prevailing low inflation. This implies that a timely response from the monetary policymaker is always important, particularly in the face of large financial disturbances and imbalances (as opposed to natural periodic financial disturbances).

For example, Schularick and Taylor [4] uses a macro-prudential model to examine the annual data from 14 developed countries from Europe and North America spanning the period 1970–2008. They find evidence that leverage in the financial sector increased substantially during this period, and they attribute this result to the decoupling of money and credit aggregates within their respective national monetary policies. Using indicators of both credit growth while controlling for the credit-to-production ratio, their research demonstrates that credit growth can be a powerful predictor of financial crises, with these measures often peaking prior to the onset of financial instability.

**Figure 1** below reveals the growth rate and leverage ratio of money and credit using the [4] database. The graph reveals how the money and credit curves have followed each other rather closely during the pre-WWII period. The only exception corresponded to the Great Depression, in which both the monetary system and credit collapsed in each country. Afterward, credit growth surpassed its previous levels, resulting in a rapid rate of growth that ultimately led to the great credit boom of 2009. The graphic shows the exponentially increasing leverage of postwar credit and the subsequent onset of financial instability that ensued. Clearly, the average ratio of bank loans to GDP doubled after 1970, while the bank asset ratio to GDP increased fourfold. This empirical evidence implies that bank asset leverage levels, along with increasing credit growth, could be used as harbingers of coming financial sector instability.

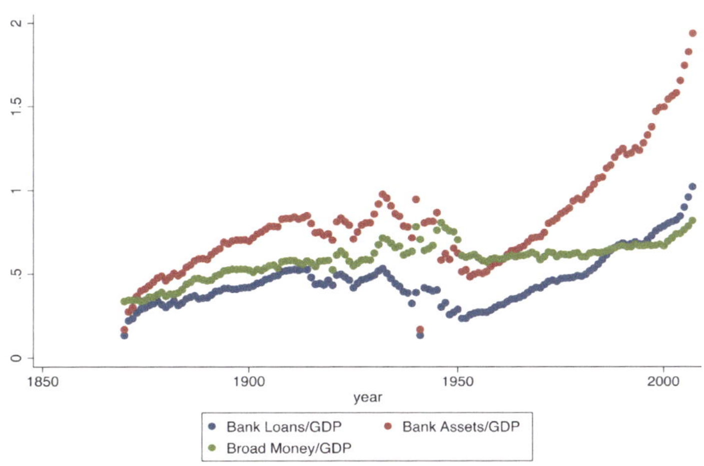


**Figure 1.**
*Money versus credit comparison in the long run. Source: [4].*

Schularick and Taylor [4] also focused on the failure of aggregate money and credit accumulated from the start of the financial crisis until 5 years after it. Their analysis revealed examples of distinct responses to a financial crisis during the two major eras considered in the study. The levels of macroeconomic factors (namely bank loans, bank assets, and broad money) before and after WWII are illustrated in **Figure 2**.

The analysis focuses on those years following various financial crises. Normal stands for the 2-year average values during normal periods that occurred before each financial crisis. Zero is the year of the actual financial crisis, followed by the subsequent 1, 2, 3, 4, and 5 years.

The left side of the graph depicts the prewar period. The data reveal that a financial crisis often leads to a "deleveraging" of the economy. Financial institutions generally reduced their levels of debt by paying off liabilities, creating a well-known V-shaped recovery, as depicted on the graph. The right side of the graph depicts the postwar era and reveals that there is no distinguishable pattern in the decline of the growth rates in both monetary and credit aggregates. This difference in response across the time periods may be attributable to the differences in the central banks' responses to monetary policy. The postwar period reflects the more common monetary policy response of monetary policy accommodation that prevented a broad money collapse in the economy. Such changes in policy focus create a higher level of bank lending activity and generate a more rapid growth of available credit.

Schularick and Taylor [4] model uses an ordinary least squares (OLS) methodology with a logit specification structure. It regresses financial ratio variables on primary macroeconomic economic variables to better understand their relationships. This allows the model to quantify the relative power of the credit ratio in predicting economic downturns, particularly in forecasting a severe economic crisis. These binary variables have been used for constructing the model-dependent variable called "financial crisis predictor." The main OLS results, coupled with another model wherein the macroeconomic variables were modified, confirm each variable's

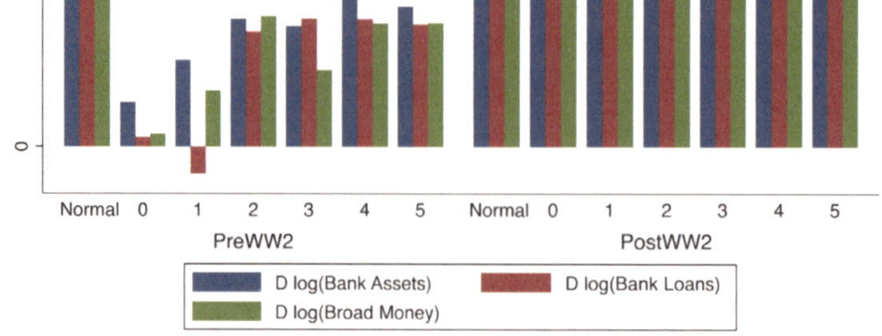


**Figure 2.**
*Aggregate reaction to the financial crisis. Source: [4].*

statistical significance. These results create evidence in support of using the credit gap, which is measured as the number of bank loans made during the postwar financial crisis, as a reliable predictor of change in a nation's economic growth.

To that end, **Figure 3** below reveals how the authors plot a curve that examines the prediction probability of their credit and monetary metrics with respect to the financial crises occurring in the baseline model. The behavioral patterns of these metrics, which are used for predicting the behavior of the financial sector, are separated into the periods before and after the war. Their model shows that the credit metric performed better than the monetary metric during the postwar period. The results of their research have helped to create a credit gap metric for predicting a future financial crisis using the observed increases in banking system credit levels.

To achieve these empirical results, Schularick and Taylor [4] use the receiver operating characteristic (ROC) methodology, which is appropriate for studying the behavior of a binary dependent variable. The results are plotted as the valid predictor

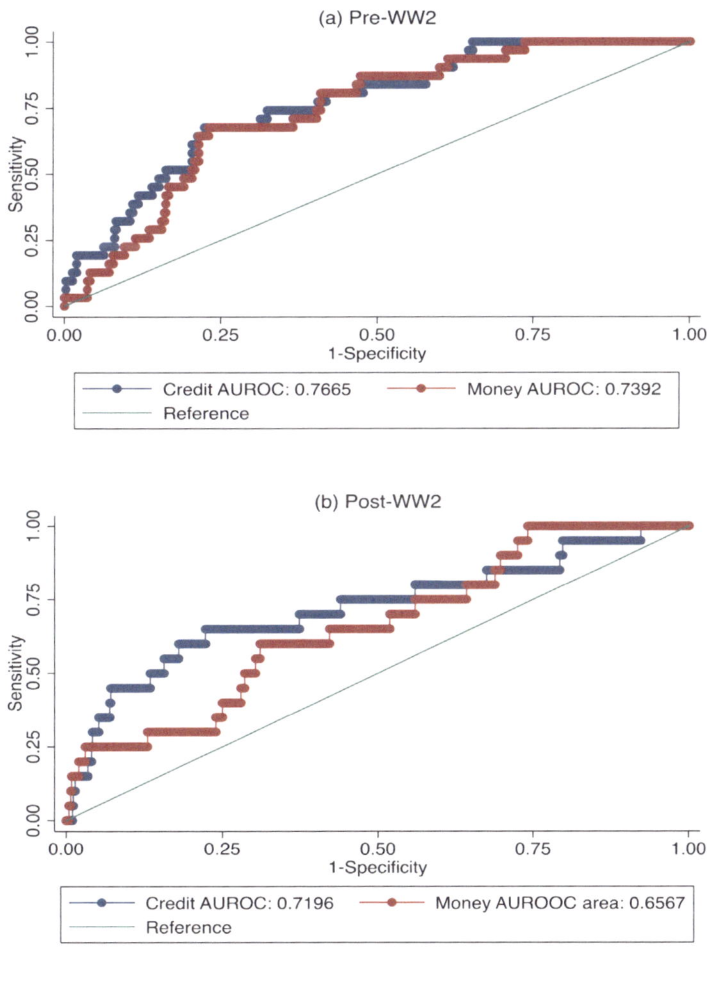


**Figure 3.**
*ROC comparisons for credit and money. Source: [4].*

versus some false one. The area under the receiver operating characteristic curve (AUROC), which represents the area under the curve of the ROC, is a measure that could be helpful in predicting the potential for a future financial crisis. An AUROC of 0.5 is equal to the probability of the reference line or "coin toss." This value would indicate that the model is effectively useless in its predictive capacity. An AUROC of 1, however, indicates the presence of a perfect predictor.

Accordingly, the AUROC must exceed 0.5 to reject the null hypothesis that the metric is useless as a predictor. In most credit estimation studies used to predict a crisis, an AUROC value around 0.7 indicates a relatively good level of predictive power. **Figure 3** above reveals the AUROC values created by Schularick and Taylor [4]. The AUROC value for the credit metric during the prewar period is 0.77, while the value for the money metric during this same period is 0.74. Further, the graphic reveals how the two metrics were highly correlated during the prewar period.

In contrast, the credit score AUROC value over the postwar period fell to 0.72, while the monetary metric AUROC value fell to 0.66. Further, the graphic reveals how the two metrics are less correlated after the war than they were before the war. This indicates that, while the two metrics were very comparable during the prewar era, the credit metric exhibited superior predictive power for forecasting future financial instability during the postwar era.

The empirical results of this study were obtained even after controlling for other crucial macroeconomic variables, such as real GDP growth, inflation, the nominal interest rate, the real interest rate, and the investment/GDP ratio. The resulting AUROC statistics did not vary significantly from that set by the AUROC factors. This increases the robustness of the claim that the credit gap metric reflects the heightened risk of the economy experiencing a financial drought.

## 2.3 Implications of the Schularick and Taylor study

The empirical research by Schularick and Taylor [4] was the first study to identify how the relationship between money, credit, and GDP was relatively more stable during the pre-WWII period but became less so afterward. Their research revealed that the predictive powers of money and credit growth metrics diverged after WWII, likely a result of ever-increasing levels of credit borrowing and bank liabilities in the postwar era.

The potential for using this relationship for developing credit-based metrics for predicting is supported in subsequent literature. Using data from a similar list of developed countries in Europe and North America, Jordà et al. [28] explored the relationship between credit growth, leverage, and financial crises using over a century of data. Their empirical analysis reveals how periods of excessive credit growth often preceded financial crises across these nations. They found that high levels of leverage amplify the business cycle of a nation's economy, making countries more susceptible to severe economic downturns whenever credit bubbles burst. Further, the resulting economic instability became increasingly severe and persistent over time, leading to sustained economic weakness. Ultimately, the authors conclude that economies exhibiting higher degrees of financial leverage tend to consistently experience deeper subsequent recessions and slower economic recoveries. Their conclusions support the theory that such a relationship could be employed to create a metric to help predict future financial crises and resulting economic recessions.

Another key contribution of the Schularick and Taylor study was that evidence of increasingly vulnerable financial systems facilitated greater real-economy risks associated with high levels of growth in the size of a nation's financial system. The robustness of their overall results supported the hypothesis that the resulting significant changes in credit gaps became a significant stimulator of the subsequent financial crises in the postwar period. They find empirical evidence that augmenting the role of the nonmonetary financial system after World War II created endogenous credit bubbles that culminated in the global financial downturn. Specifically, the increased prevalence of private credit around the globe was a strong influence on the variation in the credit metric, implying that this sector may contain valuable information about the probability of future financial crises.

Previously, Adrian and Shin [29] examined the role of leverage in exacerbating financial instability by analyzing the structural changes in financial intermediation leading up to the 2008 global financial crisis. They find that, over time, financial institutions increasingly relied on short-term wholesale funding and securitization, noting that this trend amplified systemic global financial risks. As financial institutions increased borrowing during economic booms and deleveraged during economic downturns, their reliance on short-term funding made the global system susceptible to liquidity dry-ups, which in turn triggered widespread distress when asset prices fell, and funding evaporated.

However, Schularick and Taylor suggest that, historically, some credit booms across the nations studied were not followed by a financial crisis. They found that when changes in the level of technology spurred increased financial leverage, or when changes in financial market efficiencies occurred, the resulting volatility in the credit markets resulted in greater levels of capital investment in the short run, and subsequent economic prosperity in the long run. Their research emphasizes the need to achieve a better understanding of any substantial financial market changes in creating productive versus destructive credit booms. They suggest that this necessarily requires a more holistic overview.

Further, the authors warn that the correlation between relatively accurate indicators and resulting outcomes does not necessarily imply theoretical causality. Further knowledge of how a significant change in financial markets might accurately predict a nation's coming economic vulnerability is needed before adopting the indicator as a meaningful influence over optimal public policy design and implementation. Indeed, financial stability can be a consequence of ineffective or harmful financial regulation. In such a case, changes in postwar credit growth trends might not be the best predictor of the financial crisis, but such accuracy could merely be cointegrated with poor governmental monetary, fiscal, or regulatory policy decisions.

For example, Dell'Ariccia et al. [2] examines the relationship between credit booms and financial stability across different countries. The authors find that rapid credit growth driven by financial innovation and deregulation has led to increased risks within a country's financial system, ultimately resulting in financial crises. They find that high degrees of financial leverage, and unregulated and deteriorating lending standards can result from poor regulatory frameworks, leading to broad levels of excessive risk-taking and increased financial instability.

### 2.4 Implications for optimal public policy

Ultimately, the optimal type of financial regulation and the desired structure of the financial markets require careful application of the insights gained from the research conducted by Schularick and Taylor. Their results have implications for using a credit-based metric as a forecasting tool for informing the design and implementation of a nation's financial and economic policy. Such metrics would need to be properly designed, as any significant differences in the trends between public versus private credit activity may impact the investment behavior of the private sector.

Consider the research by Dell'Ariccia et al. [30] who compare the credit booms across many different sectors of a nation's economy. They found that the construction sector exhibits a unique behavior relative to the other sectors in responding to credit booms. In such a case, this difference would be lost in a singular measure of a credit metric. In other words, the probability of a financial crisis occurring, and the capacity of a credit gap metric predicting it, could be influenced by the type of credit that is changing over time.

Gourinchas and Obstfeld [24] discuss how the global economy's increasing interconnectedness has heightened the risks of financial contagion. They highlight the importance of international financial cooperation in managing global economic stability. They state how it is imperative for countries to adopt coordinated policy responses. This implies that the capacity of a credit gap metric would be influenced by the degree of international connections between global financial institutions.

Kaminsky and Reinhart [23] examine the interplay between the "twin curses" of banking crises and currency crises. They find that misguided monetary policy can lead to false currency valuations and capital flow volatility, resulting in excessive risk-taking by financial institutions that create asset bubbles. This implies that the capacity of a credit gap metric would be influenced by the quality of a nation's monetary policy.

This begs the question: What areas of regulatory policy can be informed by an optimally designed credit metric? Adrian and Shin [26] advocate for macroprudential policies that limit excessive leverage and ensure that financial institutions maintain adequate liquidity buffers to mitigate volatile procyclical behavior. They suggest limits on leverage ratios to prevent excessive borrowing by financial institutions, minimum liquidity requirements for financial institutions, and countercyclical buffers that increase during economic booms and decrease during downturns.

Dell'Ariccia et al. [2] suggest several macroprudential policies to manage credit growth and maintain financial stability. This includes countercyclical capital buffers to absorb potential future losses, placing limits on loan-to-value and debt-to-income ratios to prevent excessive borrowing, and stress testing to detect vulnerabilities to systemic risks. Gourinchas and Obstfeld [24] highlight the importance of accounting for the global economy's increasing interconnectedness across financial markets, necessitating nations adopt coordinated policy responses to localized financial crises. They suggest strengthening international financial cooperation, implementing internationally coordinated oversight policies, and adopting countercyclical financial policies that alter capital requirements based on prevailing market conditions.

An optimally designed credit-based metric can only be useful as a forecasting tool if it can meaningfully inform the design and implementation of such financial regulations and public policies. The above literature makes it clear that any such metric must be calculated while controlling for variation across financial sectors, the degree of international financial interdependence, and the prevailing quality of a nation's monetary policy. Further, it must be understood how the metric can itself be influenced by prevailing liquidity requirements, countercyclical capital buffers, and regulatory limitations, such as debt-to-income ratios.

## 3. Conclusion

Empirical analysis by Schularick and Taylor [4] has demonstrated how the early warning signs of a pending financial crisis can be predicted by using a well-designed credit gap metric that reveals the fast growth rate of credit relative to a nation's GDP. Using the credit gap perspective in conjunction with asset prices to design measures of aggregate credit growth can be used as an important and reliable indicator to predict a pending financial crisis [28]. Schularick and Taylor have shown that when a nation's credit availability (per dollar of GDP) grew faster than a nation's monetary base during the post-WWII era was revealed to create a more volatile response in postwar bank assets and contributed to greater financial instability. Capturing this credit-based trend in a metric could provide meaningful insights for designing and implementing optimal financial market policies.

The empirical findings from the Schularick and Taylor research suggest that the amplitude, length, and disruptive power of the business cycle are all related to significant changes prior to governmental financial and monetary regimes. Those policies that appear to increase the volatility of credit markets also tend to increase financial market fragility during times of relative economic prosperity. Such periods often result in economic downturns that reduce a nation's long-run rate of economic growth. Fast credit lending by banks may generate a boom in the short run. However, such a boom can also augment a banking system's vulnerability by exposing its balance sheet to greater risks. This, in turn, can lead to the inability to handle even modest financial shocks, resulting in lower economic growth.

## Conflict of interest

The authors declare no conflict of interest.

## Author details

Jón Jónsson*, Kjartan Sigurðsson and Helga Kristjánsdóttir
University of Akureyri, Akureyri, Iceland

*Address all correspondence to: jon@unak.is

## References


[1] van der Cruijsen CAB, Eijffinger SCW, Hoogduin LH. Optimal central bank transparency. Journal of International Money and Finance. 2010;**29**(8):1482-1507

[2] Dell'Ariccia G, Igan D, Laeven L, Tong H. Credit booms and macrofinancial stability. Economic Policy. 2016;**31**(86):299-355

[3] Mishkin FS. Is monetary policy effective during financial crises? American Economic Review. 2009;**99**(2):573-577

[4] Schularick M, Taylor AM. Credit booms gone bust: Monetary policy, leverage cycles, and financial crises, 1870-2008. American Economic Review. 2012;**102**(2):1029-1061

[5] Canova F, Pappa E. Fiscal policy, pricing frictions and monetary accommodation. Economic Policy. 2011;**26**(68):555-598

[6] Filardo A. Monetary policy and asset price bubbles: Calibrating the monetary policy trade-offs. SSRN Electronic Journal. 2004;**155**:1-30

[7] Garrison R. Time and Money: The Macroeconomics of Capital Structure. London: Routledge; 2000

[8] Hayek FA. Prices and Production. London, United Kingdom: G. Routledge & Sons, Limited; 1931

[9] von Mises L. Human Action. A Treatise on Economics. New Haven, CT: Yale University Press; 1949

[10] Salerno J. A reformulation of Austrian business cycle theory in light of the financial crisis. SSRN Electronic Journal. 2011;**15**:3-44

[11] La Porta R, Lopez-de-Silanes F, Shleifer A, Vishny RW. Law and finance. Journal of Political Economy. 1998;**106**(6):1113-1155

[12] Acemoglu D, Johnson S, Robinson J. Institutions as the fundamental cause of long-run growth. In: National Bureau of Economic Research Working Paper Series. Cambridge: National Bureau of Economic Research; No. 10481. 2004

[13] Boettke PJ, Coyne CJ. Entrepreneurship and development: Cause or consequence? In: Austrian Economics and Entrepreneurial Studies. Leeds, United Kingdom: Emerald Group Publishing Limited; 2003. pp. 67-87

[14] Minsky H. A theory of systemic fragility. In: Altman E, Sametz A, editors. Financial Crises: Institutions and Markets in a Fragile Environment. New York, NY, United States: John Wiley and Sons; 1977. pp. 138-152

[15] Kindleberger C. Manias, Panics, and Crashes: A History of Financial Crises. New York: Basic Books; 1978

[16] Barberis N, Thaler R. A survey of behavioral finance. In: Handbook of the Economics of Finance. Vol. 1. Amsterdam, Netherlands. 2003. pp. 1053-1128

[17] Shiller RJ. From efficient markets theory to behavioral finance. Journal of Economic Perspectives. 2003;**17**(1):83-104

[18] Allen F, Gale D. Comparing Financial Systems. Cambridge, Massachusetts, United States: MIT Press; 2000

[19] Laeven L, Valencia F. Systemic banking crises database II. IMF Economic Review. 2020;**68**(2):307-361

[20] Taylor A. The great leveraging. In: The Social Value of the Financial Sector: Too Big to Fail or Just Too Big? Vol. 29. Singapore: World Scientific; 2014. pp. 33-65

[21] Rajan RG, Zingales L. Financial dependence and growth. The American Economic Review. 1998;**88**(3):559-586

[22] Borio C. The financial cycle and macroeconomics: What have we learnt? Journal of Banking & Finance. 2014;**45**(C):182-198

[23] Kaminsky GL, Reinhart CM. The twin crises: The causes of banking and balance-of-payments problems. American Economic Review. 1999;**89**(3):473-500

[24] Gourinchas P-O, Obstfeld M. Stories of the twentieth century for the twenty-first. American Economic Journal: Macroeconomics. 2012;**4**(1):226-265

[25] Bernanke BS, Gertler M, Gilchrist S. Chapter 21—The financial accelerator in a quantitative business cycle framework. In: Handbook of Macroeconomics. Vol. 1. Amsterdam, Netherlands: Elsevier; 1999. pp. 1341-1393

[26] Adrian T, Shin HS. Financial intermediaries and monetary economics. In: Friedman BM, Woodford M, editors. Handbook of Monetary Economics. Vol. 3. Amsterdam, Netherlands: Elsevier; 2010. pp. 601-650

[27] Mian A, Sufi A, Verner E. Household debt and business cycles worldwide*. The Quarterly Journal of Economics. 2017;**132**(4):1755-1817

[28] Jordà Ò, Schularick M, Taylor AM. Leveraged bubbles. Journal of Monetary Economics. 2015;**76**:S1-S20

[29] Adrian T, Shin HS. The changing nature of financial intermediation and the financial crisis of 2007-2009. Annual Review of Economics. 2010;**2**:603-618

[30] Dell'Ariccia G, Ebrahimy E, Igan D, Puy D. Discerning Good from Bad Credit Booms: The Role of Construction. Washington D.C., United States: International Monetary Fund; 2020

Chapter 3

# Predicting Financial Crises: The Role of Shocks to Real Interest Rates and Credit on Aggregate Economic Activity, Lessons from the Austrian Business Cycle Theory

*Yahuza Abdul Rahman*

## Abstract

This study investigates postulates of the ABCT in selected advanced and emerging economies. Specifically, using quarterly data from 1980q1 to 2023q1, it estimates a Structural Vector Autoregressive Model with exogenous variables (SVARX) based on the Stochastic Keynesian Model for 20 selected countries. Outcomes of the study suggest mixed results. First, credit expansion and contraction are indeed induced by deviations of real interest rates from the trend. However, whilst this causal relationship is positive in the West and Latin America, it is negative in East Asia, Africa, and Middle East. Second, in 11 out of the 20 countries, credit expansion leads to substantial positive gaps of real GDP per capita around its potential level. It, however, leads to negative gaps in the remaining nine countries. Third, private consumption actually falls below the trend level in response to a positive shock to credit. Finally, values of imports tend to respond positively to impulses to credit. It concludes that financial crises are due to deviations of real interest rate from the equilibrium rate, which cause the output to deviate from its trend level leading to crises. Therefore, substantial deviations of real interest rates from the equilibrium rates give signals of pending financial crisis.

**Keywords:** financial crisis, structural shocks, vector autoregression, advanced economies, emerging economies, The Austrian Business Cycle Theory, Stochastic Keynesian Model

## 1. Introduction

Analyses of historical financial time series suggest that financial crises have become regular events within the global financial markets. Recent financial crises have had a profound impact on the global economy, leading to widespread job losses, home foreclosures, and significant declines in economic growth [1–5]. From the strand of the theoretical literature, three broad forms of financial crises have been identified, and they are banking crises and panics [6, 7], credit frictions and market freezes [8–10], and currency crises [11–16]. Despite the devastating impacts of financial crises, there is little consensus on their causes, predictions, and mitigating factors.

Many theories have been propounded, and volumes of empirical studies have done in attempts at determining causes, providing early warning signals and preventing or mitigating the adverse impacts of financial crises. However, these attempts, though very informing, have not yielded the desired outcome. These attempts resulted into different theories of financial crises [17] and volumes of empirical studies [18–22] but with little consensus on how financial crises occur and how they could be tracked and mitigated.

One of these theories is the ABCT [23, 24]. It submits that the market is capable of allocating resources in conformity with intertemporal preferences on the basis of a market-determined natural rate of interest and that any extra-market forces which substantially influenced the prevailing interest rate to deviate from the natural rate leads to credit expansion and contraction, resulting in intertemporal misallocation of resources away from the potential level of output. Misallocations are then followed by self-correcting reallocations of resources which eventually correct the market back to equilibrium [25–27]. According to this theory, financial crises are results of excessive external interventions in the markets and the subsequent self-correction of the markets to restore equilibrium.

The postulates of ABCT have not been adequately investigated in empirical literature. Most of the recent empirical studies [28–37] have focused attention on other financial theories with little emphases on the ABCT. They have explored a myriad of variables and tested their significance in terms of impacts and magnitudes in inducing occurrences of financial crises. However, there still remain challenging issues in identifying the underlying economic forces that give rise to financial crises. Also, connecting individual variables to specific channels and mechanisms as identified by various theories such as the ABCT is lacking. Moreover, reconciling the estimated economic magnitudes across studies and determining the resilience of financial markets to exogenous shocks still remain a challenge. This study is aimed at investigating the postulates of the ABCT of financial crises by examining the underlying responses of aggregate macroeconomic activity to short run exogenous shocks to real interest rates and private credit in selected advanced and emerging economies.

Specifically, it estimates a Structural Vector Autoregressive Model with exogenous variables (SVAR-X) and isolates the underlying structural impulse-responses of real interest rate, private credit, real GDP per capita, private consumption, tax revenues, and import values in 20 selected advanced and emerging economies. The countries are grouped into five categories of four countries each. The categories are the West, Latin America, Africa, Middle East, and East Asia. Countries in each category are selected based on their income levels and availability of data. The groups are the United States, the United Kingdom, Canada, and Sweden from the West; Bolivia, Chile, Mexico, and Peru from Latin America; Botswana, Egypt, Mauritius, and South Africa from Africa; Bahrain, Iran, Jordan and Lebanon from Middle East; and China, Malaysia, Philippines, and Singapore.

Guided by the Stochastic Keynesian Macroeconomic Framework, the study identifies private consumption, private credit, real interest rate, tax revenues, import values, and real GDP per capita as endogenous variables and broad money supply, government consumption, export values, and real exchange rate as the exogenous variables. With the exception of the real interest rate, each of these variables was decomposed into trend and cyclical components, where the cyclical parts were used for the estimations. The study estimates, isolates, and compares the underlying structural impulse-responses of these macroeconomic variables from these countries.

For identification restrictions on the structural parameters, Cholesky decomposition method on AB-Model was used, where the variables are arranged in order of consumption, credit, tax revenues, real interest rate, imports, and real GDP per capita. Outcomes of the study lend strong support to the ABCT. The study makes contributions to knowledge by testing the ABCT and how it can be used for signaling and predicting financial crises. It also suggests a theoretical framework for operationalizing the postulates of the ABCT.

The rest of the study is organized as follows: Section 2 provides a review of the literature on theoretical and empirical studies, highlighting key theories of financial crises and some recent empirical studies. It also identifies literature gaps for further studies. Section 3 presents the methodology of the study, by highlighting the theoretical model specifications and elaborating on the empirical model specifications. It finally explains the sources of data and measurement of variables. Section 4 outlines and explains the results, and Section 5 sums it up with conclusions and recommendations.

## 2. Literature review

Financial systems are subject to periodic disturbances, leading to market crashes, panics, and recessions. Various theories attempt at explaining causes and mechanisms of financial crises. These theories help in understanding the complex factors contributing to financial crises, enabling policymakers and researchers to develop strategies for mitigating and prevention. This section presents a review of the financial literature, which, admittedly, cannot cover the entire literature due to volume and space. What it presents here is a review of three relevant theories of financial crises: the Banking Crises and Panic Model, the Moral Hazard and Adverse Selection Model, and the Austrian Business Cycle Theory. Finally, it also reviews some most recent empirical studies and identifies the study gaps.

### 2.1 The banking cries and panic model

This is a formal description of the Goldstein and Pauzner's [7] version of the Diamond and Dybvig's [6] model of banking crises and panics. It describes agents' consumption and saving behavior which may lead to financial crisis in an economy. This model is built on assumption that there are three periods (0, 1, and 2), one good, and a continuum [0, 1] of agents. Each agent is born in period 0 with an endowment of one unit. Consumption occurs only in period 1 or 2 $c_1$ and $c_2$. Each agent can be one of the two types: (1) impatient with a probability of $\lambda$ and (2) patient with a probability of 1-$\lambda$. There is no aggregate uncertainty, and agents' types are independent and identically distributed. Agents learn their type at the beginning of period 1. Impatient agents can consume only in period 1 and obtain a utility of $u(c_1)$. Patient agents can consume in both periods 1 and 2 with utility of $u(c_1 + c_2)$. $u(.)$ is twice continuously differentiable, increasing, and for any $c \geq 1$ has a relative risk-aversion coefficient: $-\frac{cu''(c)}{u'(c)} > 1$. Agents have access to a productive technology that yields a higher expected return in the long run. Each unit of input invested in period 0 generates 1 unit of output if liquidated in period 1 and R units of output with probability $p(\theta)$ or 0 units with probability $1 - p(\theta)$ if liquidated in period 2, where $\theta$ is the state of the economy with a uniform distribution of [0,1]. $p(\theta)$ is strictly increasing in $\theta$ satisfies: $E_\theta[p(\theta)]u(R) > u(1)$.

In autarky, impatient agents consume one unit in period 1, and the patient agents consume R units in period 2 with a probability of $p(\theta)$. A social planner who can verify agent's type once revealed would set the period 1 consumption level $c_1$ of the impatient agents so as to maximize the agent's ex ante expected welfare:

$\lambda u(c_1) + (1 - \lambda)\, u\left(\frac{1-\lambda c_1}{1-\lambda} R\right) E_\theta[p(\theta)]$.

The first order conditions are

$$u'\left(c_1{}^{FB}\right) = Ru'\left(\frac{1 - \lambda c_1{}^{FB}}{1 - \lambda} R\right) E_\theta[p(\theta)].$$

That is, the marginal benefit of the impatient agents equal to the marginal cost of the patient agents. Thus, there is risk sharing at the optimum.

The bank: Because the agent's type is assumed to be observable, the bank can enable risk sharing by offering a demand-deposit contract such that each agent deposits his endowment in period 0. If he demands withdrawal in period 1, he gets a fixed payment of $r_1 > 1$, but if he waits until period 2, he gets a stochastic payoff of $\tilde{r_2} = \frac{(1-nr_1)}{1-n} R$ with a probability of $p(\theta)$ and 0 with probability of $(1 - p(\theta))$. If the bank sets $r_1$ at $c_1{}^{FB}$ and only the impatient agents demand early withdrawal, the expected utility of the patient agents is $E_\theta[p(\theta)].u\left(\frac{1-\lambda r_1}{1-\lambda} R\right)$. As long as this value exceeds $u(r_1)$, there is an equilibrium in which only the impatient agents make early withdrawal. This equilibrium is optimal if the number of the impatient agents $(n)$ demanding early withdrawal is less than $\frac{1}{r_1}$. However, if $> \frac{1}{r_1}$, there will be another sub-optimal equilibrium where all agents demand early withdrawal, where period 1 payment will be $r_1$ with probability $\frac{1}{nr_1}$ or 0 with probability of $1 - \frac{1}{nr_1}$ and the period 2 payoff is zero.

Thus, the optimum equilibrium of this model is contingent on four key variables:

i. $\lambda$, the probability of the impatient type agents

ii. $n$, the number of the impatient agents

iii. $r_1$, the period 1 payoff

iv. $R$, returns on the remaining assets carried over to period 2.

The question is what factors influence dynamics of these variables? $\lambda$ and $n$ will be influenced by income levels of agents and the extent of income inequality in the country. $R$ is dependent on the state of the economy, and $r_1$ may depend on $R$. Thus, the state of the economy is at the core of bank runs.

### 2.2 The moral hazard and adverse selection model

In the above model, high probability of the impatient agents and their number may result in low level of assets with the banks for advancing long-term credits. This may result in low level of credits, hence credit rationing. To avoid credit rationing and freeze, the policy should aim at reducing the number of impatient agents to the barest minimum. This presumes that the agents' type is known as assumed in the above model. In reality, however, agents' type is not known. Also, return on investment is likely to be influenced by effort of the agents. These introduced the problems of adverse selection and moral hazards in the system.

Holmstrom and Tirole [9] developed a model to account for these issues. This model assumes that there is a continuum of entrepreneurs, with access to the same investment technology and different amounts of capital A, with a distribution function $G(A)$. The required investment is I, and entrepreneurs need to raise I –A from outside investors. Gross return on investment is either R or 0, and the probability of getting R instead of 0 depends on the type of the project the entrepreneur undertakes. There are three possible project types: (1) good with R returns, with $P_H$ probability of success (2) bad with low private benefit $b$, with $P_L$ probability of success, and (3) bad with high private benefits $B$, with $P_L$ probability of success, $P_H > P_L$ and $B > b$. All entrepreneurs seek to choose a good project. However, an entrepreneur may choose a bad project if it provides him with non-pecuniary benefit. Therefore, if unconstrained the entrepreneur may always choose a bad project with high private benefit. The rate of return demanded by outside investors is given by $\gamma$, which can either be fixed or realized from an upward slopping function $S(\gamma)$. It is assumed that only good project is viable, that is,$P_H R - \gamma I > 0 > P_L R - \gamma I + B$, ensuring that investing in a bad project generates a negative total surplus. This implies that entrepreneurs with large assets A would have easy access to external financing. Therefore, every entrepreneur needs to own A and access I –A from the bank to be able to undertake viable investment.

The question is how would the entrepreneur divide the returns R from a good investment with the bank? Let us assume that the entrepreneur would take $R_f$ and the bank gets $R_u$ such that $R_f + R_u = R$. A necessary condition for the entrepreneur to participate in a good project is

$$P_H R_f \geq P_L R_f + B$$

$R_f \geq B/\Delta P$, where $\Delta P = P_H - P_{L.}$

This is the incentive compatibility constraint, which ensures that the entrepreneur benefits more from a good project than a bad project. The maximum expected income to the bank is $P_H\left(R - \frac{B}{\Delta P}\right)$, and the participating constraint of the bank is

$\gamma(I - A) \leq P_H\left(R - \frac{B}{\Delta P}\right)$. This puts an endogenous financing constraint on the entrepreneur, which depends on how much internal capital A he has. Let the threshold amount that an entrepreneur should have to access external financing be $\overline{A}(\gamma)$ such that $\overline{A}(\gamma) = I - \frac{P_H\left(R - \frac{B}{\Delta P}\right)}{\gamma}$. Thus, only entrepreneurs with capital above this threshold can raise external funds for investment. This outcome is the classic credit rationing result [8]. Therefore, only entrepreneurs with a minimum amount of capital equal to the threshold can raise external financing.

However, if the bank can put in their own capital of $K_m$ to monitor the entrepreneur to prevent him from choosing a bad project with a high private benefit, the threshold amount can be relaxed to $\underline{A}(\gamma, \beta)$ so that entrepreneurs with a level of capital lower than the threshold $\overline{A}(\gamma)$ will be able to get financing by the bank, where $\beta$ is the return required by the bank for monitoring. It follows that

$\underline{A}(\gamma, \beta) = (I - I_m(\beta)) - \frac{P_H\left(R - \frac{b+c}{\Delta P}\right)}{\gamma}$, where $I_m(\beta)$ is the amount of capital provided by the bank, which is decreasing in the return $\beta$ demanded by the bank for monitoring.

Hence, the entrepreneur only needs to raise $(I - I_m(\beta))$ directly from the bank. The entrepreneur in that case can only promise the bank with expected payment of $P_H\left(-\frac{b+c}{\Delta P}\right)$, so that both maintain incentives to choose a good project and monitor.

Implications of this model:

i. In the presence of moral hazards, credit rationing prevails with only entrepreneurs with own internal capital above a threshold that can raise external financing.

ii. However, if the bank can invest its own capital in monitoring the entrepreneur to choose a good project and receive a return on monitoring, many entrepreneurs with capital below the threshold can participate in external financing.

This underscores the vulnerability of the financing system. Per the model, only entrepreneurs within the top income group can raise external capital. However, by assuming monitoring role, the bank opens itself to bad entrepreneurs who might choose bad project with high probability. If the proportion of this category is higher than the initial entrepreneurs, then the stability of the system will strictly depend on the monitoring technology of the bank. Any shortfall in the monitoring responsibility of the bank increases the probability of bad projects and any adverse shock to the fundamentals of the economy will increase the probability of a credit crunch.

### 2.3 The Austrian business cycle theory

Stability in the above two models depends to some extent on the fundamentals of the real economy. This brings the Austrian theory of business cycle to the fore, necessitating us to understand the real cases of changes in the aggregate economic activity.

This theory is due to Hayek [23, 24, 38, 39]. This review is based on the rendition of Snowdon and Vane [26]. According to this theory, the market is capable of allocating resources in conformity with intertemporal preferences on the basis of a market-determined natural rate of interest and that any extra-market forces which substantially influenced the prevailing interest rate to deviate from the natural rate lead to credit expansion and contraction, resulting in intertemporal misallocation of resources away from the potential level of output. Misallocations are then followed by self-correction reallocations of resources which eventually correct the market back to equilibrium. The external interventions in the market and the subsequent self-correction of the market are the causes of the cyclical movements of actual output around the economy's potential level, hence financial crisis. The model makes a distinction between saving-induced credit expansion and capital injection-induced credit expansion.

In the nut shell, according to this theory, padding the supply of loanable funds with newly created money drives a wedge between saving and investment. The immediate effects are as follows:

i. No credit shortage occurs

ii. Periods of economic expansions in which an inherent problem of mismatch between saving and investment is concealed festers.

iii. A bust which is the eventual but inevitable resolution to the problem occurs.

Any of the above theories provides some insights on sources of financial crises. However, taking them in isolations, they fall short of giving adequate explanations to sources of financial crises. A critical look at these models indicates that they are related in some key variables, albeit with varying degrees of emphasis. Model 1 is linked with model 3 through the payoff (natural interest rate) which determines the level of saving. According to both models, any distortion in the market which fixes the interest rate below or above the equilibrium level affects the availability of loanable funds. In the words of model 1, the number of the impatient agents will increase and in the words of model 3 saving will fall. Return on assets in model 1 and output fluctuations in model 3 are also related. Artificial boom causes bubbles in return on assets and market self-correction leads to bust in output and asset returns. Implicit in the model is the price level which gives signals to the real factors.

Moreover, model 2 is related to both models 1 and 3 through credit expansion. While it takes the level of credit as given and looks at the behavior of agents and their types, model 1 also takes it as given and looks at the number of agents, but model 3 examines the sources of the credit expansion, as to whether it is saving-induced expansion or money-induced expansion. Therefore, if taking any of these models in isolation fails to offer adequate explanations on the sources of financial crises, taking them together may offer some important insights on financial crises. This is what this study attempts to achieve.

Empirical literature in this regard highlights the standing level of understanding on sources of financial crises. From the perspective of the fundamentals, historical time series analysis has shown that financial crises are often preceded by a combination of factors, including excessive borrowing and debt [38], asset price bubbles [39], financial innovation and deregulation [40], and global imbalances [41]. Some studies observed rising income inequality of the top 10% category of households and low productivity growth as robust predictors of financial crisis [28, 29]. A rapid build-up of debt, whether public or private, is also observed to increase the likelihood of a financial crisis, as did a larger share of short-term external debt, higher debt service cover, and lower reserves cover [30].

Moreover, some studies [30] observed that countries that experienced financial crises frequently employed combinations of unsustainable fiscal, monetary, and financial sector policies. There is also evidence of critical slowing down of fundamentals [31], weak macroeconomic environment, particularly low output and high inflation [42] and high financial leverage [43]. Also, high interest rates are identified to be associated with systemic banking sector problems as well as vulnerability of balance of payments [21]. Joao Tovar Jalles [44] examined determinants of banking crises and observed that recent baking crises are mainly related to the asset side of bank's balance sheets and [33] summarized and analyzed the main economic and political factors of financial crises.

Other studies [34] were attempts at predicting the timing and measuring magnitudes of the impacts of financial crises. They explored how crises are measured, whether they are predictable, and why they are associated with economic contractions and concluded that crises are predictable with growth in credit and elevated asset prices playing an especially important role. It is observed that financial crises are not simply random but typically a prolonged build-up of macro-financial imbalances [28], and Greenwood et al. [35] estimated the predictability of financial crises as a function of past credit and asset price growth.

Furthermore, other studies [2] examined the post crises effects of financial crises and observed that financial crises have significant consequences, including output losses, unemployment [3], home foreclosures [4], and increased income inequality [5]. For example, Brauning and Viacheslav [19] examined the macroeconomic effects of a likely credit contraction triggered by the recent banking turmoil. They documented a sizeable and persistent decline in output and rising unemployment following non-systemic financial distress. Hardy and Sever [20] studied how financial crises affect innovative activities. They provided a link between banking crises and observed the pattern of lower long-term output growth. Frydman and Xu [18] surveyed the recent empirical literature on historical banking crises. They highlighted three overarching threats: (1) leverage in the financial system is a systematic precursor to crises, (2) crises have sizeable negative effects on the real economy, and (3) government interventions can ameliorate these effects. Romer and Romer [21] also attempted at identifying the effects of recent crises on financial performance and organizational resilience. Lower investment during financial crises is the key factor leading to permanent loss of output and total factor productivity in the wake of a crisis [22].

Policy responses to financial crises have included monetary policy [45], fiscal policy [46], financial regulation [47], and international cooperation [48]. Therefore, there is no scanty of studies with regard to determinants of financial crises. However, there still remain challenges in identifying the underlying economic forces that give rise to the relationships evidenced in theories and in historical data. Also, connecting these individual factors to specific channels and mechanisms emphasized by theory, and reconciling the estimated economic magnitudes, are currently challenging to contrast across studies. This study therefore seeks to attempt at contributing to filling some of these gaps.

## 3. Methodology

### 3.1 Introduction

This section presents the method and approach used for the analysis. It exploits features of a version of the Keynesian Stochastic Macroeconomic Model (KSMM) in a structural VARX setting. The section comprises the theoretical model specification, empirical model specification, and the data source.

### 3.2 Theoretical model specification

Empirical analysis of the dynamics of financial Markets requires strong theoretical foundation for explanations. Unfortunately, none of the above reviewed models of financial crises gives a definite structural macroeconomic framework of an economy to guide the analysis. In order to avoid spiral exercise without theory, this study is premised on a version of the Keynesian Stochastic Macroeconomic Model (KSMM). The model is an economic framework that combines elements of Keynesian economics with stochastic variables to analyze economic behavior under uncertainty. This model is suitable for studying various economic phenomena such as business cycle, monetary policy, fiscal policy, and financial markets and provides a more realistic representation of economic behavior under uncertainty, allowing for a deeper understanding of complex economic phenomena. Following the derivations of [49, 50], the structural features of the model are given by the following six structural equations:

$$C_t = c_0 + c_1(Y_{t-1} - T_{t-1}) + c_2X_t + \varepsilon_c \quad \text{(consumption)} \tag{1}$$

$$I_t = b_0 - b_1R_t + b_2Y_{t-1} + \varepsilon_I \quad \text{(investment)} \tag{2}$$

$$R_t = r_0 - r_1Z_t + r_2Y_t + \varepsilon_R \quad \text{(money market equilibrium)} \tag{3}$$

$$T_t = t_0 + t_1Y_t + t_2M_t + \varepsilon_T \quad \text{(tax revenue)} \tag{4}$$

$$M_t = m_0 + m_1Y_t + m_2R_t + m_3T_t + m_4E_t + \varepsilon_M \quad \text{(imports)} \tag{5}$$

$$Y_t = C_t + I_t + G_t + X_t - M_t = C_t + T_t + S_t \quad \text{(macro − balance)} \tag{6}$$

Here, the endogenous variables are as follows:

$C_t$ is consumption, $I_t$ is investment, $T_t$ is tax revenue, $M_t$ is imports, $Y_t$ is national income, and $R_t$ is nominal interest rate. The exogenous variables are $X_t$ is export, $E_t$ is nominal exchange rate, $G_t$ is government spending, and $Z_t$ is real money balance. $c_i$, $b_i$, $t_i$, $m_i$, and $r_i$ for $i = 1, 2, 3 \ldots$ are parameters. The shocks $\varepsilon_c$, $\varepsilon_I$, $\varepsilon_T$, $\varepsilon_M$, and $\varepsilon_R$ are normally distributed with zero means and constant variance. This model can be estimated using the SVARX approach [51, 52].

The SVAR model has become one of the major approaches for extracting information about the macro economy. It is suitable for quantifying impulse responses to macroeconomic shocks and enables for measuring the degree of uncertainty about impulses and for deciding on contributions of different shocks to business cycles as well as forecast errors through variance decompositions. However, the use of SVAR has its intricacies [53]. The major task in estimating SVAR model is how to recover the structural parameters from the reduced form of VAR.

In practice, different methods of identification restrictions have been used. They are (1) the Cowles Commission approach which assumes that the structural shocks are correlated and solves the identification problem by excluding variables from the structural equations. (2) The recursive approach assumes the structural shocks to be uncorrelated with one another such that the endogenous variables are ordered in a manner that they contemporaneously depend on others further down the system but not on those above. Thus, the system is presented in a triangular structure. (3) The long run restrictions method. (4) Parametric impulse restrictions [54]. (5) The sign restrictions method which requires the use of either the Givens transformation matrix or Householder transformation matrix [55, 56]. Each of these methods of identification has its strength and weakness, and no evidence exists to suggest preference of one approach over the other. However, the use of any of these identification restrictions must be grounded in theory and be guided by institutional knowledge.

### 3.3 Empirical model specification

Given the six variables of the KSMM, consumption $C_t$, investment $I_t$, interest rate $R_t$, tax revenues $T_t$, imports $M_t$, and real GDP per capita $Y_t$, let $Z_t = (C_t, \; I_t, R_t, T_t, M_t, Y_t)'$ be a vector of the endogenous variables and $u_t = (u_1, u_2, u_3, u_4, u_5)'$ be a vector of the structural innovations. The dynamic behavior of $Z_t$ is captured in a structural VAR-AB model as follows:

$$AZ_t = a_0 + A(l)Z_{t-1} + Bu_t \tag{7}$$

where $E(u_tu_t') = \sum_u$ and $E(u_tu_s') = 0$ for t $\neq s$. The reduced form equation is given as follows:

$$Z_t = A^{-1}a_0 + A^{-1}A(l)Z_{t-1} + A^{-1}Bu_t$$
$$Z_t = b_0 + G(l)Z_{t-1} + e_t \tag{8}$$

Here, $e_t = A^{-1}Bu_t$

The functional structural form of eq. (8) including the exogenous variables is represented as follows:

$$\begin{bmatrix} 1 & 0 & 0 & 0 & 0 & 0 \\ 0 & 1 & 0 & 0 & b_1 & 0 \\ 0 & 0 & 1 & 0 & 0 & r_1 \\ 0 & 0 & 0 & 1 & t_2 & t_1 \\ 0 & 0 & m_2 & m_3 & 1 & m_1 \\ 1 & 1 & 1 & 1 & 1 & 1 \end{bmatrix} \begin{bmatrix} C_t \\ I_t \\ R_t \\ T_t \\ M_t \\ Y_t \end{bmatrix} = \begin{bmatrix} a_{11} & a_{12} & a_{13} & a_{14} & a_{15} & a_{16} \\ a_{21} & a_{22} & a_{23} & a_{24} & a_{25} & a_{26} \\ a_{31} & a_{32} & a_{33} & a_{34} & a_{35} & a_{36} \\ a_{41} & a_{42} & a_{43} & a_{44} & a_{45} & a_{46} \\ a_{51} & a_{52} & a_{53} & a_{54} & a_{55} & c_{56} \\ a_{61} & a_{62} & a_{63} & a_{64} & a_{65} & a_{66} \end{bmatrix} \begin{bmatrix} C_{t-1} \\ I_{t-1} \\ R_{t-1} \\ T_{t-1} \\ M_{t-1} \\ Y_{t-1} \end{bmatrix} + \begin{bmatrix} d_{11} & d_{12} & d_{13} & d_{14} \\ d_{21} & d_{22} & d_{23} & a_{24} \\ d_{31} & d_{32} & d_{33} & d_{34} \\ d_{41} & d_{42} & d_{43} & d_{44} \end{bmatrix} \begin{bmatrix} X_t \\ G_t \\ E_t \\ Z_t \end{bmatrix} + \begin{bmatrix} \varepsilon_c \\ \varepsilon_I \\ \varepsilon_R \\ \varepsilon_T \\ \varepsilon_M \\ \varepsilon_Y \end{bmatrix} \tag{9}$$

And, restrictions on the parameters of $e_t = A^{-1}Bu_t$ are in the following form

$$\begin{bmatrix} \varepsilon_c \\ \varepsilon_I \\ \varepsilon_R \\ \varepsilon_T \\ \varepsilon_M \\ \varepsilon_Y \end{bmatrix} = \begin{bmatrix} 1 & 0 & 0 & 0 & 0 & 0 \\ a_{21} & 1 & 0 & 0 & 0 & 0 \\ a_{31} & a_{32} & 1 & 0 & 0 & 0 \\ a_{41} & a_{42} & a_{43} & 1 & 0 & 0 \\ a_{51} & a_{52} & a_{53} & a_{54} & 1 & 0 \\ a_{61} & a_{62} & a_{63} & a_{64} & a_{65} & 1 \end{bmatrix}^{-1} \begin{bmatrix} 1 & 0 & 0 & 0 & 0 & 0 \\ 0 & 1 & 0 & 0 & 0 & 0 \\ 0 & 0 & 1 & 0 & 0 & 0 \\ 0 & 0 & 0 & 1 & 0 & 0 \\ 0 & 0 & 0 & 0 & 1 & 0 \\ 0 & 0 & 0 & 0 & 0 & 1 \end{bmatrix} \begin{bmatrix} u_c \\ u_I \\ u_R \\ u_T \\ u_M \\ u_Y \end{bmatrix} \tag{10}$$

The impulse – response functions are then derived as follows:

$$\varepsilon_c = u_c \tag{11}$$
$$\varepsilon_I = a_{21}u_c + u_I$$
$$\varepsilon_R = a_{31}u_c + a_{32}u_I + u_R$$
$$\varepsilon_T = a_{41}u_c + a_{42}u_I + a_{43}u_R + u_T$$
$$\varepsilon_M = a_{51}u_c + a_{52}u_I + a_{53}u_R + a_{54}u_T + u_M$$
$$\varepsilon_Y = a_{61}u_c + a_{62}u_I + a_{63}u_R + a_{64}u_T + a_{65}u_M + u_Y$$

### 3.4 Data sources and measurement of variables

The data were obtained from the World Development Indicators (WDI). It comprises 10 annual time series variables spanning 1980 to 2023. In order to exploit variations in the data, the frequencies of the variables were increased by converting them from annual to quarterly using Chow-Lin method. With the exception of the real interest rate, each of the series was decomposed into trend and cyclical components using the Hedrick-Prescott (HP) filter. The cyclical components were used for the estimation. This was done to enable the assessment of deviations of the variables from the trends.

The endogenous variables are as follows:

1. Private consumption gap
2. Real GDP per capita (for output gap)
3. Import values gap
4. Credit gap (used as a proxy for investment)
5. Real interest rates
6. Tax revenues gap

The exogenous variables are proxied by

1. Government consumption gap
2. Export values gap
3. Exchange rates gap
4. Broad money supply gap

## 4. Estimation results and major findings

### 4.1 Descriptive statistics

Here, a sample descriptive statistics for three countries from each of the five groups are presented. This enables us to ascertain and exploit the variability of the raw data across the countries. **Table 1** reveals that, in the US, average real GDP per capita is $47,561 over the period under consideration, with a maximum of $65,020 and a minimum of $30,696. Private consumption avereaged around 81% of GDP. This is gauged by broad money supply which averaged around 78% of GDP. One significant thing to note is the rate of credit expansion to the private sector by financial institutions. The average credit supply is about 155% of GDP with a maximum of more than twice the GDP of the country. Also, average real interest rate is positive around 4%, and government consumption alone is about 5% higher than its generated tax revenues. In contrast to the UK, the avergae real GDP per capita is $37,369 with a maximum of $47,343 and a minimum of $23,331. Credit supply to the private sector is over

| Variable | Obs. | Mean | Std. Dev. | Min | Max |
|---|---|---|---|---|---|
| Private Consumption | 173 | 80.89 | 1.995 | 76.114 | 85.126 |
| Private Credit | 173 | 155.996 | 38.309 | 89.238 | 221.129 |
| Tax Revenues | 173 | 10.765 | 1.013 | 7.904 | 13.063 |
| Imports | 173 | 13.157 | 2.54 | 9.043 | 17.442 |
| Real Interest Rate | 173 | 4.235 | 2.262 | −1.189 | 8.595 |
| Real GDP Per Capita | 173 | 47,561 | 9651 | 30,696 | 65,020 |
| Broad Money | 173 | 78.485 | 12.789 | 59.659 | 115.406 |
| Exports | 173 | 10.42 | 1.755 | 6.988 | 13.644 |
| Govt. Consumption | 173 | 15.166 | .874 | 13.467 | 16.808 |

*Note: Data from the World Development Indicators, quarterly series from 1980q1 to 2023q1.*

**Table 1.**
*Descriptive statistics—United States.*

100% of GDP, and average real interest rate is positive and around 2%. However, whilst in the US, government consumption alone exceeds its tax revenues by 5%, and in the UK, tax revenue is rather above government consumption by 5% as shown in **Tables 2** and **3**.

This pattern is also observed in Canada with high average real income, credit supply far more above GDP, positive real interest rate, and government consumption being above its tax revenues. Thus, in the advanced countries, credit supply to the private sector is very high. In contrast to countries in Africa, average real GDP per capita is very low hovering around $4760, $2649, and $5342, for Botswana, Egypt, and South Africa, respectively. Whist in Botswana, tax revenue is below government consumption by about 2%, and it is above in Egypt and South Africa by about 4% and 5%, respectively. More noticeable is the level of credit supply to the private sector which is way below 50% of their GDP (**Tables 4–15**).

| Variable | Obs. | Mean | Std. Dev. | Min | Max |
|---|---|---|---|---|---|
| Private Consumption | 173 | 84.453 | 1.817 | 80.644 | 88.371 |
| Private Credit | 173 | 115.785 | 41.017 | 26.216 | 192.438 |
| Tax Revenues | 173 | 24.911 | 1.042 | 22.762 | 28.214 |
| Imports | 173 | 27.679 | 3.085 | 22.712 | 36.097 |
| Real Interest Rate | 173 | 2.02 | 2.745 | −4.301 | 6.72 |
| Real GDP Per Capita | 173 | 37,369 | 7601 | 23,331 | 47,343 |
| Broad Money | 173 | 102.727 | 43.539 | 30.764 | 165.625 |
| Exports | 173 | 26.863 | 2.771 | 22.163 | 33.43 |
| Govt. Consumption | 173 | 19.491 | 1.654 | 16.04 | 22.602 |

*Note: Data from the World Development Indicators, quarterly series from 1980q1 to 2023q1.*

**Table 2.**
*Descriptive statistics—United Kingdom.*

| Variable | Obs. | Mean | Std. Dev. | Min | Max |
|---|---|---|---|---|---|
| Private Consumption | 173 | 76.858 | 2.053 | 73.382 | 82.147 |
| Private Credit | 173 | 114.634 | 47.031 | 56.417 | 207.363 |
| Tax Revenue | 173 | 13.263 | .819 | 11.623 | 14.858 |
| Imports | 173 | 30.884 | 4.406 | 21.423 | 38.556 |
| Real Interest Rate | 173 | 3.788 | 2.506 | −.238 | 10.363 |
| Real GDP Per Capita | 173 | 37,113.97 | 5933.325 | 26,999.08 | 45,227.14 |
| Broad Money | 173 | 129.125 | 62.121 | 60.399 | 250.218 |
| Exports | 173 | 31.935 | 5.152 | 24.353 | 44.209 |
| Govt. Consumption | 173 | 21.119 | 1.313 | 19.076 | 24.445 |

*Note: Data from the World Development Indicators, quarterly series from 1980q1 to 2023q1.*

**Table 3.**
*Descriptive statistics—Canada.*

| Variable | Obs. | Mean | Std. Dev. | Min | Max |
|---|---|---|---|---|---|
| Private Consumption | 173 | 66.779 | 7.799 | 49.823 | 84.686 |
| Private Credit | 173 | 20.408 | 9.938 | 6.64 | 39.728 |
| Tax Revenues | 173 | 25.416 | 3.103 | 14.937 | 28.037 |
| Imports | 173 | 48.169 | 9.123 | 34.832 | 71.53 |
| Real Interest Rate | 173 | 3.185 | 5.362 | −12.114 | 19.782 |
| Real GDP Per Capita | 173 | 4761 | 1333 | 2001 | 6708 |
| Broad Money | 173 | 35.87 | 10.99 | 19.795 | 53.548 |
| Exports | 173 | 51.825 | 8.872 | 31.29 | 75.13 |
| Govt. Consumption | 173 | 27.238 | 3.551 | 19.401 | 36.143 |

*Note: Data from the World Development Indicators, quarterly series from 1980q1 to 2023q1.*

**Table 4.**
*Descriptive statistics—Botswana.*

### 4.2 Test for unit roots

Tests for stationarity of the variables revealed that the cyclical components are integrated to degree zero; thus, they are stationary at levels. Also, tests for model lags selection found models with two lags as most appropriate for the analysis. After that the estimated models were subjected to stability tests, where all the roots of the equations lied within the unit circle, indicating that they were stable. Finally, normality of the error terms were confirmed. Thus, the models were adequately specified as they meet all specification criteria.

### 4.3 Impulse response functions

Starting the analysis with **Figures 1–5**, each of the graphs represents a 1% positive impulse to real interest rate for all the 20 selected countries under consideration.

| Variable | Obs. | Mean | Std. Dev. | Min. | Max. |
|---|---|---|---|---|---|
| Private Consumption | 173 | 86.43 | 4.228 | 78.912 | 95.659 |
| Private Credit | 173 | 33.664 | 10.78 | 13.936 | 54.931 |
| Tax Revenues | 173 | 15.025 | 3.89 | 8.56 | 30.793 |
| Imports | 173 | 27.936 | 5.732 | 19.296 | 43.498 |
| Real Interest Rate | 173 | 3.445 | 3.648 | −8.758 | 17.585 |
| Real GDP Per Capita | 173 | 2649.469 | 750.642 | 1438.006 | 4177.614 |
| Broad Money | 173 | 83.656 | 7.036 | 66.423 | 98.136 |
| Exports | 173 | 20.375 | 5.879 | 10.345 | 33.043 |
| Govt. Consumption | 173 | 11.67 | 2.391 | 6.789 | 17.339 |

*Note: Data from the World Development Indicators, quarterly series from 1980q1 to 2023q1.*

**Table 5.**
*Descriptive statistics—Egypt.*

| Variable | Obs. | Mean | Std. Dev. | Min | Max |
|---|---|---|---|---|---|
| Private Consumption | 173 | 80.173 | 3.556 | 66.307 | 84.437 |
| Private Credit | 173 | 101.162 | 25.175 | 50.085 | 142.422 |
| Tax Revenues | 173 | 22.025 | 2.326 | 17.063 | 26.761 |
| Imports | 173 | 23.495 | 4.585 | 15.366 | 33.72 |
| Real Interest Rate | 173 | 4.172 | 3.278 | −11.009 | 12.691 |
| Real GDP Per Capita | 173 | 5342.987 | 678.553 | 4269.7 | 6263.104 |
| Broad Money | 173 | 56.638 | 10.349 | 41.517 | 73.97 |
| Exports | 173 | 25.469 | 3.508 | 18.955 | 33.538 |
| Govt. Consumption | 173 | 17.416 | 1.578 | 12.771 | 20.575 |

*Note: Data from the World Development Indicators, quarterly series from 1980q1 to 2023q1.*

**Table 6.**
*Descriptive statistics—South Africa.*

**Figure 1** presents the group for the advanced countries in the West. **Figure 2** presents the Latin American countries, **Figure 3** is for East Asia, **Figure 4** represents African countries, and **Figure 5** presents the countries in the Middle East. It should be observed that all the curves in the graphs slope downward from left to right touching the zero line by the end of the sixth quarter. This implies that the impacts of a temporal-induced shock to the real interest rate fizzle out completely within the horizon. With this temporal positive deviation of real interest rate from its natural rate assumed in these selected countries, we are set to examine the responses of credit by financial institutions to the private sector to these impulses.

First, **Figures 6–10** are impulse response functions for the groups. They show the responses of private credit growth to positive impulses to real inerest rates. In particular, **Figure 6** shows that, in the advanced countries, a positive shock to real interest rate leads to credit expansion. However, in terms of magnitude, the credit expansion

| Variable | Obs. | Mean | Std. Dev. | Min. | Max. |
|---|---|---|---|---|---|
| Private Consumption | 173 | 56.898 | 7.729 | 39.58 | 72.946 |
| Private Credit | 173 | 50.336 | 16.424 | 26.245 | 73.718 |
| Tax Revenues | 173 | 3.178 | 1.512 | .825 | 4.982 |
| Imports | 173 | 70.561 | 12.151 | 49.498 | 105.544 |
| Real Interest Rate | 173 | 7.378 | 6.585 | −14.146 | 31.899 |
| Real GDP Per Capita | 173 | 20,848 | 2187.329 | 16,136 | 24,734 |
| Broad Money | 173 | 67.43 | 12.948 | 28.419 | 85.812 |
| Exports | 173 | 82.93 | 11.648 | 56.817 | 115.324 |
| Govt. Consumption | 173 | 16.964 | 2.825 | 11.293 | 23.939 |

*Note: Data from the World Development Indicators, quarterly series from 1980q1 to 2023q1.*

**Table 7.**
*Descriptive statistics—Bahrain.*

| Variable | Obs. | Mean | Std. Dev. | Min. | Max. |
|---|---|---|---|---|---|
| Private Consumption | 173 | 66.393 | 10.689 | 50.902 | 90.109 |
| Private Credit | 173 | 34.047 | 13.961 | 15.177 | 60.297 |
| Tax Revenues | 173 | 5.789 | 1.278 | 3.694 | 10.158 |
| Imports | 173 | 20.786 | 4.786 | 8.727 | 30.37 |
| Real Interest Rate | 173 | −3.51 | 5.335 | −18.845 | 13.985 |
| Real GDP Per Capita | 173 | 4389.004 | 786.291 | 2986.998 | 5739.944 |
| Broad Money | 173 | 54.473 | 15.79 | 35.237 | 91.461 |
| Exports | 173 | 20.008 | 6.604 | 3.732 | 31.116 |
| Govt. Consumption | 173 | 13.553 | 2.456 | 9.477 | 21.451 |

*Note: Data from the World Development Indicators, quarterly series from 1980q1 to 2023q1*

**Table 8.**
*Descriptive statistics—Iran.*

in the US is most substantial to about 2% above its trend. In the remaining countries the UK, Canada, and Sweden, the credit response is less than 1% above the trend. Canada shows the least response among the four countries.

Also, in the Latin America, a positive deviation of real interest rate from its natural rate leads to credit expansion in all the four selected countries—Bolivia, Chile, Mexico, and Peru—as shown in **Figure** 7. Specifically, in Bolivia, after the initial rise in the first quarter, credit seems to fall below its inintial level before the shock. These findings are consistent with the postulate of the Austrian Real Business Cycle Theory, which states that a deviation of real interest rate from its natural rate leads to credit expansion. However, in Canada and the UK, there seems to be some initial drop in credit in the first quarter before picking up to a peak by the second qurter. However, in the East Asia, Africa, and the Middle East, a positive 1% deviation of

| Variable | Obs. | Mean | Std. Dev. | Min | Max |
|---|---|---|---|---|---|
| Private Consumption | 173 | 99.405 | 6.627 | 85.191 | 115.543 |
| Private Credit | 173 | 69.564 | 10.157 | 46.497 | 91.769 |
| Tax Revenue | 173 | 18.422 | 2.694 | 14.608 | 24.69 |
| Imports | 173 | 70.472 | 13.658 | 42.05 | 98.543 |
| Real Interest Rate | 173 | 5.159 | 4.184 | −11.808 | 12.747 |
| Real GDP Per Capita | 173 | 4089.31 | 504.745 | 3214.38 | 4981.998 |
| Broad Money | 173 | 112.496 | 14.33 | 81.709 | 138.877 |
| Exports | 173 | 44.095 | 7.825 | 24.227 | 59.835 |
| Govt. Consumption | 173 | 22.031 | 3.92 | 15.841 | 31.506 |

*Note: Data from the World Development Indicators, quarterly series from 1980q1 to 2023q1.*

**Table 9.**
*Descriptive statistics—Jordan.*

| Variable | Obs. | Mean | Std. Dev. | Min. | Max. |
|---|---|---|---|---|---|
| Private Consumption | 173 | 85.242 | 5.423 | 72.943 | 92.742 |
| Private Credit | 173 | 42.563 | 18.305 | 12.826 | 80.168 |
| Tax Revenues | 173 | 12.971 | 3.865 | 7.095 | 16.965 |
| Imports | 173 | 29.626 | 4.737 | 22.285 | 41.971 |
| Real Interest Rate | 173 | 17.766 | 13.17 | −3.217 | 44.408 |
| Real GDP Per Capita | 173 | 2246.107 | 523.681 | 1603.297 | 3242.949 |
| Broad Money | 173 | 56.282 | 28.714 | 10.736 | 121.501 |
| Exports | 173 | 27.605 | 8.627 | 16.881 | 47.166 |
| Govt. Consumption | 173 | 14.402 | 2.503 | 9.028 | 19.739 |

*Note: Data from the World Development Indicators, quarterly series from 1980q1 to 2023q1.*

**Table 10.**
*Descriptive statistics—Bolivia.*

real interest rate from its natural rates rather leads to credit contraction as depicted in **Figures 8–10**.

With these mixed results of the impact of a 1% positive shock to real interest rates on private credit growth, I moved on to investigate the effects of credit expansion on output growth. I induced a 1% positive shock on credit to determine its impacts on real GDP per capita, private consumption, imports, and tax revenues in the selected countries. Refer to Figures A1 to A5 in Appendix A for the graphs of impulses to credit growth. **Figures 11–15** present impulse response functions of the impacts of a 1% positive shock to private credit on real GDP per capita.

As shown in **Figure 11**, a 1% positive shock to credit leads to initial fall in real GDP per capita in all the four countries in the West, except in the United States, where an impulse to private credit leads to an increase in per capita GDP above its trend. In terms of magnitudes of the responses, the fall in real GDP per capita below its trend in

| Variable | Obs. | Mean | Std. Dev. | Min | Max |
|---|---|---|---|---|---|
| Private Consumption | 173 | 74.673 | 5.314 | 63.794 | 90.949 |
| Private Credit | 173 | 99.491 | 16.24 | 73.082 | 124.876 |
| Tax Revenues | 173 | 17.293 | 1.925 | 13.307 | 23.215 |
| Imports | 173 | 29.059 | 3.497 | 21.252 | 39.514 |
| Real Interest Rate | 173 | 5.924 | 4.935 | −3.872 | 21.555 |
| Real GDP Per Capita | 173 | 9165.917 | 3498.994 | 4047.017 | 14247.71 |
| Broad Money | 173 | 60.543 | 22.116 | 26.942 | 93.679 |
| Exports | 173 | 30.822 | 6.032 | 15.543 | 45.13 |
| Govt. Consumption | 173 | 12.368 | 1.758 | 9.666 | 16.026 |

*Note: Data from the World Development Indicators, quarterly series from 1980q1 to 2023q1.*

**Table 11.**
*Descriptive statistics—Chile.*

| Variable | Obs. | Mean | Std. Dev. | Min | Max |
|---|---|---|---|---|---|
| Private Consumption | 173 | 77.815 | 4.017 | 66.412 | 82.562 |
| Private Credit | 173 | 13.822 | 18.406 | −31.63 | 77.546 |
| Tax Revenues | 173 | 10.66 | 1.814 | 7.703 | 13.9 |
| Imports | 173 | 25.355 | 9.807 | 8.981 | 45.687 |
| Real Interest Rate | 173 | 3.482 | 3.878 | −17.249 | 14.857 |
| Real GDP Per Capita | 173 | 9137.363 | 796.882 | 7735.722 | 10343.35 |
| Broad Money | 173 | 28.412 | 6.634 | 11.13 | 43.51 |
| Exports | 173 | 24.968 | 8.607 | 9.862 | 42.761 |
| Govt. Consumption | 173 | 9.885 | 1.297 | 7.665 | 12.199 |

*Note: Data from the World Development Indicators, quarterly series from 1980q1 to 2023q1.*

**Table 12.**
*Descriptive statistics—Mexico.*

the United Kingdom is very substantial, falling to about 30%, and the fall in Sweden is over 20%. The fall in Canada is below 10%. However, in terms of resistance, GDP recovers fully by the end of the second quarter to its initial level before the shock.

Also, in Latin Amrica, a 1% positive shock to credit leads to initial fall in real GDP per capita in three out of all the countries—in Bolivia, Chile, and Peru. However, like the United States, a 1% positive shock to credit leads to increases in real GDP per capita arount the trend in Mexico. In magnitudes, just like the countries in the West, the falls in real GDP in response to the shock to credit are substantial, and they also recover fully by the end of the second quarter. These results are shown in **Figure 12**.

The fall in real GDP per capita due to a 1% shock to credit expansion is corroborated by the findings from Malaysia and China in the East Asisa, from Botswana in Africa, and from Jordan and Lebanon in the Middle East. However, findings from the

| Variable | Obs. | Mean | Std. Dev. | Min | Max |
|---|---|---|---|---|---|
| Private Consumption | 173 | 58.087 | 5.334 | 48.913 | 67.451 |
| Private Credit | 173 | 111.184 | 36.459 | 52.627 | 194.674 |
| Tax Revenues | 173 | 10.655 | 1.501 | 7.291 | 13.147 |
| Imports | 173 | 17.672 | 5.301 | 8.403 | 28.444 |
| Real Interest Rate | 173 | 2.052 | 2.747 | −7.99 | 7.356 |
| Real GDP Per Capita | 173 | 4026.822 | 3561.89 | 430.855 | 12,174 |
| Broad Money | 173 | 132.508 | 56.58 | 36.427 | 227.945 |
| Exports | 173 | 19.819 | 7.044 | 8.337 | 36.035 |
| Govt. Consumption | 173 | 14.893 | 1.197 | 12.498 | 17.13 |

*Note: Data from the World Development Indicators, quarterly series from 1980q1 to 2023q1.*

**Table 13.**
*Descriptive statistics—China.*

| Variable | Obs. | Mean | Std. Dev. | Min | Max |
|---|---|---|---|---|---|
| Private Consumption | 173 | 62.997 | 5.708 | 51.33 | 73.974 |
| Private Credit | 173 | 109.02 | 23.939 | 49.909 | 158.505 |
| Tax Revenues | 173 | 16.084 | 2.721 | 10.885 | 20.199 |
| Imports | 173 | 72.997 | 15.348 | 49.025 | 100.597 |
| Real Interest Rate | 173 | 4.444 | 3.707 | −3.903 | 22.957 |
| Real GDP Per Capita | 173 | 6828.185 | 2534.283 | 3159.743 | 11691.36 |
| Broad Money | 173 | 120.63 | 16.873 | 64.377 | 140.762 |
| Exports | 173 | 81.966 | 20.663 | 50.873 | 121.311 |
| Govt. Consumption | 173 | 13.075 | 1.835 | 9.769 | 18.321 |

*Note: Data from the World Development Indicators, quarterly series from 1980q1 to 2023q1.*

**Table 14.**
*Descriptive statistics—Malaysia.*

Philippines and Singapore in East Asia, from Egypt, Mauritius, and South Africa in Africa, and from Bahrain and Iran in the Middle East suggest that a 1% positive shock to private sector credit leads to an increase in real GDP per capita around its long run trajectory. Thus, findings on the impact of credit expansion on income produce mixed results. In 11 out of the 20 cuntries, whilst credit expansion leads to an initial fall in real GDP per capita arount its long run trend, only recovering by the second quarter, it leads to an increase in real GDP per capita in the remaining nine countries.

The fall in the real GDP in respose to the shock to credit may be due to the self-correctcing process in the market according to the postulates of the ABCT. This fact may well be explained by the Moral Hazard and adverse select model, where deviations from the equilibrium real interest rate affects the optimal level of credit rationing by opening avenues for the moral hazards and adverse selections. This fact is also

| Variable | Obs. | Mean | Std. Dev. | Min | Max |
|---|---|---|---|---|---|
| Private Consumption | 173 | 50.573 | 5.256 | 37.709 | 60.148 |
| Private Credit | 173 | 98.885 | 17.76 | 68.907 | 133.342 |
| Tax Revenues | 173 | 14.251 | 1.852 | 11.577 | 18.916 |
| Imports | 173 | 165.14 | 16.995 | 136.94 | 208.931 |
| Real Interest Rate | 173 | 4.486 | 1.938 | −3.249 | 9.726 |
| Real GDP Per Capita | 173 | 38013.305 | 16121.483 | 13953.89 | 67948.89 |
| Broad Money | 173 | 104.114 | 24.315 | 62.1 | 149.279 |
| Exports | 173 | 183.551 | 18.592 | 148.731 | 228.994 |
| Govt. Consumption | 173 | 10.072 | 1.041 | 8.171 | 13.394 |

*Note: Data from the World Development Indicators, quarterly series from 1980q1 to 2023q1.*

**Table 15.**
*Descriptive statistics—Singapore.*

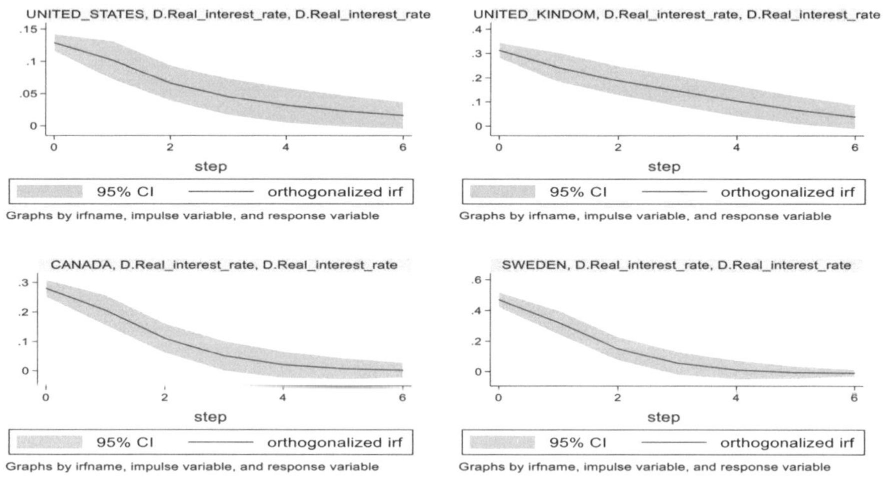


**Figure 1.**
*IRFs of real interest rate to real interest rate—The West. From the top left is for the US followed by the UK and from the bottom left is for Canada and then Sweden. The graphs show behavior of a 1% shock to Real Interest Rate. Observe that all the lines begin from a positive spike at the zero point and fall out completely along the horizontal line by the sixth quarter.*

reinforced by the extent of credit expansion evidenced in the data for advanced countries, which is more than double of the level of GDP in the countries.

The next move was to examine the nexus between credit and savings through the responses of consumption to a 1% shock to credit expanion. If consumtion actually falls in response to a positive shock to credit, it could be concluded that credit expasion is savings-induced. **Figure 16** presents impulse-response graphs for credit and consumption for the selected countries in the West. It shows that consumption indeed falls in response to a positive impulse to credit in the West. This result is

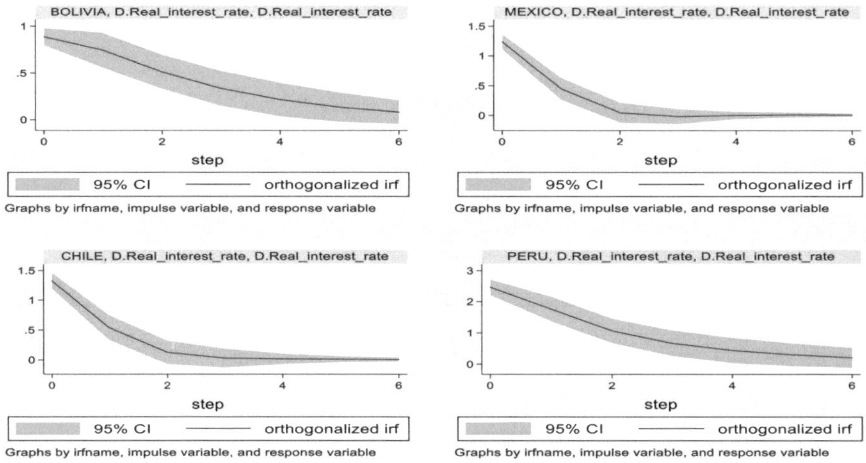


**Figure 2.**
*IRFs of real interest rate to real interest rate—Latin America. From the top left is for Bolivia followed by Mexico and from the bottom left is for Chile and then Peru. The graphs show behavior of a 1% shock to Real Interest Rate. Observe that all the lines begin from a positive spike at the zero point and fall out completely along the horizontal line by the sixth quarter.*

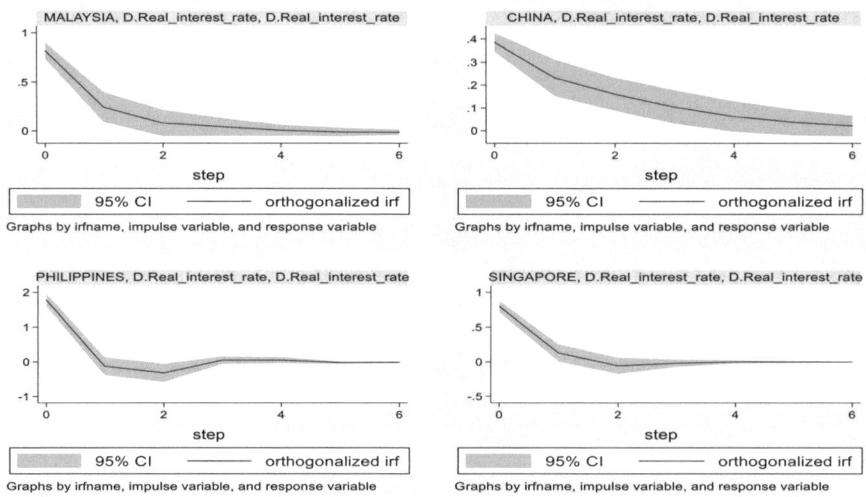


**Figure 3.**
*IRFs of real interest rate to real interest rate—East Asia. From the top left is for Malaysia followed by China and from the bottom left is for Philippines and then Singapore. The graphs show behavior of a 1% shock to Real Interest Rate. Observe that all the lines begin from a positive spike at the zero point and fall out completely along the horizontal line by the sixth quarter.*

confirmed in almost all the countries in under consideration, except in Africa where results from Mauritius and South Africa exhibit increasing consumption in response to credit expansion throughout the horizon. These results are shown by the graphs in **Figures 17-20**, respectively, for Latin America, East Asia, Africa, and the Middle East.

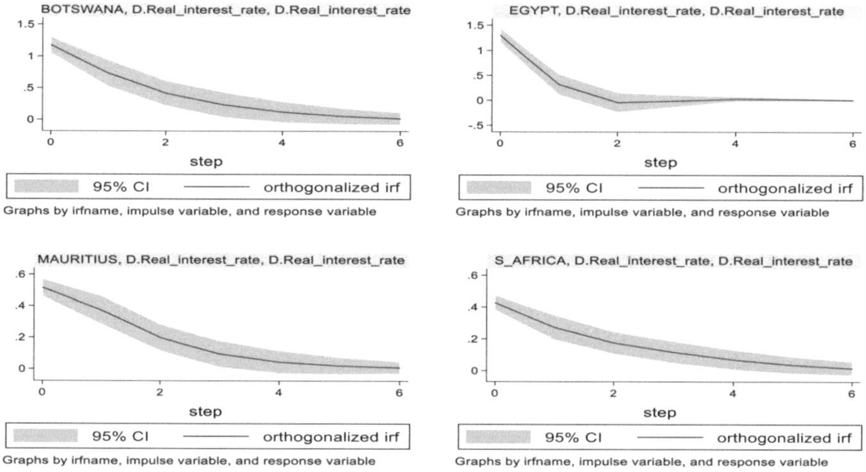


**Figure 4.**
*IRFs of real interest rate to real interest rate—Africa. From top left is for Botswana followed by Egypt and from the bottom left is for Mauritius and then South Africa. The graphs show behavior of a 1% shock to Real Interest Rate. Observe that all the lines begin from a positive spike at the zero point and fall out completely along the horizontal line by the sixth quarter.*

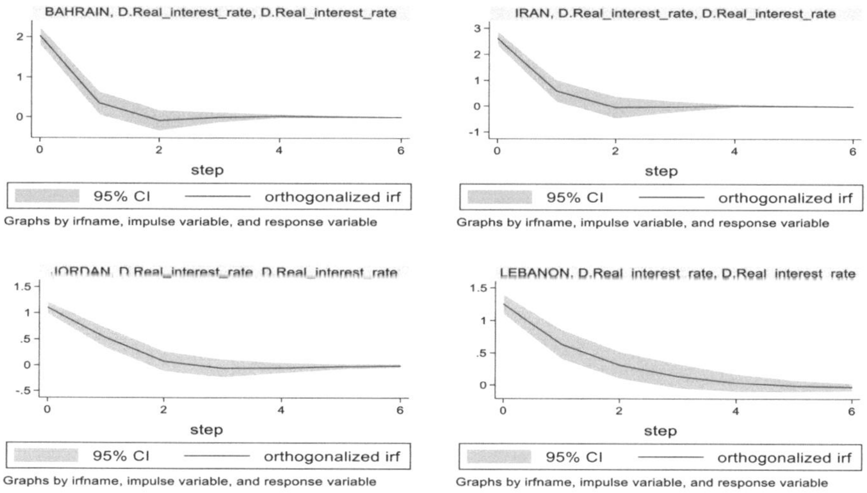


**Figure 5.**
*IRFs of real interest rate to real interest rate—Middle East. From top left is for Bahrain followed by Iran and from the bottom left is for Jordan and then Lebanon. The graphs show behavior of a 1% shock to Real Interest Rate. Observe that all the lines begin from a positive spike at the zero point and fall out completely along the horizontal line by the sixth quarter.*

Consumption, however, recovers fully from the sluck by the second quarter suggesting that consumer thriftness in resoponse to credit expansion is a temporal phenomenon.

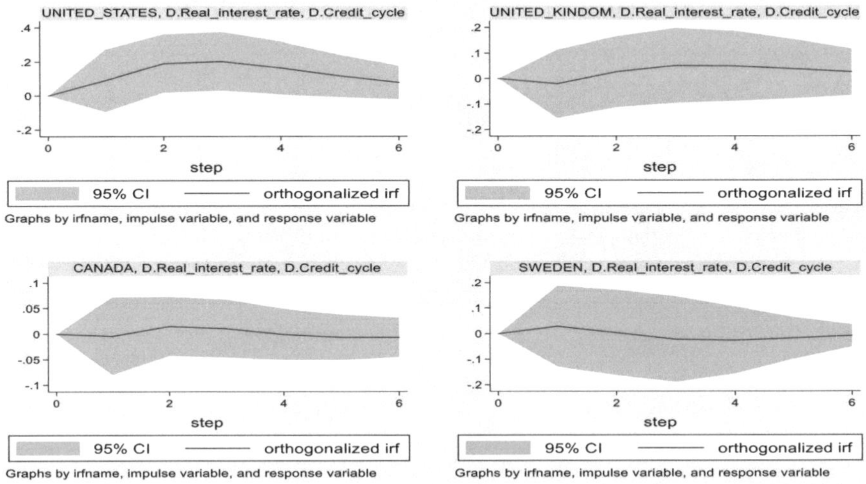


**Figure 6.**
*IRFs of real interest rate to private credit—The West. From top left is for the US followed by the UK and from the bottom left is for Canada and then Sweden. The graphs show responses of credit cycles to a 1% shock to Real Interest Rate. All begin from the zero line. The US and Sweden continue with a positive course to a peak before fizzling out. The UK followed a negative course to the first quarter before it rises to a peak and fizzle out. Canada starts with a delayed positive response.*

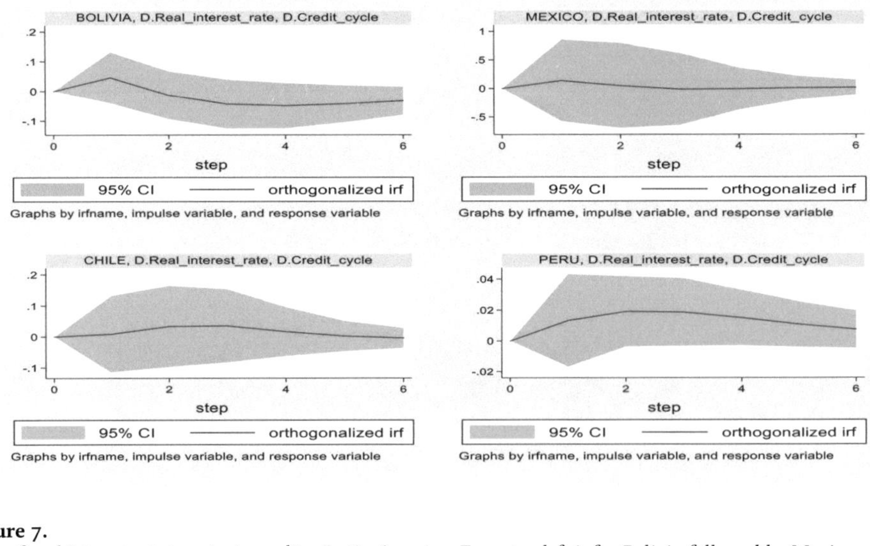


**Figure 7.**
*IRFs of real interest rate to private credit—Latin America. From top left is for Bolivia followed by Mexico and from the bottom left is for Chile and then Peru. The graphs show responses of credit cycles to a 1% shock to Real Interest Rate. All begin from the zero line and follow a positive course along the horizontal axis to a peak before fizzling out. Bolivia and Mexico attain their peaks in the first quarter but Chile and Peru had a persistent rise up to 3rd quarters.*

Finally, the study also examined the responses of import values to credit exapansion with the view to ascertaining the extent to which private credit expansion is used in support for imports in these countries. **Figure 21** presents impulse respnse

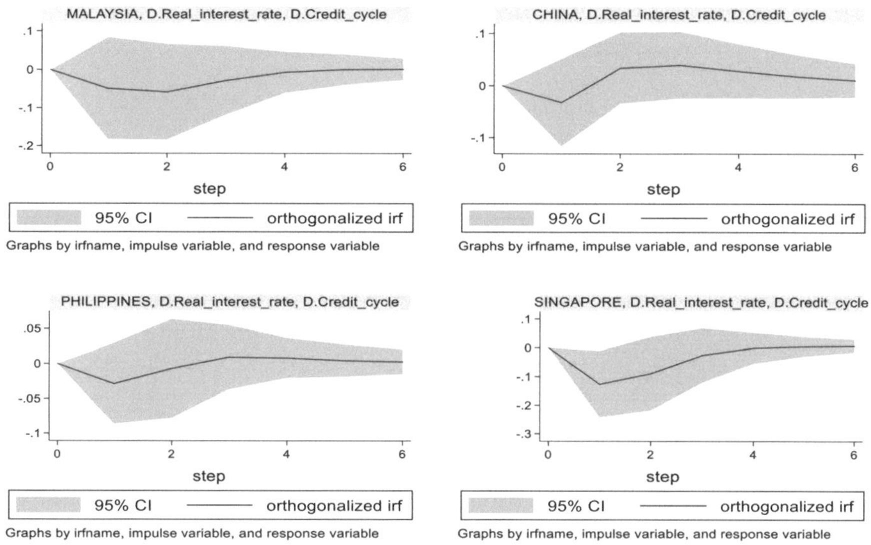


**Figure 8.**
*IRFs of real interest rate to private credit—East Asia. From top left is for Malaysia followed by China and from the bottom left is for Philippines and then Singapore. The graphs show responses of credit cycles to a 1% shock to Real Interest Rate. All begin from the zero line and follow a negative trajectory to a minimum before recovering back to the zero line by the 3rd quarters.*

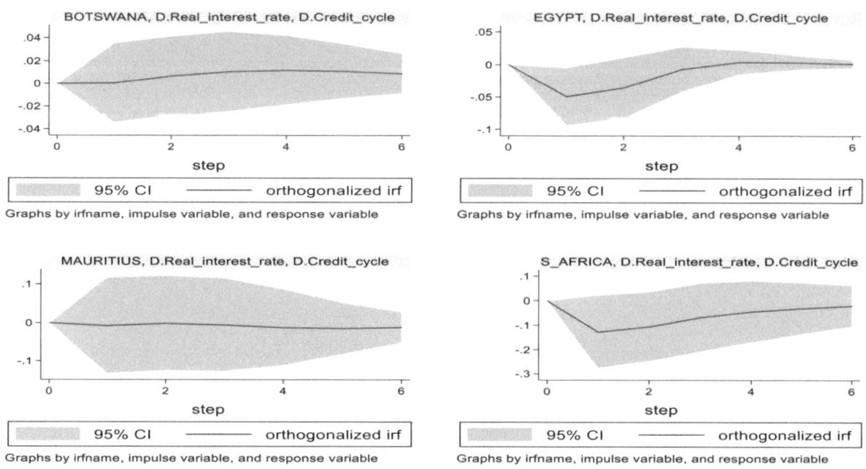


**Figure 9.**
*IRFs of real interest rate to private credit—Africa. From top left is for Botswana followed by Egypt and from the bottom left is for Mauritius and then South Africa. The graphs show responses of credit cycles to a 1% shock to Real Interest Rate. All begin from the zero line with a mixed course. Egypt and South Africa continue with a negative course to a minimum by the end of the 1st quarter before recovering. Botswana had a delayed response with mild positive course but Mauritius barely traces the zero line.*

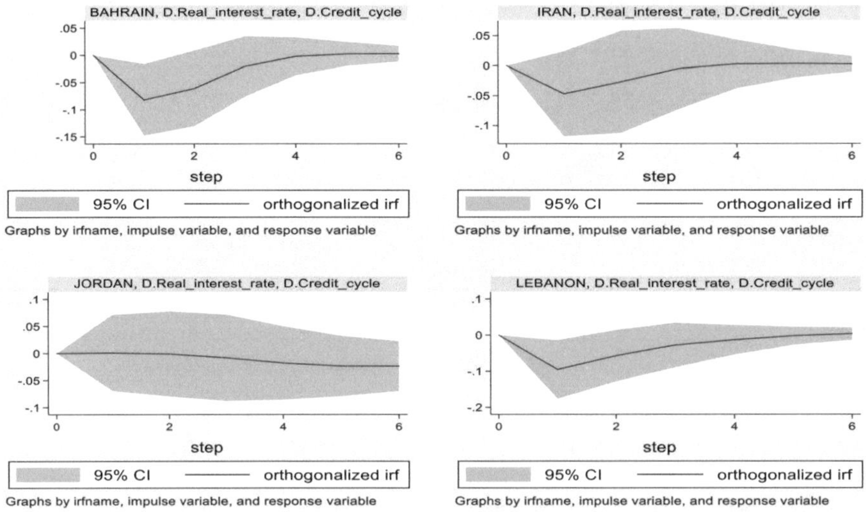


**Figure 10.**
*IRFs of real interest rate to private credit—Middle East. From top left is for Bahrain followed by Iran and from the bottom left is for Jordan and then Lebanon. The graphs show responses of credit cycles to a 1% shock to Real Interest Rate. All begin from the zero line. However, whilst Bahrain, Iran and Lebanon followed a negative trajectory before recovering after the 1st quarter, Jordan barely traces the zero line.*

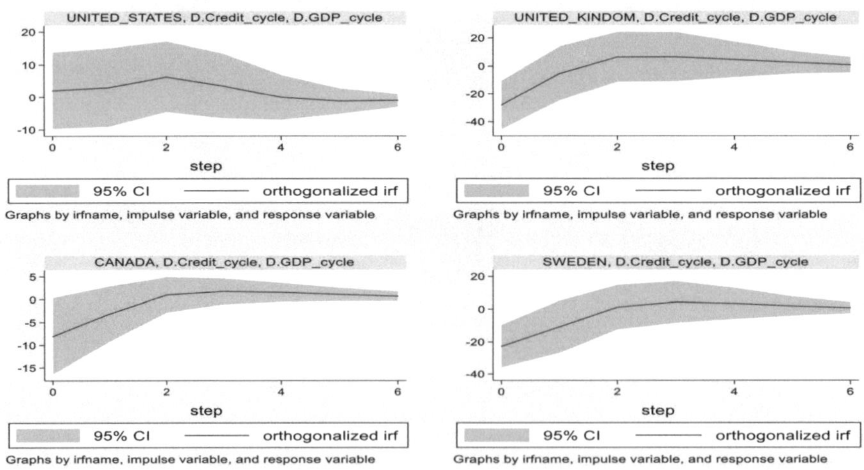


**Figure 11.**
*IRFs of private credit to real GDP per capita—The West. From top left is for the US followed by the UK and from the bottom left is for Canada and then Sweden. The graphs show responses of cycles of Real GDP to a 1% shock to private credit. Observe that apart from the US which starts with a positive spike above the zero line on the vertical axis, all the rest start with a substantial negative spike rising to recover fully to the zero line along the horizontal axis by the 2nd quarters.*

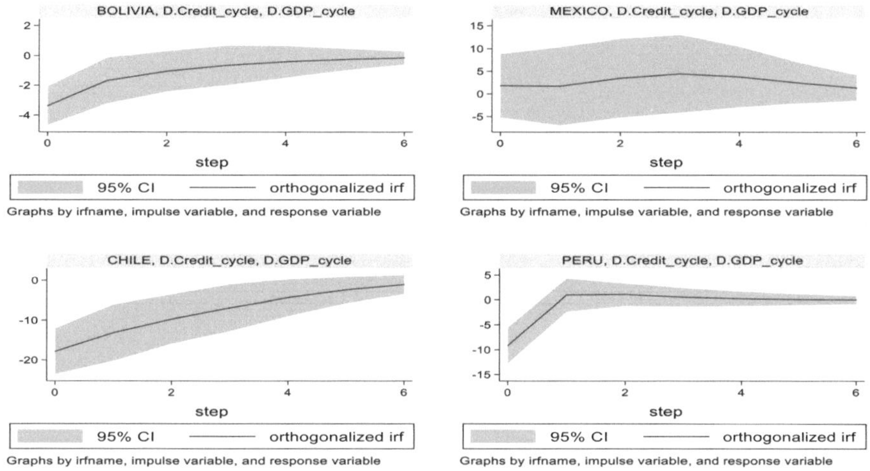


**Figure 12.**
*IRFs of private credit to real GDP per capita—Latin America. From top left is for Bolivia followed by Mexico and from the bottom left is for Chile and then Peru. The graphs show responses of cycles of Real GDP to a 1% shock to private credit. Observe that apart from Mexico which starts with a positive spike above the zero line on the vertical axis, all the rest start with a substantial negative spike rising to recover fully to the zero line along the horizontal axis.*

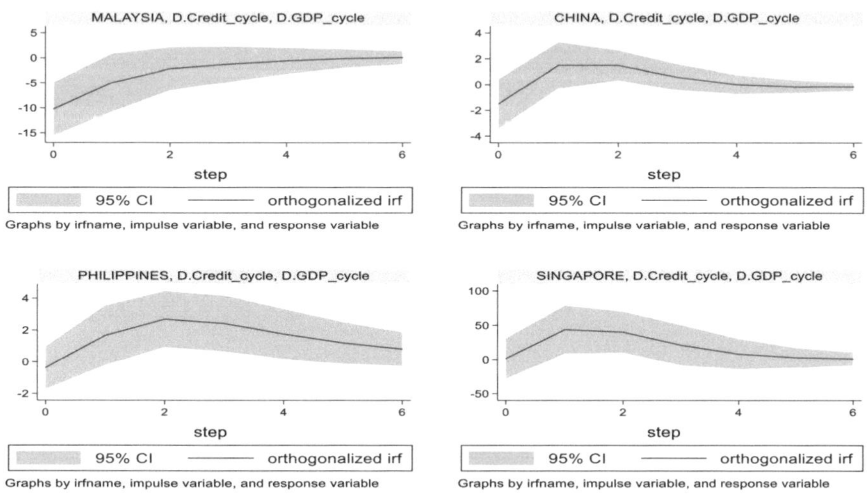


**Figure 13.**
*IRFs of private credit to real GDP per capita—East Asia. From top left is for Malaysia followed by China and from the bottom left is for Philippines and then Singapore. The graphs show responses of cycles of Real GDP to a 1% shock to private credit. Observe that whilst Malaysia and China start with a negative spike, Philippines and Singapore start from zero rising to a peak before falling back to zero by the 5th quarters.*

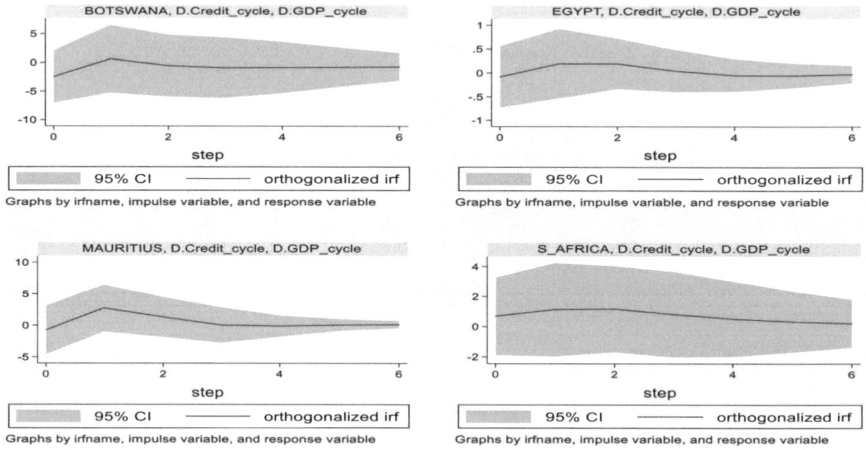


**Figure 14.**
*IRFs of private credit to real GDP per capita—Africa. From top left is for Botswana followed by Egypt and from the bottom left is for Mauritius and then South Africa. The graphs show responses of cycles of Real GDP to a 1% shock to private credit. Observe that apart from Botswana which starts a little below the zero line in a positive direction, Egypt and Mauritius start almost on the zero line in the positive direction but South Africa starts with a spike above the zero line.*

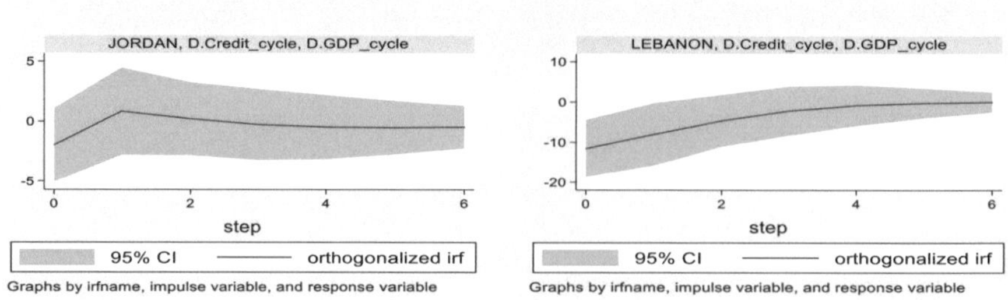


**Figure 15.**
*IRFs of private credit to real GDP per capita—Middle East. From top left is for Bahrain followed by Iran and from the bottom left is for Jordan and then Lebanon. The graphs show responses of cycles of Real GDP to a 1% shock to private credit. Observe that Bahrain starts from zero in the positive direction; Iran starts with a positive spike substantial above the zero line, Jordan starts with a mild negative spike in the positive direction, and Lebanon starts with a substantial negative spike only to recover to the zero line by the 4th quarters.*

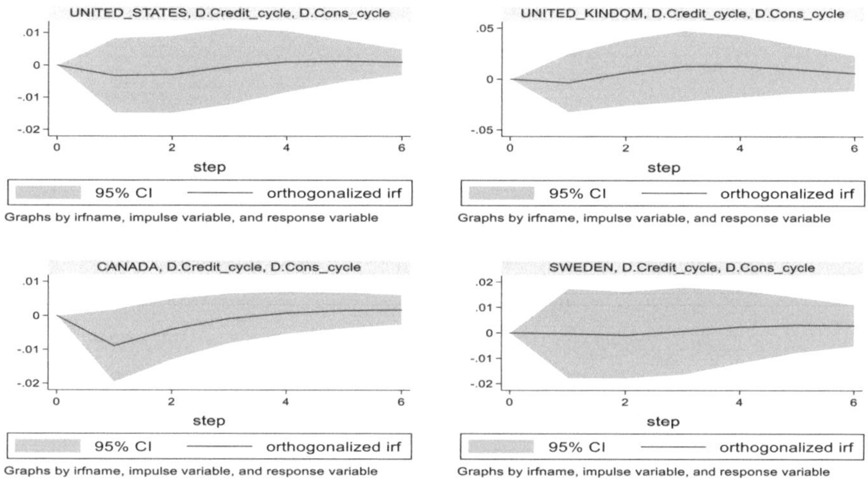


**Figure 16.**
*IRFs of private credit to private consumption—The West. From top left is for the US followed by the UK and from the bottom left is for Canada and then Sweden. The graphs show responses of private consumptions cycles to a 1% shock to private credit. Observe that all start from the zero line in the negative direction to a minimum after the 1st quarter before recovering but Sweden almost traces the zero line.*

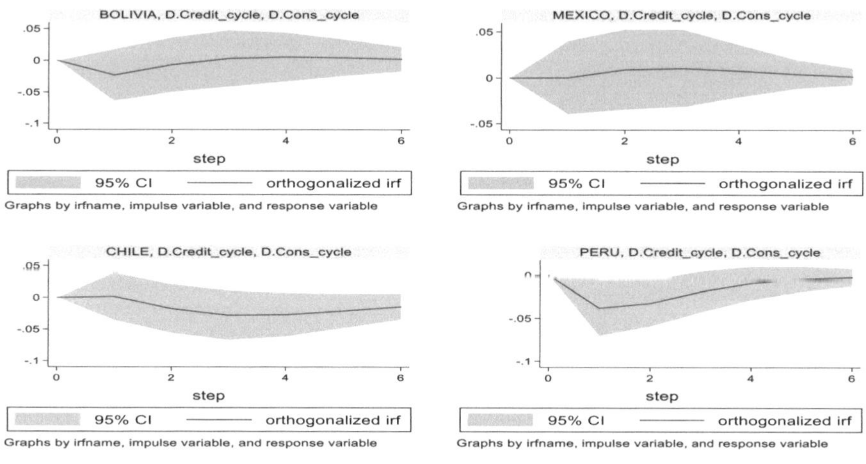


**Figure 17.**
*IRFs of private credit to private consumption—Latin America. From top left is for Bolivia followed by Mexico and from the bottom left is for Chile and then Peru. The graphs show responses of private consumptions cycles to a 1% shock to private credit. Observe that they all start from zero, but Bolivia, Chile and Peru take to the negative direction before recovering, Mexico moves in the positive direction with a delay.*

graphs for responses of imports to a 1% positive impulse to private sector credit from the countries in the West. The graphs show that except for the United States, import values increase to a maximum of about 2% in response to a positive shock to credit. This outcome is corroborated by the results in Latin America, in Africa, and some

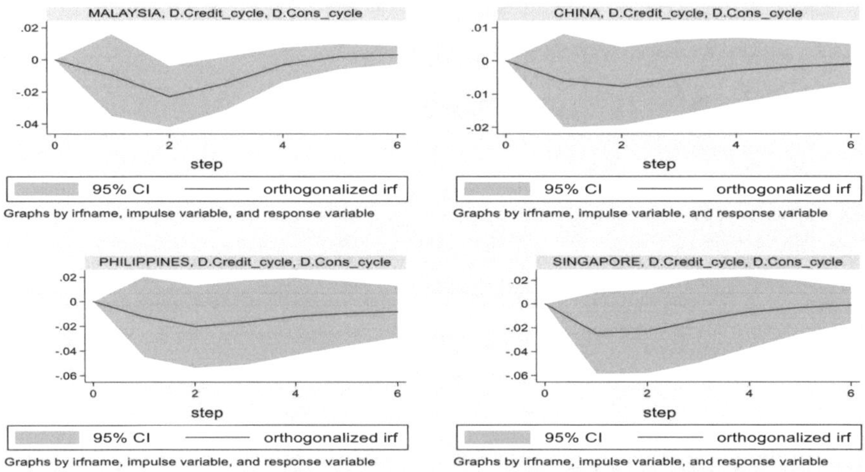


**Figure 18.**
*IRFs of private credit to private consumption—East Asia. From top left is for Malaysia followed by China and from the bottom left is for Philippines and then Singapore. The graphs show responses of private consumptions cycles to a 1% shock to private credit. Observe that they all start from zero moving in the negative to a minimum before recovering back to zero by the 4th quarters.*

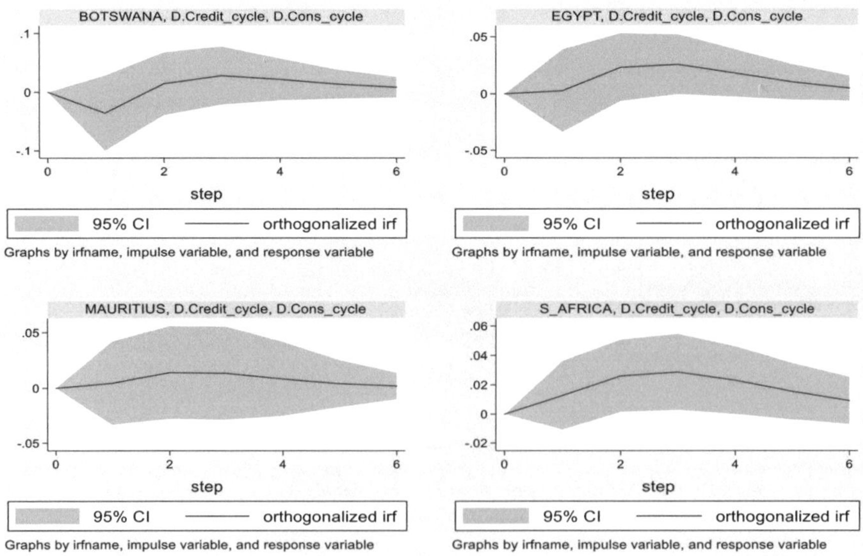


**Figure 19.**
*IRFs of RFs of private credit to private consumption—Africa. From top left is for Botswana followed by Egypt and from the bottom left is for Mauritius and then South Africa. The graphs show responses of private consumptions cycles to a 1% shock to private credit. Observe that apart from Botswana which moves in the negative direction from zero, the rest move in the positive directions from zero.*

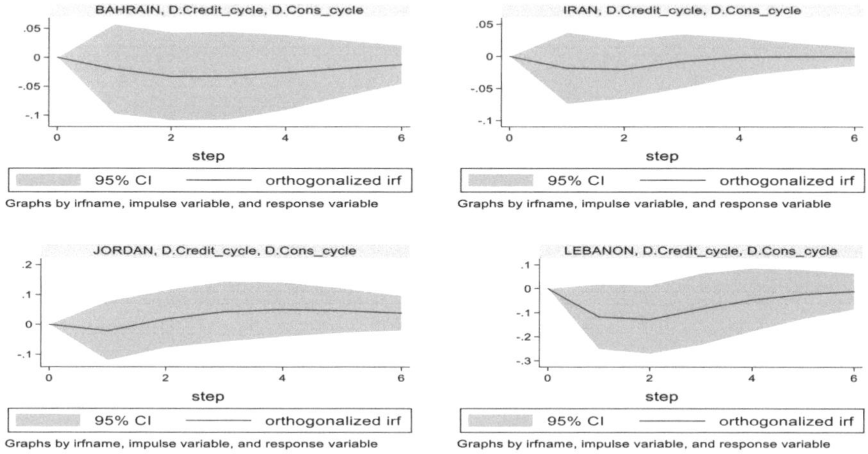


**Figure 20.**
*IRFs of private credit to private consumption—Middle East. From top left is for Bahrain followed by Iran and from the bottom left is for Jordan and then Lebanon. The graphs show responses of private consumptions cycles to a 1% shock to private credit. Observe that they all start from zero, moving in the negative direction before recovering in varying degrees to zero.*

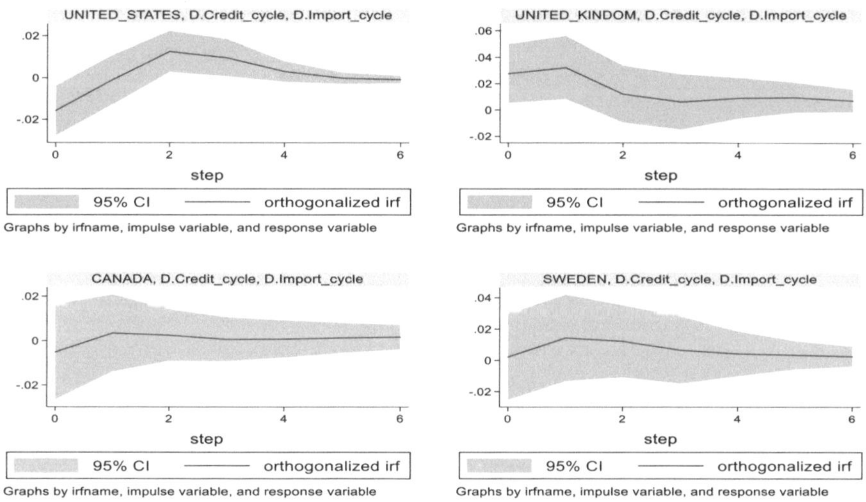


**Figure 21.**
*IRFs of private credit to imports—The West. From top left is for the US followed by the UK and from the bottom left is for Canada and then Sweden. The graphs show responses of import cycles to a 1% shock to private credit. Observe that they all move in the positive directions however, the US and Canada start with a negative spikes in varying magnitudes.*

countries in the East Asia. However, in the United States, values of imports initially fall by more than 1% in response to a credit expansion before recovering to a peak of about 1.5% by the second quarter (**Figure 22**).

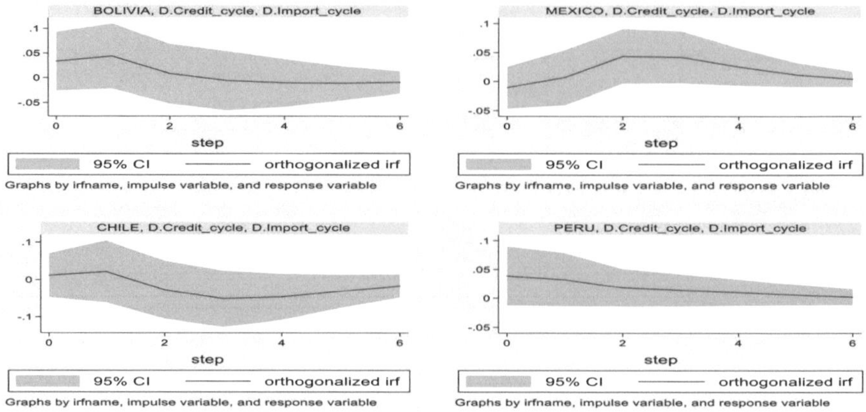


**Figure 22.**
*IRFs of private credit to imports—LatinAmerica. From top left is for Bolivia followed by Mexico and from the bottom left is for Chile and then Peru. The graphs show responses of import cycles to a 1% shock to private credit. Observe that they all start with a positive spike from zero except Mexico that starts below the zero line.*

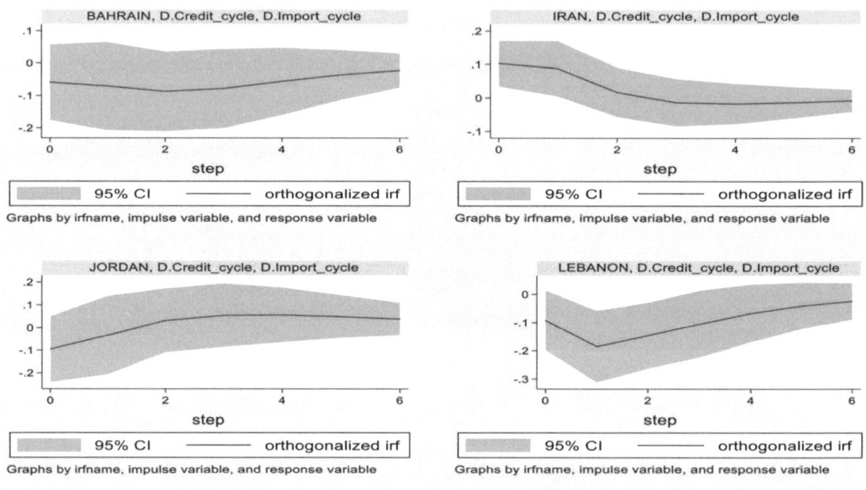


**Figure 23.**
*IRFs of private credit to imports—Middle East. From top left is for Bahrain followed by Iran and from the bottom left is for Jordan and then Lebanon. The graphs show responses of import cycles to a 1% shock to private credit. Except Iran that starts with a positive spike, all start with a negative spike.*

The result for the United States is corroborated by the results from the Middle East countries, in **Figure 23**, where import values fall in response to credit expansion. The only exception from the region is Iran which exhibits postive import values from the onset of the shock to credit. Also, Malaysia and Singapore in the East Asia in **Figure 24** and South Africa in **Figure 25** show negative import values at the onset of the credit shock before recovering to positive trajectory by the second quarter.

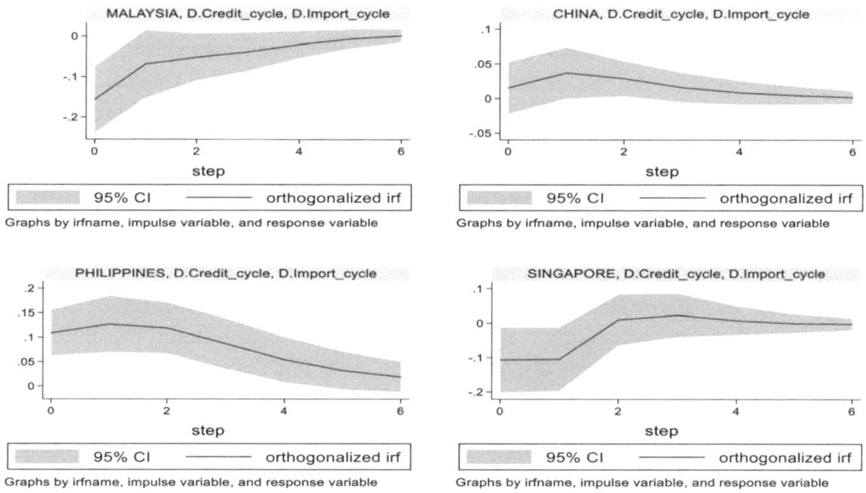


**Figure 24.**
*IRFs of private credit to imports—East Asia. From top left is for Malaysia followed by China and from the bottom left is for Philippines and then Singapore. The graphs show responses of import cycles to a 1% shock to private credit. Malaysia and Singapore starts with a negative spike and China and Philippines start with a positive spike.*

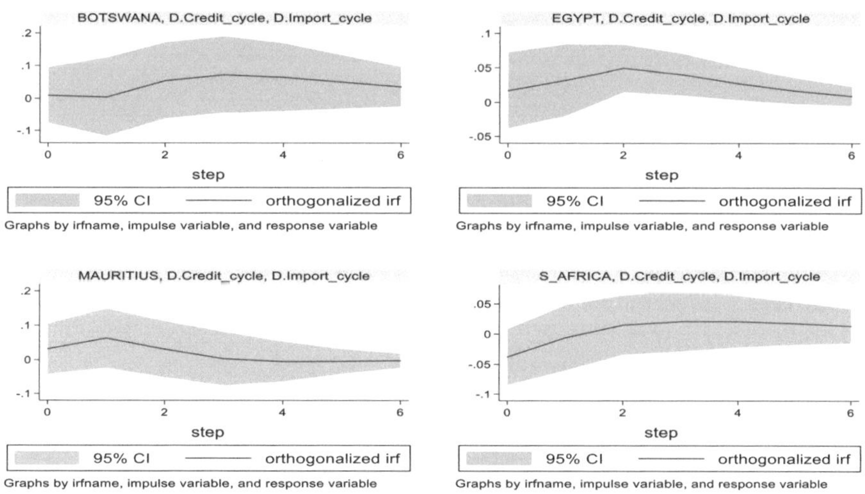


**Figure 25.**
*IRFs of private credit to imports—Africa. From top left is for Botswana followed by Egypt and from the bottom left is for Mauritius and then South Africa. The graphs show responses of import cycles to a 1% shock to private credit. All of them start with a positive trajectory except South Africa which starts with a negative spike.*

## 4.4 Limitations of the study

There are problems of empirical analysis with the postulates of the ABCT. The ABCT puts emphasis on the microeconomic structure of production over time, so it is susceptible to aggregation problem [57]. It envisions different equilibra for a given variable in different markets, with the implication that empirical analysis of the ABCT should explore less aggregated macroeconomic data. Thus, when observing empirically, the ABCT is aware of many exogenous variables that may confound the theorized relationship because the empirical field is not a contrived setting. For example, the natural interest rate is the equilibrium rate for demand for loanable funds which may exist in different markets for different parties in a given economy. The bank's rate may diverge from the natural rate as a result of credit expantion.

Therefore, first, there is a problem in defining the natural rate of interest for empirical purposes. This study uses the real interest rate, so the outcome that "credit expansion and contraction are indeed induced by deviations of real interest rate fron trends" should be analyzed within this limitation. Also, the finding that "whilst this causal relationship (between real intererst rate and credit) is positive in the West and Latin America, it is negative in East Asia, Africa, and Middle East could be as a result of exogenous confounding factors that are not included in this model.

Second, the finding of this study "in 11 out of the 20 cuntries, whilst credit expansion leads to an initial fall in real GDP per capita arount its long run trend, only recovering by the second quarter, it leads to increase in real GDP per capita in the the remaining 9 countries" does not confirm nor negate the ABCT. This may be again be due to confounding exogenous factors not captured in this model because the empirical setting is not a contrived field.

Third, the finding that "private consumption actually falls below the trend level in response to a positive shoc to credit, suggesting that credit expansion may be savings – induced" does not confirm nor negate the ABCT and may be attributed to the same empirical challenges aluded to above. Therefore, findings of this study should be analyzed within the above limitations.

## 5. Concluding remarks

In the nutshell, this study examined the postulates of the Austrian theory of business cycle in some selected advanced and emerging economies. Using quarterly data from 1980q1 to 2023q1, it estimated the SVAR-X model based on the Stochastic Keynesian Open Macroeconomic framework for 20 selected countries and found a mixed result in support of the ATBC. Outcomes of the study indicate that, first, credit expansion is indeed induced by deviations of real interest rates from the trend. However, whilst this causal relationship is positive in the West and the Latin America, it is negative in East Asia, Africa, and the Middle East. In particular, a 1% positive shock to real interest rate leads to private credit expansion in the West and Latin America. It however leads to credit contractions in the East Asia, Africa, and the Middle East. The real causes of this mixed responnse in terms of direction are yet to be ascertained, but it could be attributable to regional characteristics.

Second, findings on the impact of credit expansion on real GDP per capita produced a mixed results. In 11 out of the 20 cuntries, whilst credit expansion leads to an initial fall in real GDP per capita arount its long run trend, only recovering by the second quarter, it leads to an increase in real GDP per capita in the the remaining nine countries. Also, on the dynamics of private consumption, the results indicate that private consumption falls in response to a positive shock to credit. This suggests that savings rises in the course of credit expansion; thus, credit expansion may be savings-induced. A further research into the sources of credit expansion, either interest rate-induced or savings-induced, would be interesting and might explain why real GDP per capita responds differently to credit expansion in different regions.

Third, the results further indicate that, in most of the countries under study, values of imports tend to increase in response to credit expansion. The only exception comes from the United States and the Middle East, where values of imports tend to decrease in response to credit expansion. Thus, credit expansion goes to support imports in most of the countries in the world. Finally, the study sought to determine the impact of credit expansion on tax revenues. It indicates that, generally, credit expansion leads to increases in tax revenues in most of the countries under study. However, for want of space, these results are not displayed here.

## Acknowledgements

I acknowledge the reviewer(s) for the swift response, valuable comments, and suggestions which helped in improving this study.

## Additional information

**JEL code**: B 53, E 12, E 14, G 01

## Declaration of conflicting interests

The author declares no potential conflicts of interest with respect to the research, authorship, and/or publication of this article.

## Author details

Yahuza Abdul Rahman
Department of Economics, Kwame Nkrumah University of Science and Technology, Kumasi, Ghana

*Address all correspondence to: yahuzaar@gmail.com

## References


[1] World Bank. Global Economic Prospects, 2010: Crisis, Finance, and Growth in Developing Countries. 2010. Available from: https://documents.worldbank.org [Accessed: 2 August 2024]

[2] Benetrix AS, O'Rourke KH, Williamson JG. The spread of manufacturing to the periphery, 1870-2007. Journal of Economic Perspectives. 2012;**26**(2):151-170

[3] ILO. Global Employment Trends 2013. Recovering from a Second Jobs Dip/ International Labour Office. Geneva: ILO; 2013. p. 2013

[4] Quecia RG, Stegman MA. Residential mortgage lending in the United States, 1992-2008. Journal of Housing Economics. 2010;**19**(2):151-163

[5] Stiglitz JE. The Price of Inequality. How Today's Divided Society Endangers our Future. W.W. Norton & Company; 2013. Available from: https://wwnorton.com

[6] Diamond DW, Dybvig PH. Bank runs, deposit insurance, and liquidity. Journal of Political Economy. 1983;**91**(3): 401-419

[7] Goldstein I, Pauzner A. Demand-deposit contracts and the probability of Bank runs. The Journal of Finance. 2005; **60**(3):1293-1327

[8] Stiglitz JE, Weiss A. Credit rationing in markets with imperfect information. The American Economic Review. 1981; **71**(3):393-410

[9] Holmstrom B, Tirole J. Financial intermediation, loanable funds and the real sector. The Quarterly Journal of Economics. 1997;**112**(3):663-691

[10] Ivashina V, Scharfstein D. Bank lending during the financial crisis of 2008. Journal of Financial Economics. 2010;**97**(3):319-338

[11] Krugman P. A model of balance of payments crises. Journal of Money, Credit and Banking. 1979;**11**(3):311-325

[12] Flood RP, Garber PM. Collapsing exchange-rate regimes: Some linear examples. Journal of International Economics. 1984;**17**(1–2):1-13

[13] Obstfeld M. Models of currency crises with self-fulfilling features. European Economic Review. 1996;**40**(3–5):1037-1047

[14] Wilm P, Swank J, de Haan J. Determinants of the real impact of banking crises: A review and new evidence. The North American Journal of Economics and Finance. 2018;**43**: 54-70

[15] Caballero RJ, Krishnamurthy A. International and domestic collateral constraints in a model of emerging market crises. Journal of Monetary Economics. 2001;**48**(3):513-548

[16] Schneider M, Tornell A. Balance sheet effects, bailout guarantees and financial crises. The Review of Economic Studies. 2004;**71**(3):883-913

[17] Goldstein I, Razin A. Three branches of theories of financial crises. In: NBER Working Paper Series, WP 18670. Vol. 10(2). Finance: Foundations and Trends (R); 2015. pp. 113-180

[18] Frydman C, Xu C. Banking crises in historical perspective. In: NBER Working Paper Series 31092. National Bureau of Economic Research, Inc.; 2023

[19] Brauning F, Viacheslav. The Historical Effects of Banking Distress on Economic Activity. Federal Reserve Bank of Boston Research Paper Series, Current Policy Perspectives 96216. Federal Reserve Bank of Boston; 2023

[20] Hardy B, Sever C. Financial crises and innovation. In: Bank for International Settlements (BIS) Working Papers No. 846. Bank for International Settlements; 2020

[21] Romer CD, Romer DH. New evidence on the impact of financial crises in advanced countries. In: NBER Working Paper No. 21021. National Bureau of Economic Research, Inc.; 2015

[22] Cerra V, Hakamada M, Lama R. Financial crises, investment slumps and slow recoveries. In: IMF Working Paper WP/21/170. International Monetary Fund. 2021

[23] Von Mises L. The Austrian Theory of the Trade Cycle and Other Essays. Ludwig von Meses: Institute of Auburn University, 1996. 1978. ISBN: 094566218, 9780945466215

[24] Hayek FA. The use of knowledge in society. The American Economic Review. 1945;**35**(4):519-530

[25] Goldstein I. Fundamentals or Panic: Lessons from the Empirical Literature on Financial Crises. (October 26, 2010). 2011. Available from: https://ssrn.com/abstract=1698047 [Accessed: 12 September 2024]

[26] Snowdon B, Vane HR. Modern Macroeconomics, its Origins, Development and Current State. West Street, USA: Edward Elgar Publication Inc. 136; 2005

[27] Quah CH. Austrian Economics in One Lesson. Munipal: Manipal Universal Press; 2021. ISBN 13:9788195399093

[28] Paul P, Pedtke JH. Pedtke. Historical patterns around financial crises. FRBSF Economic Letter, Federal Reserve Bank of San Francisco. 4 May 2020;**2020**(10): 1-5

[29] Paul P. Historical patterns of inequality and productivity around financial crises. Journal of Money, (Credit and Banking, Blackwell Publishing). 2023;**55**(7):1641-1665

[30] Koh WC, Kose MA, Nagle PS, Ohnsorge FL, Sugawara N. Debt and financial crises. In: World Bank Group Policy Research Working Paper 9116. 2020

[31] Diks C, Hommes C, Wang J. Critical slowing down as an early warning signal for financial crises? Empirical Economics. 2019;**57**(4):1201-1228

[32] Ari A. Determinants of Banking Crises in: Elgar Encyclopedia of Financial Crises. 2023. Elgar Online. Available from: https://www.elgaronline.com

[33] Xuan S. The determinants of financial crises. In: 4th International Conference on Global Economy, Finance and Humanities Research (GEFHR 2021). Beijing Institute of Technology, Clausius Scientific Press; 2021

[34] Sufi A, Taylor AM. Financial crises: A survey. In: NBER Working Papers 29155, National Bureau of Economic Research, Inc.; 2021

[35] Greenwood R, Hanson SG, Shleifer A, Sorensen JA. Predictable financial crises. Journal of Finance, American Finance Association. 2022;**77**(2):863-921

[36] Capiro Jr. G, Vincenzo D, Giovanni F, Walter GP. Macro Financial Determinants of the Great Financial Crisis: Implications for Financial Regulations. 2014. Available from:

https://mpra.ub.uni-muenchen.de/26088/ [Accessed: 2 September 2024]

[37] Pereira CP, Joaquim JSR, Vidigal da Silva J. The Main determinants of banking crises in OECD countries. Review of World Economics. 2018;**154**: 203-227

[38] Reinhart CM, Rogoff K. The aftermath of financial crises. American Economic Review. 2009;**99**(2):466-472

[39] Kindleberger CP, Aliber RZ. Manias, Panics, and Crashes: A History of Financial Crises. Basingstoke [u.a.]: Palgrave Macmillan; 2011. ISBN: 978-0-230-36535-3

[40] Johnson S. The quiet coup. The Atlantic. 2010;**305**(4):46-49

[41] Obstfeld M, Rogoff K. Global imbalances and the financial crisis. Journal of International Economics. 2009;**80**(1):1-14

[42] Demirguc-Kunt A, Detragiache E. The determinants of banking crises in developing and developed countries. IMF Staff Papers. 1998;**45**(1): 81-109

[43] Neacsu M, Eugenia IG. Analysing the impact of crises on financial performance: Empirical insights from tourism and transport companies listed on the Bucharest stock exchange (during 2005-2022). Journal of Risk Financial Management. 2024;**17**(2):80

[44] Jalles JT. Financial crises and climate change. Comparative Economic Studies. 2023;**2024**(66):166-190

[45] Bernanke BS, Gertler M, Gilchrist S. The financial accelerator in a quantitative business cycle framework. Handbook of Monetary Economics. 2011;**3**:1345-1371

[46] Blanchard O, Dell'Ariccia G, Mauro P. Rethinking macroeconomic policy. Journal of Money, Credit and Banking. 2010;**42**(1):199-215

[47] Dodd-Frank Act. Public Law 111-203. 2010

[48] G20. Communiqué. Leaders' Summit- Cannes—3-4 November 2011. 2011. Available from: https://www.unodc.org [Accessed: 20 August 2024]

[49] Jemovic M, Marinkovic S. Determinants of financial crises—An early warning system based on panel logit regression. International Journal of Finance & Economics. 2019;**26**(1): 103-117

[50] McCallum BT, Nelson E. An optimizing IS-LM specification for monetary policy and business cycle analysis. Journal of Money, Credit and Banking. 1999;**31**(3, Part 1):296-316

[51] Warsono R, Wamiliana W, Usman. Vector autoregression with exogenous variables model and its application in modelling and forecasting energy data: Case study of PTBA and HRUM energy. International Journal of Energy Economics and Policy. 2019;**9**(2): 390-398

[52] Ocampo S, Rodriguez N. An introductory review of a structural VAR-X estimation and application. Revista Colombiana de Estadistica. Dec 2012;**35**(3):479-508

[53] Rothenberg TJ. Identification in parametric models. Econometrica. 1971; **39**(3):577-591

[54] Pagan A, Robertson J. Structural models of the liquidity effect. Review of Economics and Statistics. 1998;**80**(2): 202-217

[55] Fry R, Pagan A. Sign restrictions in structural vector autoregressions: A critical review. Journal of Economic Literature. 2011;**49**(4):938-960

[56] Ruhio-Ramirez JF, Waggoner DF, Zha T. Structural vector autoregression: Theory of identification and algorithms for inference. The Review of Economic Studies. 2009;**2009**(77):665-696

[57] Garrison RW. The theory of the Austrian business cycle. In: Glasner D, editor. Business Cycle and Depression. Vol. 1997. New York: Garland Publishing Co; 1997. pp. 23-27

Chapter 4

# Perspective Chapter: An Overview of Time Series Decomposition and Its Applications

*Pankaj Das and Samir Barman*


## Abstract

Time series (TS) data is ubiquitous in various fields such as finance, economics, meteorology, and engineering. The analysis of TS data aims to understand the underlying patterns, make predictions, and inform decision-making. One of the fundamental techniques in TS analysis is decomposition, which breaks down a TS into its constituent components: trend, seasonality, and residuals. This chapter provides a comprehensive overview of TS decomposition, breaking down data into trend, seasonality, and residuals. It covers classical methods, such as additive and multiplicative models, advanced techniques like X-12-ARIMA and Seasonal-Trend decomposition using LOESS (STL), and recent approaches, including machine learning (ML) based decompositions. Practical applications in agriculture, meteorology, and economics, along with challenges like non-stationarity and nonlinear behavior, are discussed. The chapter offers guidelines for selecting appropriate methods and includes case studies for real-world insights. It is a valuable resource for researchers, data scientists, and professionals analyzing complex TS data.


**Keywords:** decomposition methods, residuals, seasonality, statistical analysis, time series analysis, trend analysis

## 1. Introduction

TS analysis is a fundamental tool in understanding and predicting temporal data, where observations are collected sequentially over time. One of the most critical techniques within this domain is TS decomposition. TS decomposition involves breaking down a complex TS into its underlying components: trend, seasonality, and residuals (or noise). This process provides a clearer understanding of the patterns within the data, enabling more accurate forecasting and analysis [1]. Decomposition is essential for several applications. It enhances the accuracy of predictive models by isolating and understanding each component separately. Additionally, it aids in anomaly detection, where deviations from expected patterns are more easily identified [2]. In various industries, from finance to healthcare, TS decomposition helps identify and interpret trends, optimize resource allocation, and improve decision-making processes. Decomposition techniques help analysts and researchers to gain deeper insights into their data, leading to more informed and effective strategies.



IntechOpen

## 2. What is time series decomposition?

Decomposition is a technique that breaks down complex structures or processes into simpler subcomponents. In the realm of data analysis, it specifically involves separating various factors that influence the behavior of a dataset. TS decomposition is a particular application of this technique, concentrating on TS data. It involves breaking down a TS into several key components to better understand its underlying patterns and behaviors in the data and enhance forecasting accuracy. The primary objective of TS decomposition is to isolate the different factors influencing the data, allowing for more effective modeling and interpretation of the TS.

A TS can be divided into four key components: the trend, seasonal component, cyclic component, and the residual or irregular component.

The trend (T) is a fundamental aspect of TS data, indicating the long-term movement or direction of the data over a specific period. It illustrates whether the data is increasing, decreasing, or remaining stable. Trends can be discerned through graphical representations, line graphs, or statistical techniques like moving averages or regression analysis. There are three trends: upward trend, characterized by an increase over time; downward trend, characterized by a decrease over time; horizontal trend, indicating little to no change, reflecting stability.

The seasonal component (S) highlights regular patterns over fixed intervals (e.g., monthly or quarterly). These patterns manifest consistently due to periodic occurrences such as holidays, climate variations, or business cycles. For instance, retail jacket sales typically rise during the winter season annually, showcasing this cyclical nature of seasonality. Techniques such as seasonal decomposition of TS, seasonal indices, or statistical methods like Fourier analysis and periodograms can help identify seasonal components.

The cyclic component (C) reflects long-term oscillations in the data, often influenced by economic, business, or environmental factors. Unlike seasonality, these cycles vary significantly in duration and do not adhere to fixed periods. They may extend over multiple years and are frequently associated with economic trends. An example would be the fluctuations in business performance during recession or boom periods. Advanced statistical tools, such as regression or spectral analysis, are employed to find these long-term variations and differentiate them from trends and seasonal effects. In many decompositions, the cyclic component is grouped with the trend or considered part of the residuals, depending on the method.

Finally, the residual or noise (R) component represents random fluctuations in the data stemming from unpredictable events, which cannot be accounted for by the trend, seasonality, or cyclic components. These short-term variations may arise from sudden market shifts, natural disasters, or random errors during data collection. The random component is derived by isolating the other components (trend, seasonal, and cyclic) from the data, enabling analysts to pinpoint the remaining random variations.

## 3. Types of time series decompositions

TS decomposition can be approached using different methods, depending on the data's nature and the analysis's specific objectives. The primary types of TS decomposition are [1, 3].

### 3.1 Additive decomposition

In additive decomposition, a TS is assumed to be the sum of its components:

$$Y(t) = T(t) + S(t) + R(t) \tag{1}$$

Trend ($T(t)$): indicates the long-term progression or data direction.

Seasonality ($S(t)$): captures regular, repeating patterns within specific intervals, viz. daily, weekly, or annual cycles.

Residual ($R(t)$): accounts for random noise or irregular variations not explained by trend or seasonality.

Additive decomposition is particularly useful for TS, where the seasonal and irregular fluctuations are consistent over time. This method is often applied in scenarios where the data does not exhibit exponential growth or where the impact of seasonal variations is independent of the overall series level.

### 3.2 Multiplicative decomposition

In multiplicative decomposition, the TS is assumed to be the product of its components:

$$Y(t) = T(t) \times S(t) \times R(t) \tag{2}$$

Trend ($T(t)$): as in additive decomposition, this reflects the underlying direction or pattern.

Seasonality ($S(t)$): here, seasonal variations are proportional to the level of the trend, meaning they increase or decrease in magnitude as the trend changes.

Residual ($R(t)$): represents the random or irregular fluctuations in the data.

Multiplicative decomposition is used when the magnitude of seasonal and irregular variations is related to the trend level. This method is well-suited for TS, where fluctuations increase or decrease proportionally to the trend. For instance, a multiplicative model is more appropriate in economic data such as GDP, where higher GDP levels might coincide with larger seasonal effects.

### 3.3 Log transformation and decomposition

Sometimes, TS data are neither purely additive nor purely multiplicative. In such cases, a log transformation can be applied to convert a multiplicative model into an additive one:

$$\log(Y(t)) = \log(T(t)) + \log(S(t)) + \log(R(t)) \tag{3}$$

In cases where a TS does not fit neatly into either an additive or multiplicative model, a log transformation can be employed. Applying a logarithm to the data transforms a multiplicative series into an additive one, making it easier to decompose and analyze. This approach is instrumental in financial data, such as stock prices or sales figures, where the data might exhibit additive and multiplicative effects. After decomposition on the log-transformed data, the components can be exponentiated to revert to the original scale.

### 3.4 STL decomposition (seasonal and trend decomposition using loess)

STL is a robust and versatile method of decomposing TS into trend, seasonality, and residual components. It is beneficial for handling complex TS with multiple seasonal cycles or irregular patterns.

Seasonal: extracted using LOESS (Locally Estimated Scatterplot Smoothing), which can adapt to changing seasonal patterns.

Trend: also smoothed using LOESS, providing a flexible approach to capturing the long-term movement.

Residual: the remaining component after removing the seasonal and trend effects.

STL decomposition offers a flexible and robust way to break down TS data, particularly when dealing with complex or irregular seasonal patterns. Unlike classical methods, STL does not assume that seasonality and trend are constant over time, making it adaptable to changes in the underlying data structure. STL is particularly effective for analyzing TS with multiple seasonal components, such as daily and yearly cycles in climate data, or for data with nonlinear trends. Customizing the smoothing parameters allows analysts to capture subtle variations in the data, making STL decomposition a powerful tool for both exploratory data analysis and forecasting.

### 3.5 Classical decomposition

Classical decomposition methods are based on simple moving averages to estimate trends and seasonality.

Trend: estimated by smoothing the series using a moving average filter, removing short-term fluctuations.

Seasonality: determined by subtracting the trend from the original series and isolating the seasonal pattern.

Residual: represents the difference between the original series and the combined trend and seasonality components.

Classical decomposition methods are based on moving averages and are among the earliest techniques developed for TS analysis. While simple, they are effective for TS with clear and stable seasonal patterns. In classical decomposition, the trend is typically extracted using a centered moving average, which smooths out short-term fluctuations.

The seasonal pattern is identified by calculating the average of the detrended data for each season. The remaining part, the difference between the original data and the combined trend and seasonal components, is considered the residual. This method is useful for its simplicity and ease of interpretation, making it a good starting point for TS analysis.

### 3.6 X-11 and X-13-ARIMA-SEATS decomposition

These are advanced statistical techniques used mainly for economic and financial TS. They provide detailed seasonal adjustments and are widely used by government agencies for official statistics.

X-11: an earlier method that adjusts for seasonal effects and trading days.

X-13-ARIMA-SEATS: a more advanced approach that integrates ARIMA modeling with the decomposition process to improve forecasting accuracy.

These methods are particularly valuable when dealing with the data's complex seasonal patterns and irregularities. These methods are particularly valuable in official statistics, where accurate seasonal adjustment is crucial for making informed policy decisions and economic analyses.

## 4. Importance of time series decomposition

TS decomposition is a critical technique in TS analysis that plays a fundamental role in understanding, interpreting, and forecasting temporal data. Here are the key reasons why TS decomposition is important [1:3].

### 4.1 Enhanced understanding of data

TS decomposition breaks down a complex TS into its basic components—trend, seasonality, and residuals. This separation provides a clearer picture of the underlying hidden patterns in the data. By differentiating these individual components, analysts can better understand the long-term trend, cyclical patterns, and random variations within the series. This understanding is essential for making informed decisions based on the data.

### 4.2 Improved forecasting accuracy

One of the primary applications of TS decomposition is forecasting. A breakdown of the TS allows for the analysis and forecasting of each component separately. Combining these predictions allows forecasting models to generate more precise and trustworthy forecasts. For instance, understanding seasonal patterns allows for more precise predictions during peak periods, while trend analysis can provide insight into long-term growth or decline.

### 4.3 Facilitating seasonal adjustment

Eliminating seasonal effects from TS data reveals the underlying trend in many fields, especially in economics and finance. This process is known as seasonal adjustment. It plays an important role in accurate analysis and decision-making. For example, unemployment rates often vary seasonally, and decomposing the series helps analysts remove these fluctuations to focus on the true trend.

### 4.4 Detection of anomalies or outliers

Decomposing a TS makes detecting anomalies or outliers in the data easier. Analysts can identify unusual deviations from expected patterns by isolating the residual component, which represents the noise or unexplained variation. This is particularly valuable in fields like finance, where detecting anomalies can signal fraud or errors, or in manufacturing, where it can indicate quality control issues.

### 4.5 Better model selection and validation

Understanding a TS's components helps select the appropriate models for analysis and forecasting. For instance, knowing whether a series has a strong seasonal component might suggest using models like seasonal ARIMA (SARIMA) or exponential smoothing methods. Additionally, decomposition allows for better validation of models by comparing how well they capture each component, leading to more robust and reliable models.

### 4.6 Simplifying complex data

Real-world TS data can be complex, with multiple overlapping patterns. Decomposition simplifies this complexity by breaking the series into manageable components. This simplification not only aids in analysis but also in communicating insights to stakeholders who may not be familiar with advanced statistical methods. Analysts can convey key insights more effectively by presenting the data in terms of trend, seasonality, and residuals.

### 4.7 Guiding business strategy

Understanding the components of a TS can inform strategic decisions for businesses. For example, identifying a strong upward trend might lead to increased investment in capacity, while understanding seasonal patterns can guide marketing and inventory decisions. By decomposing TS data, businesses can align their strategies with the underlying dynamics of their market.

### 4.8 Noise reduction

Decomposition helps in filtering out noise from the TS data. The residual component, which represents the noise, can be isolated and analyzed separately. This noise reduction is particularly important in sensitive applications, such as control systems or real-time monitoring, where noise can obscure important signals.

### 4.9 Supporting multivariate analysis

In cases where multiple TS are being analyzed simultaneously, decomposition can compare trends and seasonal patterns across different series. This is particularly useful in economic analysis, where different indicators may need to be compared, or in marketing, where sales data across different regions or products might be analyzed in parallel.

## 5. Recent developments in time series decompositions

TS decomposition has evolved significantly in recent years with the advancements in computational methods, the availability of big data, and the growing complexity of real-world applications. These developments have introduced new techniques and improved existing methods, making TS decomposition more powerful, flexible, and applicable to a broader range of problems [4]. Here are some of the key recent developments in TS decomposition.

### 5.1 Advanced machine learning techniques

Recent innovations in ML have led to the development of novel decomposition methods that leverage deep learning architectures and advanced algorithms.

For instance, techniques like long short-term memory (LSTM) networks and Convolutional Neural Networks (CNNs) have been adapted to TS decomposition. These can read complex, nonlinear patterns and interactions in TS data that traditional methods might miss. For an example:

Seasonal-Trend decomposition using LSTM (STL-LSTM): This approach combines the power of LSTM networks with traditional STL decomposition, allowing for the modeling of nonlinear trends and seasonality. The LSTM component captures long-term dependencies and nonlinearities, while the STL part handles the decomposition of the TS into TS components, viz. trend, seasonal, and residual.

### 5.2 Bayesian time series decomposition

Bayesian methods have been increasingly applied to TS decomposition. These methods allow for the incorporation of prior knowledge and estimating uncertainty in the decomposition process. For example, Bayesian Structural Time Series (BSTS): This framework uses Bayesian inference to decompose TS into components such as trend, seasonality, and regression effects while also accounting for the uncertainty in each component. BSTS is particularly useful for scenarios where data is sparse or noisy, providing more robust and interpretable decompositions.

### 5.3 State-space models and Kalman filtering

State-space models have seen renewed interest in TS decomposition, particularly with the integration of Kalman filters. These models provide a dynamic and flexible way to model TS data, allowing for real-time decomposition as new data becomes available. For an example:

Dynamic linear models (DLMs): A specific type of state-space model, DLMs allow for the dynamic updating of trend and seasonal components over time. Kalman filtering estimates these components in real time, making this approach particularly useful for applications like financial forecasting, where data arrives continuously.

### 5.4 Empirical mode decomposition (EMD) and variants

Empirical mode decomposition (EMD) has been increasingly used in TS analysis, especially in applications where the data is nonlinear and nonstationary. EMD decomposes a TS into intrinsic mode functions (IMFs) without assuming a specific model structure. For an example:

Ensemble Empirical Mode Decomposition (EEMD): EEMD, an improved version of EMD, solves the issue of mode mixing by adding random noise to the data before breaking it down into its components. This approach is particularly useful in biomedical signal processing and climate science, where data can be highly irregular and complex.

### 5.5 Robust decomposition methods

Robust decomposition methods have gained popularity due to the growing need to handle outliers and noise in TS data. These methods are designed to be less sensitive to anomalies, ensuring that the decomposition process remains stable and reliable despite irregularities. Example:

RobustSTL: An extension of the classical STL (seasonal-trend decomposition using LOESS), RobustSTL is designed to handle outliers and noise more effectively. It achieves this by incorporating robust statistical techniques into the decomposition process, making it suitable for TS with significant noise or irregular fluctuations.

## 5.6 Frequency domain decomposition

Recent developments have also focused on frequency domain approaches to TS decomposition, which involve analyzing the spectral properties of the data. These methods are particularly useful for identifying underlying periodic patterns and separating components in the frequency domain. Example:

Wavelet decomposition: This method decomposes a TS into components at different scales, allowing for the analysis of both high-frequency (short-term) and low-frequency (long-term) patterns. Wavelet decomposition is widely used in fields like finance and engineering, where understanding multi-scale phenomena is crucial.

## 5.7 Tensor decomposition for multivariate time series

Tensor decomposition methods have emerged as powerful tools for scenarios where multiple TS are analyzed simultaneously. Tensor decomposition originates from multilinear algebra (a generalization of matrix decomposition). Tensors, or multidimensional arrays, extend matrices to higher dimensions and can capture complex relationships across multiple factors or modes (e.g., time, space, and variables). Tensor decomposition is a mostly used technique when we collect time series data across multiple variables or dimensions (e.g., time, location, and variable type). Tensor decomposition helps find out important components from high-dimensional data. Tensor decomposition is suitable for capturing patterns, identifying underlying factors, or reducing dimensionality.

These methods extend traditional decomposition techniques to handle multidimensional data, capturing complex relationships across multiple TS. An example is canonical polyadic (CP) decomposition: applied to TS data organized in a tensor format, CP decomposition separates the data into components that capture trends, seasonality, and interactions across different dimensions. This approach is increasingly used in recommendation systems and social network analysis, where multivariate TS data is common. Tensor decompositions can enhance model interpretability, make high-dimensional data more manageable, and improve predictive performance by focusing on the most significant patterns in the data. Tensor decomposition in multivariate time series is widely used in fields such as finance, neuroscience, and sensor networks, where understanding time-dependent relationships across multiple variables is critical.

## 5.8 Seasonal hybrid extreme decomposition (SHED)

Seasonal hybrid extreme decomposition (SHED) is a technique that analyzes complex seasonal patterns and trends in time series data. SHED is a recent approach combining decomposition techniques to handle complex TS data. It is also known as the ensemble hybrid decomposition technique. In short, SHED combines traditional decomposition methods with advanced hybrid approaches to effectively separate a time series into different components: seasonal, trend, and extreme events. The primary goal of SHED is to enhance forecasting accuracy, especially for data that exhibits seasonal variations and sudden, extreme fluctuations (e.g., spikes or dips). The critical components of SHED are seasonal (daily, weekly, or yearly patterns), trend (the long-term progression or general direction of the data), and extreme components (sharp peaks, anomalies, or outliers that do not fit into regular seasonal or trend patterns). The approach integrates wavelet transform, EMD, and other methods to separate a TS into more granular components, enhancing the accuracy of subsequent analysis and forecasting. SHED is applicable in fields requiring both regular pattern recognition and robustness to anomalies, ultimately enhancing forecasting and decision-making in dynamic environments like energy demand forecasting, financial market analysis, etc.

## 6. Application of time series decompositions in agriculture

In agriculture, it has several applications. Agricultural commodity prices are highly volatile, mostly nonlinear and nonstationary, due to several factors like uncertainty in production, demand-supply imbalances, government policy interventions, and others. These make the forecasting of agricultural commodity prices more challenging to the investigators. Among the different methods available in the literature, decomposition-based methods are more important and popular due to their "divide and conquer" principle. The evolutions and uses of decomposition methods mainly depend on several data properties, like seasonal patterns, heterogeneity, linearity, and the stationarity of data.

The STL, a versatile and robust decomposition-based method, is popularly used for agricultural price forecasting [4–7] and for forecasting the commodity prices. First, deseasonalized the series by extracting the seasonal component calculated by STL decomposition. Second, point forecasting of price values is done by constructing statistical models, like ARIMA, ETS, and others, on a seasonally adjusted series. Finally, the integration of seasonal components to get the final forecast value [6]. However, the main challenges for forecasting through simple STL decomposition are mainly due to assumptions of linear trend, additive seasonality, choice of the seasonal cycle length and smoothing parameters, and proper choice of model for forecasting different components.

Several hybrid methods combining STL with ML techniques have been developed and used for forecasting to deal with such problems. For instance, recent developments in STL with ELM (extreme learning machines) are used for seasonal agricultural commodities, particularly for vegetable market price forecasting [5]. Complete detail can be found in a study by Jaiswal et al. [7], where the seasonal TS has been first decomposed into a trend, seasonal, and remainder components. Secondly, each component has been individually forecasted using ELM. Finally, the forecasts of individual components (trend, seasonal, and reminder) were added to produce the final estimates for the original series. A schematic diagram is presented in **Figure 1**. The outputs of the empirical results are best compared to traditional methods for forecasting.

High-frequency TS data often exhibit nonlinear and nonstationary behavior with fluctuations. Methods based on EMD and its variants (hybrid models) are widely used to address these characteristics in agricultural data [8–12]. Analytical R packages for

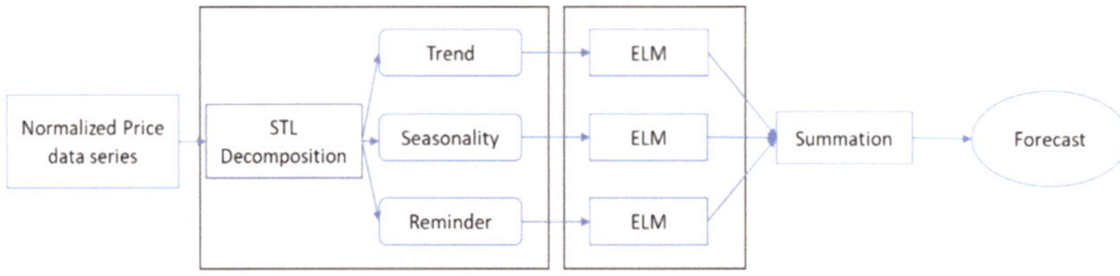


**Figure 1.**
*STL-ELM method for agricultural commodity price forecasting.*

EMD variants, such as EMD-ANN and EMD-SVR, are available in the literature. In a study by Das et al. [10], they applied EMD-ANN and EMD-SVR to forecast the monthly price index of vegetables. Initially, the EMD technique decomposes the original nonlinear and nonstationary data into a limited number of independent sub-series, including k intrinsic mode functions (IMFs) and a residual. These IMFs and the residual are then modeled and predicted using ANN or SVR. The forecasted values of the IMFs and the residual are summed to produce an ensemble forecast for the original series. When comparing the performance of EMD-based hybrid models with standard models like ANN and SVR, the results indicated that while ANN and SVR are commonly used for nonlinear data, they struggled with the nonstationary nature of the dataset. In contrast, the hybrid models EMD-ANN and EMD-SVR performed better due to their ability to capture both nonlinear and nonstationary patterns, making them a viable alternative for forecasting volatile agricultural price series (**Figure 2**).

Recently, variational modal decomposition (VMD) and its variants have been widely used to address the challenges of highly volatile, nonlinear, and nonstationary agricultural commodity price data [13]. Zhang et al. [14] applied VMD variants to forecast volatile agricultural commodities such as lean hog prices, soybean meal prices, and soybean oil prices in China. They achieved promising results. **Figure 3**

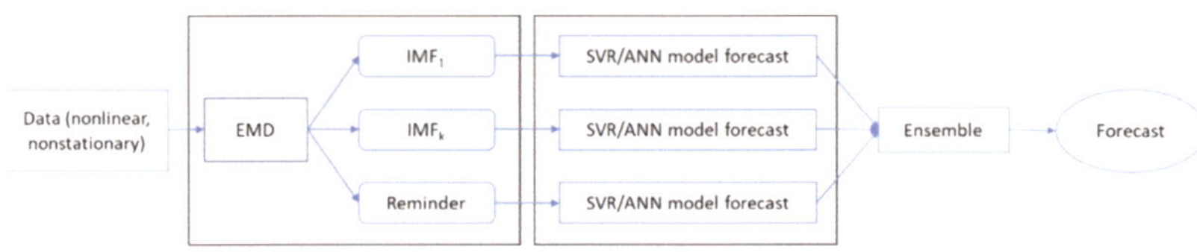


**Figure 2.**
*Hybrid model EMD-SVR/EMD-ANN for agricultural price forecasting.*

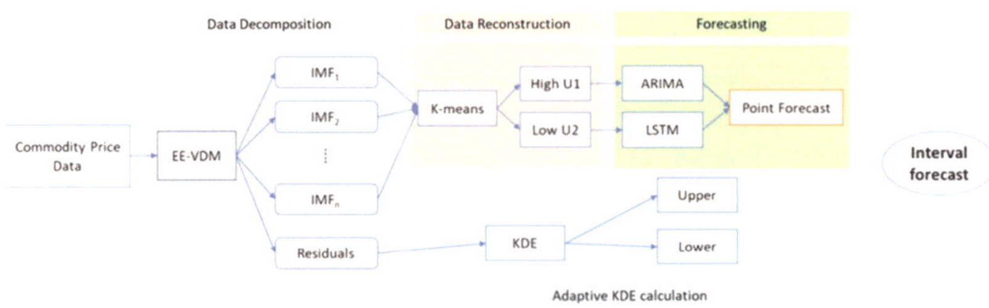


**Figure 3.**
*Hybrid model VMD-ARIMA-LSTM for lean hog prices, soybean meal prices, and soybean oil prices in China.*

provides a schematic representation of this hybrid forecasting approach. This study compares a hybrid model's effectiveness (VMD-ARIMA-LSTM) to seven other forecasting models. These include single models (RF, LSTM, BP), models using EMD decomposition (EMD-ARIMA-SVM, EMD-BP), and models using VMD decomposition (VMD-LSTM, VMD-ARIMA-BP). The results showed that VMD-based models, particularly VMD-ARIMA-LSTM, significantly outperform EMD-based models due to VMD's ability to resolve modal confusion and end effects, enhancing decomposition performance. In forecasting experiments on three datasets, VMD-ARIMA-LSTM showed improvements in RMSE by 5.46%, 14.68%, and 10.28% for 1-step, 3-step, and 6-step ahead predictions, respectively, and similarly improved MAPE results. It has been concluded that decomposing and reconstructing the original sequence and selecting an appropriate forecasting model based on sequence complexity leads to better predictions for highly volatile agricultural commodities. This highlights the advantages of the decomposition-integration strategy. A Diebold-Mariano (DM) test further confirmed the superiority of VMD-ARIMA-LSTM. However, due to its lower complexity, no significant improvement has been observed for lean hog price data in certain steps. Overall, the decomposition-based models are practical and applicable to agricultural price forecasting.

## 7. Applications of time series decompositions in other sectors

The TS decomposition methods are widely applied in various fields beyond agriculture, like Environmental Science, Meteorology, and Climate Science [3, 15–18], Economics and Finance [1, 19], Marketing and Sales, Engineering, and Manufacturing [20–22], Healthcare and Epidemiology [23, 24], and many other fields, to understand forecast, and control time-dependent data.

The uses of TS decomposition in environmental science are to forecast key variables like temperature, rainfall, pollution levels, or other meteorological parameters. These parameters are the key indicators of climate change, and the TS decompositions are used for accurate forecasting. In recent times, hybrid methods have been more popularly used, rather than the traditional TS decomposition methods, like the DL-MEMD model for hourly global horizontal irradiance forecasting [25], Hybrid DL-MVMD model for estimating daily solar radiation [26], Hybrid gray-STL with Gaussian process for CO2 emissions forecasting [18]. Decomposition techniques like STL and its variants are commonly used to forecast temporal features of meteorological data. A study by Liu and Zhang [27] used a decomposition-based prediction model combining STL and gated recurrent units (STL-GRU) for forecasting the surface temperature of various regions in China. This method analyzed these regions' patterns and long-term trends in temperature data.

The decomposition techniques are also popularly used for precipitation forecasting, especially when the chances of erroneously mixing future information into the training data occur. Jiao and He [28] effectively employed the VMD-BiLSTM-based stepwise decomposed ensemble method to overcome the mixing problem for practical forecasting of reciprocation. A study by Parviz and Ghorbanpour [29] improved hybrid models by integrating linear and nonlinear approaches focusing on signal decomposition for complex nonlinear components. It evaluates the effectiveness of combining SARIMA with EMD and maximal overlap discrete wavelet transform (MODWT) utilizing monthly rainfall data from Iran. The process involved using

SARIMA to model the data, decomposing its error series into IMFs with EMD, and then forecasting these IMFs using support vector regression.

TS decomposition is widely used to forecast economic indicators such as inflation, GDP, and unemployment rates. Analysts can make more precise predictions about future economic conditions by separating the trend (long-term growth), seasonal effects (like holiday impacts), and random variations. For instance, tools like ARIMA and seasonal decomposition of time series (STL) filter out the seasonal component and capture core economic trends. In stock market forecasting, decomposition methods help identify the underlying price trend, seasonal behavior (such as quarterly earnings reports), and residual noise. For example, EMD has been used in currency exchange forecasting to identify local trends and reduce the noise before applying predictive models like least squares support vector regression [30]. A study by Sohrabbeig et al. [31] extended beyond single-seasonal patterns, incorporating methods like Multiple Seasonal-Trend Decomposition using Loess (MSTL). MSTL can handle complex datasets with multiple seasonal cycles, such as daily and weekly patterns in financial TS. This is particularly useful for high-frequency trading, where market behavior follows distinct patterns over different time horizons. The multiresolution analysis through wavelets is increasingly popular for nonstationary TS, as is stock prices and volatility [30, 32]. By decomposing the series into different frequency components, this method helps capture both short-term fluctuations and long-term trends, enabling robust modeling of dynamic financial systems.

TS decomposition is a versatile technique with applications across multiple fields. Breaking down complex data into components provides insights into long-term trends, cyclical variations, and irregularities, supporting better decision-making and planning in various industries.

## 8. Packages/software of TS decomposition

R/RStudio, Python, and MATLAB are software that is primarily used for TS decomposition. There are packages in the software for applying a specific TS decomposition technique (**Table 1**).

| Method | R package |
|---|---|
| VMD | VMDecomp |
| EMD | EMD |
| EEMD | EMD |
| Wavelet | wavelets |
| Fourier decomposition | swdft |
| Tensor decomposition | rTensor |
| Seasonal and Trend decomposition | stl |
| Kalman filter | Rcpp |
| Bayesian time series decomposition | Rbeast |

**Table 1.**
*Some decomposition techniques and required R packages for their application.*

## 9. Conclusions

In conclusion, TS decomposition is a critical technique for understanding and analyzing complex data across various fields, including finance, economics, meteorology, and engineering. This chapter has outlined both classical and advanced decomposition methods, such as additive, multiplicative, STL, and newer ML approaches, highlighting their practical applications in diverse domains like agriculture and economics. Additionally, the chapter addresses key challenges, such as non-stationarity and nonlinearities, offering a thorough guide for selecting appropriate methods and understanding real-world TS data through case studies. In the end, this chapter provides a complete overview of TS decomposition and its practical applications for forecasting to inform data-driven decision-making.

## Acknowledgements

The authors thank the editor and the anonymous reviewers for their comments and suggestions on improving the manuscript.

## Conflict of interest

The authors declare no conflict of interest.

## Author details

Pankaj Das[1*] and Samir Barman[2]

1 ICAR-Indian Agricultural Statistics Research Institute, New Delhi, India

2 ICAR-Indian Grassland and Fodder Research Institute, Jhansi, India

*Address all correspondence to: pankaj.iasri@gmail.com

## References


[1] Box GE, Jenkins GM, Reinsel GC, Ljung GM. Time Series Analysis: Forecasting and Control. 5th ed. New Jersey: Wiley; 2015

[2] Shumway RH, Stoffer DS. Time Series Analysis and Its Applications With R Examples. 4th ed. Switzerland: Springer; 2017

[3] Chatfield C. The Analysis of Time Series: Theory and Practice. London: Chapman and Hall; 2013

[4] Cleveland RB, Cleveland WS, McRae JE, Terpenning IJ. STL: A seasonal-trend decomposition procedure based on loess. Journal of Official Statistics. 1990;**1**:3-33

[5] Xiong T, Li C, Bao Y. Seasonal forecasting of agricultural commodity price using a hybrid STL and ELM method: Evidence from the vegetable market in China. Neurocomputing. 2018;**275**:2831-2844

[6] Ouyang Z, Ravier P, Jabloun M. STL decomposition of time series can benefit forecasting done by statistical methods but not by machine learning ones. Engineering Proceedings. 2021;**5**(1):42

[7] Jaiswal R, Choudhary K, Kumar RR. STL-ELM: A decomposition-based hybrid model for price forecasting of agricultural commodities. National Academy Science Letters. 2022;**45**(6):477-480

[8] Das P. Study on machine learning techniques based hybrid model for forecasting in agriculture [thesis]. New Delhi: Graduate School, Indian Agricultural Research Institute; 2019

[9] Das P, Jha GK, Lama A, Parsad R, Mishra D. Empirical mode decomposition based support vector regression for agricultural Price forecasting. Indian Journal of Extension Education. 2020;**56**(2):7-12

[10] Das P, Jha GK, Lama A. Empirical mode decomposition based hybrid machine learning models for agricultural commodity price forecasting. Statistics and Applications. 2023;**21**(1):99-112

[11] Choudhary K, Jha GK, Jaiswal R, Kumar RR. Decomposition-based long short-term memory model for price forecasting of agricultural commodities. Iran Journal of Computer Science. 2024;**2**:1-3

[12] Ghose B, Pandit P, Mazumder C, Sinha K, Sahu PK. Comparative study of EMD based modelling techniques for improved agricultural price forecasting. Journal of the Indian Society of Agricultural Statistics;**78**(1):53-62

[13] Das P, Jha GK, Lama A. Variational mode decomposition based machine learning models optimized with genetic algorithm for price forecasting. Journal of the Indian Society of Agricultural Statistics. 2022;**76**(3):141-150

[14] Zhang D, Zhang X, Hu H, Zhang B, Ling L. A hybrid model for point and interval forecasting of agricultural price based on the decomposition-ensemble and KDE. Soft Computing. 2024;**28**(17):10153-10176

[15] Chatfield C, Yar M. Holt-winters forecasting: Some practical issues. Journal of the Royal Statistical Society Series D: The Statistician. 1988;**37**(2):129-140

[16] Zhang X, Zwiers FW, Li G. Monte Carlo experiments on the detection of trends in extreme values. Journal of Climate. 2004;**17**(10):1945-1952

[17] Moreno-Carbonell S, Sanchez-Ubeda EF, Muñoz A. Time series decomposition of the daily outdoor air temperature in Europe for long-term energy forecasting in the context of climate change. Energies. 2020;**13**(7):1569

[18] Yuan H, Ma X, Ma M, Ma J. Hybrid framework combining grey system model with Gaussian process and STL for CO2 emissions forecasting in developed countries. Applied Energy. 2024;**360**:122824

[19] Souropanis I, Vivian A. Forecasting realized volatility with wavelet decomposition. Journal of Empirical Finance. 2023;**74**:101432

[20] Montgomery DC. Introduction to Statistical Quality Control. United Kingdom: John Wiley & Sons; 2013

[21] Hyndman RJ. Forecasting: Principles and Practice. USA: OTexts; 2018

[22] Qiu Y, He Z, Zhang W, Yin X, Ni C. MSGCN-ISTL: A multi-scaled self-attention-enhanced graph convolutional network with improved STL decomposition for probabilistic load forecasting. Expert Systems with Applications. 2024;**238**:121737

[23] Nsoesie EO, Brownstein JS, Ramakrishnan N, Marathe MV. A systematic review of studies on forecasting the dynamics of influenza outbreaks. Influenza and Other Respiratory Viruses. 2014;**8**(3):309-316

[24] Baharom M, Ahmad N, Hod R, Abdul Manaf MR. Dengue early warning system as outbreak prediction tool: A systematic review. Risk Management and Healthcare Policy. 2022;**15**:871-886

[25] Gupta P, Singh R. Combining a deep learning model with multivariate empirical mode decomposition for hourly global horizontal irradiance forecasting. Renewable Energy. 2023;**206**:908-927

[26] Band SS, Qasem SN, Ameri R, Pai HT, Gupta BB, Mehdizadeh S, et al. Deep learning hybrid models with multivariate variational mode decomposition for estimating daily solar radiation. Alexandria Engineering Journal. 2024;**105**:613-625

[27] Liu X, Zhang Q. Combining seasonal and trend decomposition using LOESS with a gated recurrent unit for climate time series forecasting. Vol. 12. IEEE Access; 2024. pp. 85275-85290

[28] Jiao X, He Z. A novel coupled rainfall prediction model based on stepwise decomposition technique. Scientific Reports. 2024;**14**(1):10853

[29] Parviz L, Ghorbanpour M. A hybrid EMD and MODWT models for monthly precipitation forecasting using an innovative error decomposition method. Stochastic Environmental Research and Risk Assessment. 2024;**14**:1-24

[30] Rabbouch H, Rabbouch B, Saâdaoui F. Multiresolution data analytics for financial time series using MATLAB. In: Data Analytics for Management, Banking and Finance: Theories and Application. Switzerland: Springer Nature; 2023. pp. 113-134

[31] Sohrabbeig A, Ardakanian O, Musilek P. Decompose and conquer: Time series forecasting with multiseasonal trend decomposition using loess. Forecasting. 2023;**5**(4):684-696

[32] Berger T. Forecasting based on decomposed financial return series: A wavelet analysis. Journal of Forecasting. 2016;**35**(5):419-433

Chapter 5

# A Decade of Machine Learning Applied to Management and Economics: Learning through a Case Study of Corporate Resilience

*Jacques Bughin*


## Abstract

Econometrics has traditionally focused on statistical regression-type methods for analysing economic data, but is increasingly integrating techniques from data science, using sophisticated machine learning (ML) models, both to improve predictive accuracy and to develop non-parametric inference, for example with new feature importance techniques such as Shapley values. While development has been rapid and exciting, significant efforts are still required to achieve full convergence between traditional and new data methods. This research examines a decade of progress in ML, focusing on its application to predicting and explaining the drivers of business resilience during crises, such as the COVID-19 pandemic. It is shown that ML uncovers significant non-linearities in the way capabilities, such as innovation, ecosystem play or agility, have been able to stimulate resilience. Empirical results show that gradient boosting and random forests outperform traditional econometric models in predictive accuracy by margins of over 10%, while maintaining interpretability through feature importance metrics. This study highlights the strengths and trade-offs of ML methods and provides practical insights into their computational underpinnings. By comparing traditional econometric methods with ML techniques, we illustrate the promise and challenges of convergence between these fields.


**Keywords:** econometrics, machine learning, Shapley values, permutation, accuracy, resilience

## 1. Introduction

Big data, with their unique ability to discover subtle population patterns and heterogeneities not possible with small-scale data, have been powering many business domains for several years—enabling Moderna's discovery of an RNA-based vaccine for COVID-19 in weeks [1], improving Netflix personalisation for two thirds of video consumption [2], or supporting responses to user queries for OpenAI's ChatGPT model trained on billions of tokens [3, 4].

In parallel, big data and their associated classification methods, such as machine learning (ML) and deep learning (DL), have also gained traction in many scientific fields, including more recently in economics. These methods are particularly recognised for their enhanced ability to model complex, non-linear systems and to make more accurate predictions than traditional econometric techniques. In addition, although still emerging, inference tools from ML are refining traditional econometrics and addressing the need for better model explainability and interpretability [5–7].

The current study provides a summary of the development of supervised machine learning methods as applied to the field of economics. It starts with a chronology of their developments, then discusses the types of methods, together with examples of applications and related findings. While ML models have been designed to excel in predictive accuracy in the context of complex data generation processes, a corollary of these classification methods is that they tend to be less interpretable than linear models, while it is often crucial to uncover the mechanisms that these models capture, especially when it comes to fairness, welfare or policy validation.

We then discuss so-called "explainable" machine learning methods, such as permutations, attribution importance, or Shapley values, and comment on how the need for such methods has evolved, including a new literature on (causal) inference, both in terms of model specifications ("feature importance") and how those features marginally affect model output.

Adding to an emerging literature [8, 9], we finally illustrate the relevance of ML methods in the context of predicting firm resilience. We pick this topic for the reason that corporate resilience—that is, the ability to endure and survive—is still poorly understood, and is likely affected by multiple attributes, and in a non-linear fashion. However, most studies related to firm resilience tend to produce linear analyses one feature at a time [10, 11]. Using the shock of the 2019 pandemic, we demonstrate the added value of ML techniques in these circumstances, while a final section concludes and highlights new avenues of research.

## 2. Data science methods

### 2.1 Evolution of machine learning into economics

Applied economics has long been dominated by econometrics, which relies on statistical techniques, such as regression, time series models and hypothesis testing. These techniques assume strong parametric relationships, making them suitable for small and structured datasets, but they are limited in flexibility and fragile if they deviate from their parametric assumptions.

Machine learning was introduced in 1959 by Arthur Samuel, an IBM employee, to define the pattern recognition tasks that provided the "learning" component of early artificial intelligence (AI) expert systems [12]. However, machine learning techniques did not gain attention in economics until the early twenty-first century, when their application became possible without major computational constraints and large datasets became more available.

According to Gogas and Papadimitriou [12], the most obvious case of the use of ML in economics is in finance and its abundance of available data, with the aim of predicting financial health or prices made possible by it. The pioneering use of ML in economics is a study by Wang et al., which demonstrated its usefulness in the context of credit scoring, while White's paper used ML with the aim of better predicting IBM's daily stock returns [13, 14].

Hal Varian, formerly of Berkeley and by then the chief economist at Google, also published a research entitled "Big Data: New Tricks for Econometrics", which highlighted the potential of ML to revolutionise empirical research in economics [15]. Varian emphasised early on that the main strength of supervised machine learning is its focus on predictive accuracy. Econometrics has traditionally focused on estimating causal effects and testing economic theories, while machine learning excels at finding patterns in data that lead to better predictions.

Varian's research caught the ear of many fellow economists, as many researchers in applied economics began to incorporate machine learning techniques into their toolkits. According to Nosratabadi et al. [16], the number of ML applications in economics started to skyrocket around 2016–2017. This is also confirmed by a bibliometric analysis of the published literature from Web of Science (WoS) and Scopus on machine learning in economics and econometrics, where the total number of studies in machine learning and economics was in the low twenties in 2010 to reach almost 1000 research papers 10 years later, or a 50-fold increase [17].

### 2.2 Supervised ML techniques

From White's paper on stock returns, supervised machine learning models have expanded into areas, such as commerce [18], consumer behaviour and social media [19, 20], macroeconomics and health economics [21, 22], agricultural and development economics [23, 24]; labour economics [25]; organisation science [26]; or even energy economics and industrial economics [27, 28].

These studies have also used different classification algorithms, of which the most common and popular methods are support vector machines (SVMs), decision trees (DTs), neural networks (NNs), random forests (RFs) and gradient boosting (GBM). Appendix 1 describes the process of running those algorithms, but what needs to be kept in mind is the trade-off between simplicity and accuracy of results, with ensemble models being more effective than others. Among others;

1. Decision tree (DT) (or classification tree) is a classification method that constructs decision rules organised in tree-like structures, where at each node the dataset is partitioned to maximise the best classification/purity, starting at the root node of the tree and then moving down the tree branch corresponding to the attribute value. Decision trees have high interpretability, but predictive results are sensitive to sample selection and tree branch hierarchy.

2. As an alternative to DT, a support vector machine (SVM) constructs a hyperplane or a set of hyperplanes. Intuitively, the hyperplane that has the greatest distance from the nearest training data points in any class achieves a strong separation, since in general, the larger the distance, the lower the generalisation error of the classifier. It is effective in high-dimensional spaces and can behave differently based on different mathematical functions known as the kernel. However, when the dataset contains more noise, such as overlapping target classes, SVM does not perform well.

3. Neural networks (NNs) mimic the interconnected neurons of the human brain. Deep learning (a subset of NN) involves multiple layers that can capture

complex patterns and interactions. "Inspired by biological networks" [28], any artificial neural network consists of at least one input layer with feature information, one or more hidden layers and an output layer that returns the predicted values. Each layer consists of nodes (neurons) connected by edges across layers, which are strengthened according to their ability to transmit information. Deep learning models also excel at handling highly non-linear and unstructured data. However, they require large datasets and are prone to overfitting without careful regularisation.

4. Random Forest (RF) is an ensemble classification technique that, instead of estimating a single DT, resamples the observations in the training set to estimate multiple trees independently. These trees are merged as a combination of bootstrap aggregation (bagging) and random feature selection. The final prediction is then based on averaging the results of all the trees. As an ensemble, the multi-decision tree RF learning model is typically more accurate than a single decision tree model. However, due to their complexity (hundreds or thousands of trees), it is not easy to understand how individual features contribute to a prediction.

5. Gradient boosting (GB), like Random Forest, is an ensemble learning algorithm based on a series of decision trees, but unlike RF, it builds trees sequentially, with each new tree attempting to correct the errors of the previous trees. The gradient is used to minimise the loss function, similar to how neural networks use gradient descent to optimise weights. Random forests tend to be faster to train because the trees are built independently, while gradient boosting is slower due to its sequential nature. Gradient boosting is more prone to overfitting, but can achieve higher accuracy than RF due to its built-in correction process, if tuned properly.

**Table 1** provides a high-level synthesis of the relative strengths of the different methods. DT, while simple and easy to interpret, is prone to overfitting. SVM, while excellent on high-dimensional data, struggles with scalability and requires careful tuning of the kernels. RF is a strong all-round performer, with less risk of overfitting, but less interpretable, while, say, NN is highly flexible, powerful for complex data types, but computationally expensive and data hungry.

In general, RF and then NN have been the most widely used methods in applied economics to date. NNs are known to be the best at dealing with non-linear (hidden) effects, but at the expense of interpretability [29]. They tend to outperform other models in areas such as asset pricing and climate change impact prediction when large datasets are available, but their performance can suffer with small datasets or simpler tasks. RFs also tend to perform very well in terms of in-sample accuracy [5] as well as (out-of-sample) predictive accuracy, especially when dealing with large datasets and high-dimensional data. GB models such as XGBoost (XB) often outperform Random Forests in terms of predictive accuracy, especially for financial market predictions and high-dimensional datasets. Nevertheless, RF seems to be increasingly preferred because of its stability, less sensitivity to overfitting and because the relative contribution of the tree's regressors to the prediction can be easily calculated using various direct techniques in tree-based models, such as Gini importance or mean decrease impurity (MDI) [30].

DOI: http://dx.doi.org/10.5772/intechopen.1008856

| Criterion | Decision trees (DTs) | Random forests (RFs) | Gradient boosting (GBoost) | Neural networks (NNs) | Support vector machines (SVMs) |
|---|---|---|---|---|---|
| Interpretability | Very High (easy to visualise) | Moderate (aggregated trees) | Low (many trees) | Low (black-box model) | Low to moderate (linear okay, but kernel SVM is not) |
| Performance | Moderate (prone to overfitting) | High | Very High (often top-performing) | High (especially deep models) | High (particularly with kernels) |
| Overfitting Risk | High (without pruning) | Low | Medium | High | Moderate (especially with kernels) |
| Scalability | High (for small datasets) | Moderate (slower training) | Moderate (slower, but handles large data) | Very High (can scale with graphics processing units (GPUs)) | Low (scales poorly to large datasets) |
| Training Speed | Very fast | Moderate (many trees) | Slow (sequential training) | Slow (deep networks take time) | Slow |
| Handles Missing Data | Yes (some implementations) | Yes | Yes | No | No |
| Handles Non-linearity | Poor (linear splits) | Good (ensemble of linear splits) | Excellent (boosting corrects non-linearity) | Excellent (intrinsically non-linear) | Excellent (with kernel tricks) |
| Works with Categorical Features | Yes (with specific implementations) | Yes (automatically with RF) | Yes (automatically with CatBoost) | No | No |

**Table 1.**
*Machine learning algorithms: Pros and cons.*

## 3. Towards explainable AI

The work of Hal Varian also had emphasised that machine learning and econometrics are complementary, not substitutes. Economists care deeply about causality—determining the direction of cause and effect—which machine learning algorithms are not primarily designed to uncover. At a technical level, econometrics aims at statistical inferential analysis, such as "estimating the coefficient associated with a variable and its confidence level with respect to a hypothesis (often the null), while machine learning models are mostly nonparametric [31]".

As many phenomena are driven by complex data processes, linear approximation can be a risky shortcut. The rise of big, granular and unstructured data provides an opportunity to use ML to study such phenomena, but preferably if there is a way to make some causal inference [7]. Importantly, one reason for models to be interpretable is the importance of ethical concerns, as opaque models could be misused. These concerns require parallel ML guidelines, especially around the ideas of "fairness", "safety", "trustworthiness" and "transparency'" [32]. The first institutionally based publication on ML and AI guidelines was the "Ethics Guidelines for Trustworthy AI" by the Independent High-Level Expert Group on Artificial Intelligence, organised by the European Union (EU), in 2019. This was the first step towards the first regulatory framework announced by 2021 and finally passed by the European Union under the European "AI Act", by March 2023, as a law governing the development and deployment of AI systems in the European Union [33, 34].

Accordingly, in recent years, economists and data science researchers have developed approaches that attempt to bridge the gap between data science and econometrics [35]. Indeed, two questions arise for effective models of an empirical phenomenon: first, whether the model is well specified and, if so, what is the impact of the features specified in the model on the emergence and pattern of the empirical phenomenon (see [5], p. 4). The second question is akin to determining the marginal effect of features on output in econometrics. The first question is also akin to the issue of adequate model specification, since in traditional econometrics missing variables can lead to poor marginal inference, and multicollinear variables can lead to large inference imprecisions. We address explainability of ML models hereafter, first by discussing model features' relevance, and then, inference.

### 3.1 Attributes' importance

Ways to address model specification are variable attribution via the decomposition of individual predictions (so called, "local attribution") and importance scores for the model as a whole ("global attribution") [36]. In general, local attribution techniques can be re-aggregated to global attribution.

#### *3.1.1 Global approaches (at model level)*

Global methods seek to explain the behaviour of the full model and the global importance of features/variables. Methods include

1. The permutation importance of a variable measures the change in model performance when the values of that variable are "randomly permuted". The underlying logic is that if the ML model has learned a strong dependency between the model outcome and a given variable, permuting the value of the variable will lead to

very different model predictions and thus affect performance. A variable is therefore defined as important if the test error after permuting a feature is substantially higher than the test error using the original value for that feature. While permutation is simple and intuitive, as it directly shows how model performance is affected when information from a feature is removed, it is computationally expensive, as it requires retraining or testing the model multiple times with shuffled data, especially for large datasets. In addition, estimates of interaction effects may be both unstable and fail to correctly account for interaction effects between features, especially when correlated features are shuffled independently.

2. The jackknife method (and its extension, jackknife plus) assesses the importance of features by systematically removing (or masking) one feature at a time and assessing how the performance of the model changes [37]. In practice, jackknife uses the residuals from one (or all) leave-one-out predictions to estimate how much deviation we can expect from new predictions. While the method is model agnostic and fairly simple and intuitive (removing a feature and observing the change in performance give an easy-to-understand measure of importance), it is computationally intensive. Like permutation importance, jackknife may underestimate the importance of features involved in complex interactions, as removing a single feature does not fully capture its interaction effects.

3. In tree-based ML models (DT, XB, RF), measures of global importance derived directly as a by-product of the learning step include GINI importance; MDI/MDA (MDI: mean decrease impurity; Breinman et al. [38] and MDA: mean decrease accuracy [39]. Gini is a measure of how much a variable contributes to optimising the objective function, while MDI, like Gini, evaluates impurity as the entropy of the distributions of the input variables in sample, while MDA does so out of sample. As the impurity decreases, the feature is considered more important.

   Assuming a sufficiently high level of trees, MDI/A has desirable properties such as consistency with the notion of feature relevance, or the ability of a variable to convey additional information about the output [40]. As the importance of a feature is calculated based on the reduction in some impurity criterion (e.g., Gini impurity or entropy) or the increase in information gain when that feature is used to partition the data during the model training process, there is no need for additional passes through the data. These measures also capture complex interactions between features without requiring explicit feature engineering, but may be biased for features measured as continuous variables, while the importance of correlated features may be unevenly distributed across correlated features.

4. Another global approach is SAGE ("Shapley Additive Global importance"), a model-agnostic method that uses Shapley values to assess the global importance of features, based on a set of input data for a scenario that implies a regression model output, which is then used to quantify the contribution of the features to the global model prediction.

   Shapley scores (and their close variants) are a tool borrowed from game theory to allocate credit to players in coalitional games; hence, the idea of using Shapley scores in a supervised learning method is to treat each feature as a "player" in a cooperative game, where the "game" is the model prediction and the payoff is the predicted value. Applied to ML, Shapley scores provide a fair way of allocating the overall model performance to different features, treating them as "players" in a cooperative game. Appendix 2 provides some extra details on how Shapley scores are derived.

SAGE can account for interactions between features because it considers how groups of features work together to influence model predictions. This ensures that the importance of a feature reflects both its individual contribution and its role in interactions with other features. However, as the calculation of the Shapley value must take into account all combinations of games/coalitions, the process can be computationally expensive—and in most cases prohibitive—requiring the development of approximations. In general, SAGE rigorously handles feature interactions using Shapley values, but it is a cumbersome method that often requires approximation in multi-feature models.

**Table 2** summarises the different methods, and the trade-off to be made between computing resources, interpretability, or still handling of complex non-linear relationships. For instance, feature importance based on tree-based models is directly computable, even if computation is a struggle in complex non-linear models. The SAGE method is robust to non-linearity but is complex to implement and not easily interpretable. Jackknife methods do not handle non-linearities easily and are resource-costly.

In practice, however, the performance of ensemble tree models is increasingly recognised, leading practitioners to favour methods, such as GB and RF. Furthermore, Sutera et al. [40] have recently pointed out that, under some reasonable conditions, MDI scores derived from tree-based ML models can match Shapley values, both theoretically and empirically. MDI scores are thus a simple built-in alternative to SHAP ("SHapley Additive exPlanations") approximations of Shapley values for assessing the global importance of features in ML models.

### *3.1.2 Local approaches*

The main advantage of local methods is that they reveal the functional form of the association between a feature and the outcome as learned by the model, which

| **Criteria** | **Permutation importance** | **Jackknife** | **MDI (mean decrease in impurity)** | **SAGE (shapley additive global importance)** |
|---|---|---|---|---|
| Model-agnostic | Yes | Yes | No | Yes |
| Handles interactions | Partially (depends on correlations) | No | No | Yes (fully considers interactions) |
| Computational efficiency | Moderate (re-evaluation per feature) | Low (retrain/ evaluate per feature) | Very high (computed during training) | Very low (computationally expensive) |
| Interpretation simplicity | High (clear performance drop) | Moderate (performance change upon removal) | Moderate | Low (complex interpretation of Shapley values) |

**Table 2.**
*Global importance metrics: Pros and cons.*

global methods cannot do. Approaches that are also agnostic to model type include DeepLIFT (for "Deep Learning Important FeaTures") [41], as well as among the most widely used: LIME (for "Local Interpretable Model-Agnostic Explanations" [42];) and SHAP (for "SHapley Additive exPlanations" [43]).

1. DeepLIFT is a model-specific method designed primarily for deep learning models. It explains a model's prediction by comparing the activation of each neuron in the model to a reference activation, and assigns importance scores to each input feature based on how much it contributed to the deviation from the reference. For each input, DeepLIFT selects a reference input (e.g., a "neutral" baseline input) and calculates the activation of each neuron in the network for both the input and the reference. DeepLIFT then propagates these differences back through the network to assign attribution scores to the input features, showing how much each input contributed to the difference in the final prediction compared to the reference. DeepLIFT is faster than methods such as SHAP because it avoids the combinatorial complexity of evaluating multiple subsets of input features. Because it uses deep neural networks, DeepLIFT is able to handle complex, non-linear relationships in the data. A key weakness is that the choice of reference point can affect the attributions, and selecting an appropriate reference is often not straightforward [44].

2. LIME is based on the construction of a simplified replacement model for the model under investigation (the "replacement model"). The surrogate model is based on the predictions of the base model computed on variations of the input data randomly perturbed, and is thus able to quantify the importance of the different features that make up the unperturbed data; on the prediction of the surrogate model.

3. Unlike LIME, SHAP is based on an approximation of the calculation of Shapley values [45]. Unlike LIME, and as noted above in relation to SAGE, the Shapley value assigns a fair contribution to each feature based on its marginal effect across all possible feature combinations, and is also a unique solution to the credit allocation problem, as defined by several other desirable properties such as symmetry and linearity [46]. SHAP is an approximation to Shapley scores, as the exact calculation of the Shapley score is computationally expensive because there is a combination of $2^n$ possible coalitions of n feature values, and the 'absence' of a feature has to be simulated by drawing random instances, which increase the variance for the estimate of the Shapley score.

**Table 3** is a summary of the local importance methods. LIME is probably the most useful method when a quick, interpretable explanation of a prediction from any type of model is needed. However, LIME can be unstable and computationally expensive for complex models. Designed specifically for deep learning models, DeepLIFT is best when dealing with neural networks. It provides efficient and interpretable attributions, but requires careful selection of a reference point.

Although additional questions remain about how Shapley values truly measure feature importance [47, 48], Lundberg and Lee [43] had shown that Shapley values provide a unifying framework for many attribution schemes. As for global measures, Sutera et al. [40] had pointed out that, under some reasonable conditions, local MDI scores derived from tree-based ML models can also match Shapley values, both theoretically and empirically.

| Criteria | LIME | SHAP | DeepLIFT |
|---|---|---|---|
| Model compatibility | Model-agnostic | Model-agnostic | Model-specific (primarily with NN) |
| Theoretical foundation | Heuristic-based | Grounded in game theory (Shapley values) | Difference from reference activation |
| Computational efficiency | Moderate to high | Low to high (approximate methods like SHAP) | Very efficient for neural networks |
| Stability of results | Can vary between runs (random perturbations) | Consistent and stable explanations | Stable, depends on reference choice |
| Computational complexity | Linear with respect to the number of samples | Exponentially complex | Relatively low, especially for NN |
| Applicability to deep models | Works with deep models but only by approximating locally | Can handle deep models (but may be slow) | Specifically designed for deep neural networks |
| Choice of reference point | No reference required | No reference required | Requires a reference input |

**Table 3.**
*Local importance metrics: Pros and cons.*

In addition to providing local, accurate, linear and consistent attributions, Shapley values provide a granular approximation of a possible feature across all observations, allowing the functional form learned by the model to be visualised. Based on this, and as discussed below, one can also formulate a more comprehensive statistical inference framework—the so-called Shapley regression that provides a clear bridge to traditional econometrics [49].

## 3.2 Attributes inference

In recent years, a number of breakthroughs have been made for the convergence of inference between ML and econometrics, from a variety of studies, such as Athey [50], Athey et al. [51, 52], Athey and Imbens [53], Athey and Wager [54]; Chernozhukov et al. [55, 56]; Davis, and Heller [57] or Nazemi and Fabozzi [58].

### *3.2.1 Attribute global significance*

Here are some examples of notable advances in statistical inference using ML models:

1. Regarding the relevance of attributes for model specification, an important avenue, based on bagged trees as in RF, is that the combination of models can give an idea of the uncertainty in the estimates of attributes. From this perspective, Wager et al. (2014) were among the first to construct asymptotic confidence intervals for random forests via infinitesimal jackknifes and combinations of models [59]. Their basis for this inference is the concept of an honest forest, where trees in a random forest are divided into one group used to select splits and another group used to make predictions, preventing the same data from being used for both model training and evaluation. This "honest" structure reduces

bias in tree predictions and ensures that the predictions are statistically valid for inference. Under certain conditions, the predictions made by honest random forests follow a normal distribution as the number of trees increases. This in turn allows the calculation of confidence intervals for predictions based on the Central Limit Theorem (CLT).

2. Mentch and Hooker in 2016 introduced a statistical inference framework for machine learning models, specifically focusing on random forests and other ensemble methods [60]. The method involves creating multiple subsets of the training data (similar to subsampling) and building decision trees on these subsets. The key difference from traditional random forests is that the trees are grown on different random subsamples rather than full bootstrap samples. The authors derived the U-statistic, which is computed for the predictions generated by individual decision trees built from subsampled data, and for which the distribution approaches normality as the number of trees grows large, allowing the use of standard confidence intervals and hypothesis tests.

However, the method involves repeated subsampling and fitting of decision trees, which can be computationally expensive, especially for large datasets. Finally, if the subsamples are too small, the trees may not adequately capture the underlying relationships in the data; and if the subsamples are too large, the trees may become too similar, reducing the variability needed for inference.

1. A more recent study by Coleman et al. [61] points out that the formal hypothesis testing procedure of Mentch and Hooker for assessing the importance of variables is computationally prohibitive. In contrast, their method is based on a permutation scheme that avoids the need for explicit covariance estimation and thus does not require a larger number of trees for larger datasets. In particular, they show that the difference in the mean squared error in out-of-sample prediction accuracy between the intact variable and the same variable permutated in tree-based models follows an asymptotically normal distribution with mean zero and finite variance.

2. Another route taken by Buckmann et al. [62] is to use the framework of Shapley regressions, which can indeed be seen as a natural extension of regression-based inference to the general non-linear model. The main difference is that inference is often only valid locally, i.e. within a region of the input space, due to the potential non-linearity of the model plane. A slightly modified null hypothesis is introduced to test the statistical significance of variables, where the difference between the coefficients of a linear model and the Shapley share coefficients is essentially the normalisation of the latter, as non-linear models have no "natural scale" to measure variation. In their study, Buckmann et al. (2021), using Shapley regressions to assess attributes to predict changes in US unemployment, show that the latter is also significantly predicted by the 3-month Treasury bill, the oil price level and the slope of the yield curve; these effects are often not captured by traditional linear econometric models—making these linear models misspecified.

Yamaguchi also refers to Shapley regression as "Shapley values project unknown (but learned) functional forms into linear space" ([63], p. 29). Using the SHAP simplification of Shapley value, it is shown that the long-term stock price changes of global automakers such as Toyota and electronics companies such as Sony in the last decade of the twentieth century were significantly related to firm factors such as sales growth and inventory ratio, while these attributes were not obvious attributes in linear models.

### *3.2.2 Attribute marginal significance*

Finally, it should be noted that in addition to the general significance, the marginal effect of attributes on the output prediction can also be made, with standard errors derived from bootstrapping. As discussed by Zhao and Hastie [64], one of the most used visualisation tools of ML models is the "partial dependence plot" (PDP) of an attribute. Not only is the PDP the same fitting formula as in Pearl [65] to identify the causal effect of an attribute on Y from observed data, but the slope of this PDP relationship is also what traditional multiple regression coefficients capture as a marginal effect under a linear model—but now extended to any model [7].

## 4. A case study on corporate resilience

### 4.1 Scope

To illustrate the current convergence between ML models and traditional econometrics, we use an analysis of firm resilience.

While economic theory has often focused on firm's performance, resilience appears to be both a critical and a strategic attribute. Indeed, valuable firms are those that survive for a long time as a result of their resilience to a variety of adverse shocks: during the last major recessions, studies of listed firms found that only 20% of firms were able to return to pre-recession performance 3 years after the onset of the crisis. In the most recent global shock we study here (the COVID-19 pandemic), about one third of listed firms had not returned to the same level of profitability 2 years after the start of the pandemic [66].

In particular, we draw on the large existing literature on strategic resources and dynamic capabilities to predict the performance trajectory of firms during COVID-19 as a function of four firm internal capabilities [67, 68]: agility [69], innovativeness [70], digitalisation and ecosystem play [71].

The resilience problem of this research would traditionally be estimated by relating the probability of resilience to indicators of these four capabilities, using parametric techniques such as logistic regression. However, one can easily hypothesise that strong non-linearities, such as a lack of digitisation, may dramatically damage firms fighting the pandemic and its social distancing measures, compared to a firm that is already digitised but not fully digitised. Similarly, firms that are able to play an important orchestrating role in ecosystems may benefit more proportionally from the ecosystem than a firm that is only passive in an ecosystem—especially at the time, during the pandemic, of major supply chain disruptions, for example.

As an alternative to least-squares techniques, one resorts here to more general Machine Learning models to predict resilience, as well as the relative importance of its antecedents. This analysis is part of recent trends of using ML models to predict organisational resilience via bundle of firm inertial capabilities. The novelty is to leverage an array of models, from artificial neural networks (NNs), to SVM, gradient boosting (GBM) and random forests (RFs), while we also produce inferences as to the significance of attributes as well as their marginal impact (through partial marginal effects (PMEs)) on resilience probability.

### 4.2 Conceptual model: The importance of four capabilities

A large number of studies on corporate resilience are prevalent, with the majority relying on the resource-based view and dynamic capabilities theory [72]. Accordingly, we rely on the same theoretical foundations and hypothesise a conceptual model, in which corporate resilience is essentially driven by four main capability factors: innovation, agility, digitisation and business ecosystem play as key drivers of resilience (see **Figure 1**).

This conceptual model can be validated by integrating several studies of resilience, as the vast majority of research has examined the resilience effect of a single capability, with a relatively limited number of studies examining a bundle of capabilities as a vector of resilience. Regarding the latter, Battisti and Deakins highlight the critical aspect of both agility and ecosystem play to leverage resilience [73]. More recently, Dyduch et al. found that firm resilience during the COVID-19 pandemic was enhanced by innovation capability, agility, as well as digitalisation [74].

Further following the dynamic capability literature, each capability reflects three general types (sensing, exploiting and transforming capabilities [75]). Following this classification, we measure each dynamic capability as follows. First, following the innovation literature, Research and Development (R&D) intensity and its change is a proxy for sensing and exploiting capabilities, while innovation-transforming capabilities are reflected by the part of R&D that goes beyond mere incremental innovation [76]. Regarding agility, we follow Mohammad [77] who emphasises a culture of agility that is able to sense the need/opportunities for adaptation; while we measure

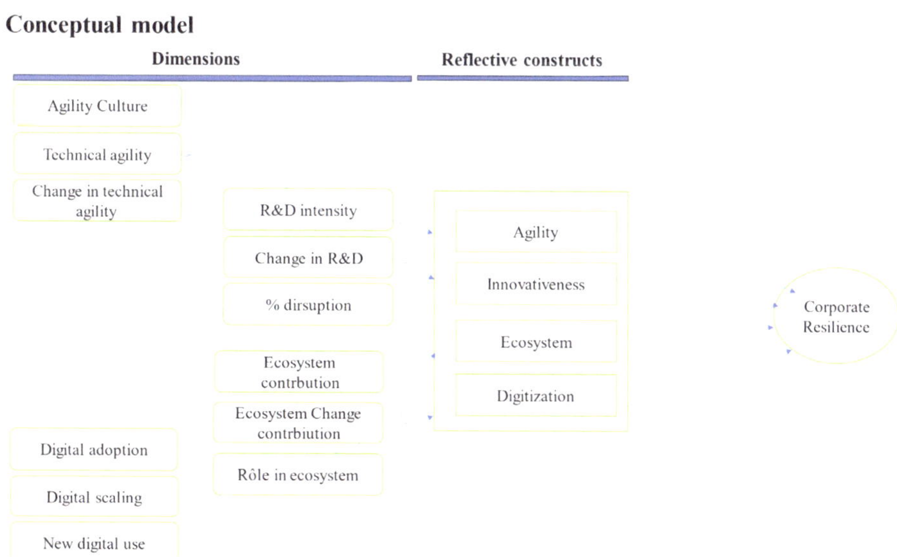


**Figure 1.**
*Conceptual model of capabilities-driven resilience.*

the exploitation of agility through three technical elements: speed, flexibility and risk taking in resource reallocation [78]. Transformative capability is measured by the degree of change in those technical elements at the time of the pandemic. In terms of ecosystem play, the literature emphasises the dominant ecosystem's contribution, as a measure of the firm's belief in its importance, and the depth of that contribution, as an indicator of the exploitation of ecosystem benefits. The literature also emphasises the firm's role in this ecosystem as a reflection of its transformative nature; in particular, the firm's orchestrator role in the ecosystem is important as a transformative capability [79]. Finally, with respect to digitisation, the literature has often measured the adoption, but especially the full exploitation (as opposed to experimentation) of technologies as an indicator of exploitable capabilities [80]. Success in digital transformation capabilities is a clear symptom of transformation capabilities, according to Ellström et al. [81].

### 4.3 Sample procedure and statistics

#### *4.3.1 Data collection*

The sample comes from an online executive survey structured by Accenture Research to explore how global companies around the world perceive and respond to the COVID-19 pandemic in late 2020/early 2021. The survey was designed by an external research firm, taking into account the dimensions of resilience capabilities from our conceptual model outlined in **Figure 1**, in line with the literature. The wording and questions were reviewed for consistency and readability by a number of external consulting experts.

The full sample was drawn from 14 representative countries. North America was represented by the United States and Canada (32 and 5% of the sample, respectively), Europe by the top five countries (5% of the sample each), Asia by Japanese and Chinese companies (9% of the sample each) and Singapore. The remaining enterprises were located in the Middle East (United Arab Emirates (UAE) and Saudi Arabia). The scope covered 18 private NACE 2 (Statistical Classification of Economic Activities in the European Community) industries, each represented by the same sample size.

Respondents were selected from the market research database of the C-suite, mostly Chief Executive Officers (CEOs), Chief Strategy Officers (CSOs) or Chief Information Officers (CIOs). The sample response rate was approximately 15% for a total sample of 4300 companies. To minimise general response bias and noisy responses, confidentiality of responses and the option not to answer questions were guaranteed [82]. Tests for possible response bias were carried out. As the study collected informants' days, early and late responses were tested for significant differences in responses after 2–4 weeks. No real difference between respondents was found, while Harman's main principal factor also accounted for 22% of the variance, well below the 50% threshold where the variance is mostly driven by respondent style.

#### *4.3.2 Data statistics*

We use profit recovery as a reflexive measure of resilience and consider a window of 18 months after the pandemic to test recovery, based on classifying a firm according to whether or not its profit has returned to pre-pandemic levels by September 2021. The 18-month window is consistent with the typical duration of crisis absorption [83]. Sixty-eight per cent of the firms in the sample did not recover their pre-pandemic revenue level by September 2021. Average revenue calculated for the full sample fell by 30% relative to 2019 at the peak of the pandemic, and "recovered" by 15% on average in the second period, but remained below 15% of their original pre-pandemic revenue by 2019. This gap is consistent with those of other studies [84].

**Table 4** provides a company perspective throughout the (peak) pandemic. While two thirds of companies pride themselves on having an agile culture, speed/flexibility and risk-taking practices are only average, although companies accelerated their investment in these practices somewhat during the pandemic. In terms of the ecosystem, 6 out of 10 companies have more than 5% of revenue coming from the ecosystem, and the same proportion sees this revenue increasing over the years—however, only 14% play an orchestrating role. Innovation intensity is typically below 5%, and one third of companies reduced R&D during the pandemic—while digital maturity was 50% of the frontier of full digitalisation, with barely 4 out of 10 companies recognising the success of their digital transformation.

Nevertheless, we observe a larger deviation from the average firm. Using a simple K-means clustering technique, we find about five clusters of firms, as in the silhouette/elbow techniques. At one extreme of the least resilient firms, we find the largest cluster, consisting of 37% of firms that are hardly innovative, reduce their expenditure during the pandemic, and are considered culturally and technically not agile. At the other extreme, we find a cluster of 11% of companies that are quite agile and digitally mature, while orchestrating an increasingly large ecosystem and increasing their R&D intensity during the pandemic. Another segment of 22% of companies, which also showed better than average resilience, is characterised by accelerated participation in ecosystems and strong non-incremental innovation capabilities during the pandemic—in contrast to the majority of companies that froze investments as a result of the pandemic risk. Two other segments (each with around 15% of firms) are closer to the average firm, but stand out for their success in digital transformation and technical (change) agility.

These different clusters clearly show non-linearity in how firms use capabilities and how this can affect recovery; they still do not say anything about how capabilities themselves can affect resilience across their full range of use. We therefore use more general machine learning techniques to capture this diversity of impact on resilience in the next subsection.

### 4.4 Results

#### *4.4.1 Predictive method selection*

**Table 5** presents predictive accuracy, via the area under the curve (AUC) with all industries pooled. One notices that the logistic regression method is systematically dominated by at least one advanced ML technique. Based on the AUC and the versatility of the technique, random forests (RFs), then GB are the most powerful methods, but all ML models provide better predictive performance than the logistic model. Given the better performance of RF, we select RF as the ML method in the rest of this research.

| Agility | Average | Innovation | Average | Ecosystem play | Average | Digitisation | Average |
|---|---|---|---|---|---|---|---|
| Agile method-speed (0 = no, 1 = medium; high = 2) | 1,49 | R&D spent (0,=0%, 1 = 1–5%, 2 = 5–10%; 3 above 10%) | 1,1 | Ecosystem revenue>5% (1,0) | 15% | Technology adoption (total): 1 to 10) | 7,9 |
| Agile method-flexibility (0 = no, 1 = medium; high = 2) | 1,2 | Change in R&D (yes = 1; 0, no; −1; reduction) | −0,2 | Ecosystem revenue increase (yes = 1; 0 otherwise) | % | Technology scaling (total): 1 to 10 | 6,5 |
| Agile method-risk taking (0 = no, 1 = medium; high = 2) | 0,93 | Share outside incremental innovation (1 = 1–20%, 2; 20–40%, 3: 40—60%; 4 > 60%) | 3,2 | Role in ecosystem: orchestrator (yes: 1; 0: no) | 14% | Increase in digital spending (yes: 1; 0; otherwise) | 66% |
| Investing further in agile method (yes = 1; 0 = no per type) | 37% | | | Role in ecosystem:major node (yes:1; 0: no) | 14% | | |
| Agile culture (1 = agree; 0 otherwise) | 67% | | | Role in ecosystem:major node (yes: 1; 0: no) | xx% | | |

**Table 4.**
*Sample statistics.*

| **AUC** | | |
|---|---|---|
| **Methods** | **In-sample** | **Out-sample** |
| Logistic regression | 0,78 | 0,71 |
| Random forests | 0,92 | 0,87 |
| GB | 0,86 | 0,77 |
| ANN | 0,78 | 0,74 |

**Table 5.**
*ML model fitness.*

### *4.4.2 Global importance*

We assess the global contribution of each capability dimension to recovery prediction through the Mean Decrease Impurity (MDI) and SAGE procedures, which are based on Shapley values. As discussed earlier, MDI is a global importance approach, essentially the average across all trees of the capability feature's ability to reduce noise at each node, while SAGE is a global measure as an aggregate to local fair measure of how a particular capability feature contributes to resilience. Shapley scores are calculated from RF, which is considered to be the best fitting model.

Importantly, it is reminded that MDI values derived from randomised trees are asymptotic Shapley values. Note that a classic drawback of the MDI method, that it can overweight cardinal values relative to others, is not relevant in our case, as all variables are categorical as derived from the survey.

#### *4.4.2.1 RF performance versus linear model performance*

**Table 6** provides the results per capability dimensions for both metrics of MDI and Shapley, including the importance based on the logistic model forecasts.

The first observation is that all dimensions are statistically significant with the RF model, whether the metric is used in MDI or through simple values, but this is not the case with the logistic model—in particular, the latter is unable to capture any significant relevance for digitisation and for R&D intensity. This reflects the fact that RF can exploit non-linear relationships that the linear regression cannot account for. The second observation is also that the linear model overweights the importance of variables such as changes in technical agility and non-incremental R&D or full commercial exploitation of digital technologies compared to other MDI/SAGE metrics. This clearly reinforces the validity of using more flexible models than linear models for the case of resilience.

#### *4.4.2.2 RF-based attribute importance rank and significance*

Focusing on the RF model, it is clear that MDI and SAGE also provide roughly the same ranking of capabilities ($r = 0.89$).

Based on **Figure 2**, which visualises both metrics by ranking the dimensions from highest to lowest global importance, SAGE underweights importance over MDI in the specific case of the impact of investment on technical agility, while SAGE overweights importance over MDI in the case of R&D intensity and digital transformation success. Notably, both metrics agree on the importance of both cultural and technical

| RForest ML model | | | |
|---|---|---|---|
| **Capability** | **Dimensions** | **MDI** | **SAGE** |
| Agility | Cultural agility | 22%*** | 24%*** |
| | Technical agility | 21%*** | 15%** |
| | Technical agility change | 12%** | 6%* |
| Innovation | R&D intensity | 4%* | 7%* |
| | R&D intensity change | 3%** | 5%** |
| | % of non-incremental R&D investment | 14%*** | 14%** |
| Ecosystem | Ecosystem revenues | 5%*** | 4%*** |
| | Ecosystem revenue change | 3%** | 3% |
| | Ecosystem play | 6%** | 7%*** |
| Digitalisation | Digital adoption | 1%* | 0% |
| | Full digital commercialisation | 4%** | 5%** |
| | Digital transformation success | 5%** | 10%*** |

*Note: *; **; ***: p < 0,01, p < 0,05; p: 0,1-tests produced as per the main text.*

**Table 6.**
*Attributes impact on resilience: Global importance.*

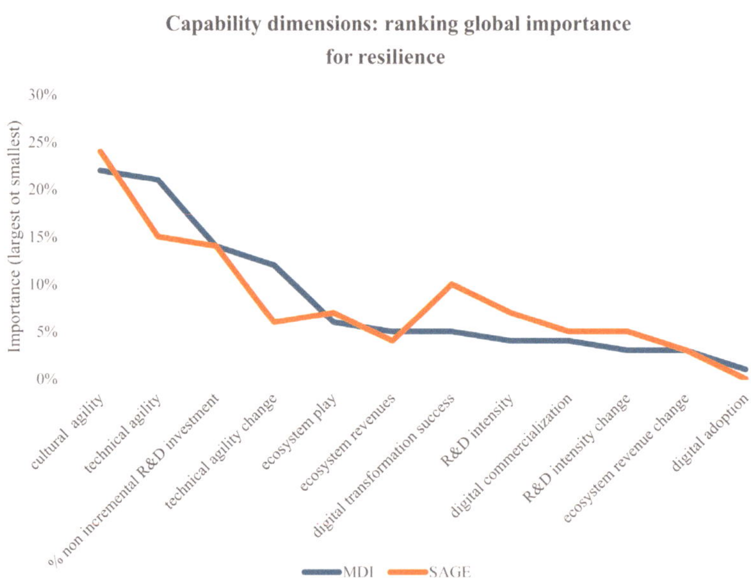


**Figure 2.**
*Global importance ranking.*

agility, non-incremental innovation, ecosystem play and digital transformation success as strong attributes affecting resilience. These nuances regarding capabilities are relatively new findings in the literature.

**Table 7** shows the contribution of the four capabilities after aggregating the importance of each dimension. Not only do the p values demonstrate that each capability significantly affects resilience, but that there is also a clear ranking, with

| **Relative importance** | | | | |
|---|---|---|---|---|
| **Capabilities** | **MDI** | | **SAGE** | |
| | **importance** | ***p*-value** | **Importance** | ***p*-value** |
| Agility | 55% | 0,1% | 45% | 0,5% |
| Innovation | 21% | 1,2% | 26% | 0,2% |
| Ecosystem | 14% | 3,0% | 14% | 1,7% |
| Digitisation | 10% | 2,5% | 15% | 2,3% |

*Note: Random forest as underlying ML.*

**Table 7.**
*Capabilities depicting global importance significance.*

agility contributing up to half the importance of predicting resilience, innovation half the effect of agility, and ecosystem and digitisation contributing 25–30% of the total, depending on the method of importance used.

Compared to the existing literature on resilience, a number of studies related to financial crises or major economic disruptions had already emphasised the importance of firm agility to "roar out" of the crisis but the importance of technical elements, such as speed/flexibility/risk taking in influencing resilience, had not been discussed [85].

Second, innovation has long been seen as critical to resilience, but the details here suggest that innovation orientation also affects resilience. Third, the pandemic has provided a clear use case for digitisation. The linear approach to linking digitalisation to resilience turned out to be insignificant, but not in the case of a more non-linear approach. In this latter case, investment in technology is also not seen as a strong contributor to differentiating resilient from non-resilient firms, as the key is how digital technologies are used for business transformation. This is in line with findings from the digital transformation literature, which emphasises that digital performance depends on transformational rather than technological change [86].

Finally, in relation to the emerging literature on ecosystems [87], the orchestrator is often described as playing a key role as the actor responsible for designing the alignment structure, as well as the main decision maker within an ecosystem [88]. In times of crisis, the orchestrator can be an important catalyst for ecosystem adaptation and is often the first beneficiary of change.

### *4.4.3 Marginal (local) importance*

So far, we have presented the relative importance of the capability dimensions on resilience, but we still do not know the magnitude and direction of the impact on resilience. For this, we rely on the PME estimates based on the RF model.

**Table 8** shows the direction of the effects—in line with the idea that capabilities should support resilience, all dimensions exert a positive push on resilience, except for two variables for which higher intensity leads to lower resilience: non-incremental innovation and investment in technical agility.

The latter, while perhaps puzzling, may reflect the fact that companies that invest in agility at the time of the pandemic are just trying to catch up, but this may be too late, given the magnitude of the shock. Indeed, we find that firms with strong technical agility do not invest more in technical agility at the time of the pandemic ($r$ = 0.58), while the ability to be technically agile before the pandemic has a strong

| Agility | Sign | Innovation | Sign | Ecosystem play | Sign | Digitisation | Sign |
|---|---|---|---|---|---|---|---|
| Agile method-technical | positive | R&D intensity | positive | Ecosystem revenue >5% | positive | Technology adoption | positive |
| Investing further in tech agile methods | **negative** | Change in R&D intensity | positive | Ecosystem revenue increase | positive | Technology scaling | positive |
| Agile culture | positive | Share outside incremental innovation | **negative** | Role in ecosystem: | positive | Digital transformation success | positive |

*Note: Sign derived from plotting the minimal detectable effect (MDE) of each dimension on resilience probability, from low to high value range of each dimension. We observe same directional effects from the probit model.*

**Table 8.**
*Direction of effects on resilience, derived from Shapley values.*

positive effect on resilience in our marginal impact assessment. Regarding innovation, the fact that more disruptive R&D is negatively associated with resilience should be seen with two nuances. First, the marginal effect is rather small, i.e. the effect on the probability of resilience decreases by only 2 points for a firm moving from no disruptive R&D to fully disruptive R&D. Finally, it should be remembered that resilience is measured here as recovery in 18 months (our cut-off for resilience)—disruptive R&D often takes longer to show results [89].

Finally, **Table 9** presents the PME profiles for some of the key variables for the RF model, in addition to a visualisation of the evolution of the marginal effect through the deciles of the range of each attribute (**Figure 3**). One can see the high non-linearity of the marginal effect, as well as a non-significant sweet spot area where attributes do not affect resilience at the margin; this sweet spot often appears around the second to fourth decile of the distribution, or around Q1-Q2

| | Technical agility | | Change in technical agility | | Ecosystem play | |
|---|---|---|---|---|---|---|
| | Prob resilience | | Prob resilience | | Prob resilience | |
| Decile | Cumulative | Marginal | Cumulative | Marginal | Cumulative | Marginal |
| 0 | −3,0% | | 46,0% | | −2,0% | |
| 1 | −6,0% | −3,0% | 51,0% | 5,0% | 4,0% | 6,0% |
| 2 | −1,5% | 4,5% | 52,6% | **1,6%** | 8,9% | 4,9% |
| 3 | −0,8% | **0,7%** | 52,1% | **−0,5%** | 8,3% | **-0,6%** |
| 4 | 1,2% | **2,0%** | 51,0% | **-1,1%** | 7,8% | **-0,5%** |
| 5 | 2,3% | **1,1%** | 45,0% | −6,0% | 17,0% | 9,2% |
| 6 | 14,8% | 12,5% | 40,0% | −5,0% | 21,4% | 4,4% |
| 7 | 30,8% | 16,0% | 31,7% | −8,3% | 23,2% | 1,8% |
| 8 | 52,2% | 21,4% | 21,8% | −9,9% | 40,7% | 17,5% |
| 9 | 72,4% | 20,2% | 19,6% | −2,2% | 45,8% | 5,1% |
| 10 | 84,8% | 12,4% | 18,9% | −0,7% | 53,9% | 8,1% |

| | Technical agility | | Change in technical agility | | Ecosystem play | |
|---|---|---|---|---|---|---|
| | Prob resilience | | Prob resilience | | Prob resilience | |
| Decile | Cumulative | Marginal | Cumulative | Marginal | Cumulative | Marginal |
| | Digital adoption at scale | | Innovation | | | |
| | Prob resilience | | Prob resilience | | | |
| Decile | Cumulative | Marginal | Cumulative | Marginal | | |
| 0 | −8,5% | | −5,1% | | | |
| 1 | −4,1% | 4,4% | −4,5% | **0,6%** | | |
| 2 | 2,2% | 6,3% | −4,0% | **0,5%** | | |
| 3 | 5,8% | 3,6% | −2,4% | **1,6%** | | |
| 4 | 8,9% | 3,1% | −0,6% | **1,8%** | | |
| 5 | 15,6% | 6,7% | 3,7% | 4,3% | | |
| 6 | 24,9% | 9,3% | 8,9% | 5,2% | | |
| 7 | 37,2% | 12,3% | 16,6% | 7,7% | | |
| 8 | 46,8% | 9,6% | 27,8% | 11,2% | | |
| 9 | 45,9% | **-0,9%** | 45,8% | 18,0% | | |
| 10 | 42,7% | −3,2% | 66,8% | 21,0% | | |

*In bold: non-significant using bootstrapped standard errors for RF.*

**Table 9.**
*Marginal effect dynamics and significance based on RF.*

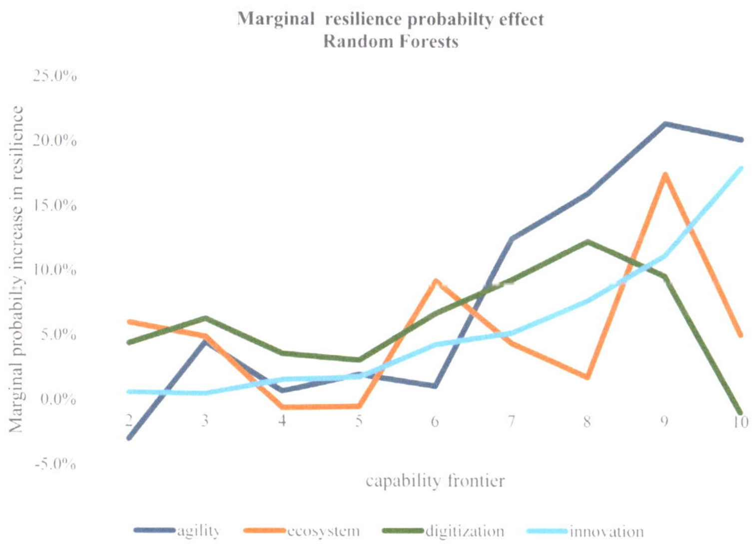


**Figure 3.**
*Marginal effect evolution of capabilities on resilience. Note: Agility: technical agility embeddedness before COVID-19 only; ecosystem: role only.*

of the attributes. In this zone, firms are not resilient—and any marginal effect will not make them better off. The largest marginal effect occurs at the late stage of the distribution, confirming that resilience depends on a strong accumulation of capabilities.

## 5. Conclusion

There is great potential to expand data science approaches, both to exploit a growing amount of very diverse and complex data, and to better capture the non-linear dynamics of how attributes affect economic phenomena. In this paper, we have shown how data science has made tremendous progress—with a wealth of new machine learning methods, as well as inference techniques based (or not) on these models—and how this has led to an important convergence between data science and traditional parametric econometrics in recent years.

We have illustrated this convergence with an empirical analysis of firm resilience associated with firm capabilities at the time of the recent pandemic crisis. The results suggest that machine learning techniques, such as Random Forest, can provide more robust yet transparent results to explain economic phenomena. It illustrates the richness of non-linearities and how these linearities can be crucial to more accurately predict resilience. Techniques such as Shapley values not only show that capabilities are positively associated with resilience, as one can capture with linear models, but also that the association is volatile and not always true—while it may even become stronger and more impactful for firms with a significant portfolio of capabilities prior to the pandemic.

There is still a lot of controversy about how ML works and how to use metrics to make inferences non-parametrically from data alone. But the path is promising—and we definitely agree with Atley's statement ([50], p. 507) that "*machine learning [could] have a dramatic impact on the field of economics within a short period of time*".

## Appendix

Computational methods of machine learning models

This appendix provides a detailed overview of the machine learning models methods (**Table A1**).

## A.1 Decision trees

Decision trees are constructed by recursively partitioning the dataset into subsets based on feature purity. At each node, the algorithm selects the feature and threshold that maximises a partitioning criterion, such as Gini impurity or information gain. Their strengths are simplicity and interpretability. Decision trees provide a

| Method | Methodology and core hypothesis |
|---|---|
| Decision trees | Recursive partitioning based on feature purity. Assumes splits maximise predictive power. |
| Random forests | Bagging of decision trees; assumes averaging reduces variance. |
| Gradient boosting | Sequential correction of prediction errors through gradient optimisation. Assumes additive error correction and improves performance. |
| Neural networks | Layered transformation of input data; assumes data relationships are hierarchical and non-linear. |
| Support vector machines (SVMs) | Maximises margin between data classes; assumes kernel transformations map data to separable spaces. |

**Table A1.**

clear visual representation of decision rules; however, they are prone to overfitting, especially in deep trees.

How it works:

- Start with the entire dataset at the root.
- For each feature, evaluate the potential split using the chosen criterion.
- Select the best split and create child nodes.
- Repeat until a stop condition is met (e.g., maximum depth, minimum samples per sheet)

## A.2 Random forests

Random forests combine multiple decision trees through a process called bagging. Each tree is trained on a bootstrapped sample of the data, and predictions are aggregated by averaging (regression) or majority voting (classification). Their strengths are stability, reduced overfitting and robustness to noise, but this comes at the cost of reduced interpretability due to the ensemble nature.

How it works:

- Generate several bootstrapped samples from the original dataset.
- Train a decision tree on each sample, using a random subset of features at each split.
- Aggregate the predictions from all the trees.

## A.3 Gradient boosting

Gradient boosting builds an ensemble of weak learners (e.g., shallow decision trees) sequentially. Each new learner attempts to correct the errors of the previous ones by optimising a loss function. If gradient boosting provides high predictive accuracy and flexibility, the method is computationally expensive, with a clear risk of overfitting without proper tuning.

How it works:

- Initialise the model with a simple prediction (e.g., the mean of the target variable).
- Calculate residuals based on the current model predictions.
- Fit a new learner to the residuals.
- Update the model by adding the predictions of the new learner, scaled by a learning rate.
- Repeat for a fixed number of iterations or until convergence.

## A.4 Support vector machines (SVMs)

SVM finds a hyperplane that separates data points into classes with the maximum margin. Non-linear relationships are captured using kernel functions. The method is effective for high-dimensional spaces and non-linear boundaries, but relies on careful kernel selection and parameter tuning.

How it works:

- Transform the input features using a kernel function (e.g., linear, polynomial, radial basis function (RBF)).
- Solve a quadratic optimisation problem to maximise the distance between classes.
- Use support vectors (data points closest to the hyperplane) to define the decision boundary.

## A.5 Neural networks

Neural networks (NNs) consist of layers of interconnected nodes (neurons) that transform input features through weighted connections and activation functions. While capable of capturing complex, non-linear relationships, NNs operate on large datasets and therefore require large computational resources; NNs are also prone to overfitting.

How it works:

- Randomly initialise weights and biases.
- Perform forward propagation to compute predictions.
- Compute loss using a predefined loss function (e.g., mean squared error).
- Use backpropagation to calculate gradients of loss with respect to weights.
- Update the weights using an optimisation algorithm (e.g., stochastic gradient descent).
- Repeat until convergence or a predefined number of epochs.B.Appendix 2: Shapley value derivation

## B.1 Shapley value: Origin and leverage in ML

Shapley values come from cooperative game theory, developed by Lloyd [45]. They offer a fair way to distribute the total gain (or cost) generated by a coalition of players based on each player's contribution. In the context of machine learning (ML), and the trend towards responsible ML (Bughin, 2024b), Shapley values have been widely adapted, which give three important features:

1. Explainability: Shapley values help make machine learning models more interpretable by showing how individual features affect a model's prediction. This is particularly important for complex models like neural networks or ensemble methods (e.g., random forests, gradient boosting), which are often considered "black boxes".

2. Fairness and transparency: Since Shapley values fairly distribute the contribution of each feature, they are widely used to address concerns about bias and fairness in AI. This is crucial in sectors like healthcare, finance or law, where model decisions must be explained to avoid unfair treatment based on sensitive features (e.g., gender, race).

3. Global and local explanations: Shapley values can provide both local (individual prediction) and global (overall model behaviour) insights. This allows users to explain why a model made a specific decision in one instance and how different features generally influence predictions.

In addition, Shapley values have some uniquely desirable properties, such as (1) efficiency: The sum of the contributions across all features equals the difference between the model's prediction and a baseline value, (2) symmetry: If two features contribute equally, they receive the same Shapley value and (3) additivity: For models combining multiple components, the Shapley value for the combined model is the sum of the Shapley values for the individual components.

## B.2 Shapley value: Definition and computation

Shapley values, 's, are a solution to how they should share the total profit in a cooperative game between acting players, N. By analogy with machine learning, suppose there are $N$ features (instead of players) that cooperate to obtain a better output prediction (instead of profit) than one alone.

The given data are characterised by a function g of a prediction by any subset $S$ of $N$ features; the interpretation of g is that for any subset $S$ of $N$, $g(S)$ is the extra prediction gain that the members of $S$ should share among themselves. The only constraint on g is that $g(S \cup T) \geq g(S) + g(T)$, which implies that the value of the coalition is at least equal to the value of its parts acting separately.

Assuming the three features described above, that is

1. The sum of the Shapley values of all attributes is equal to the value of the total attribute coalition, so that all the gain is distributed among the attributes ("efficiency" axiom).

2. If attributes $i$ and $j$ are equivalent in the sense that $g(S \cup \{i\}) = g(S \cup \{j\})$ for any subset $S$ of $N$ containing neither $i$ nor $j$, then the values for $i$ and $j$ are equivalent $\phi i(g) = \phi_j(g)$ ("symmetry" axiom).

3. For two output functions, g and h, $\phi(g) + \phi i(h) = \phi_i(g + h)$ for all $i$ in $N$, where the game $[g + h]$ is defined by $[g + h](S) = g(S) + hw(S)$ for any coalition $S$ ("additivity axiom").

Then there is a unique solution, called the Shapley value and as shown by Shapley [45], the attribute $i$ Shapley value satisfies:

$$\Phi_i = \sum_{S \subseteq N \setminus \{i\}} {}^{|S|!\,(|N|-|S|-1)!}/_{|N|!} \cdot [g(S \cup \{i\}) - g(S)] \quad (1)$$

As g is not known automatically, (A1) is estimated as:

$$\sum S_{\subseteq F \setminus \{i\}} {}^{|S|!\,(|F|-|S|-1)!}/_{|F|!} \cdot [f_{S\{i\}}(xs_{\cup\{i\}}) - fs(x_s)] \quad (2)$$

where the term $[fS_{\cup\{i\}}(xS_{\cup\{i\}}) - fS(xS)]$ is the marginal contribution of player $i$ to coalitions $S$; $F$ is a set of players and $S$ is a subset of $F$ that does not include the $i$th player $S \subset F \setminus \{i\}$, while$|F|!$ are the permutations of the number of $F$.

As an example (see Yamaguchi [63]), suppose three features with same equally likely probability to be activated in sequence and influence the outcome. Given (A2), we first compute the probabilities $({}^{|S|!\,(|F|-|S|-1)!}/_{|F|!}$, then the marginal function $[f_{S\cup\{i\}}(xS_{\cup\{i\}}) - fS(x_S)]$.

1. We thus have $F = 3 = \{X1, X2, X3\}$ and $i = 1$ are given, while the number of permutations is $|F|! = 6$, and $S$ are the following four subsets: {{none}, $\{X2\}$, $\{X3\}$, $\{X2, X3\}$}, Cases {none} and $\{X2, X3\}$ imply S = 2,and$|S|!(|F| - |S| - 1)!/|F|! = 2/6$, while the two other cases lead to a probability of 1/6 each.

2. Then, one needs to compute each company characteristic function g using the regression model $(X)$. When finding g, each characteristic value is fixed to find the value of $g(x)$. S one uses the expected value (the average value) of the feature instead of the missing feature, that is for the four possibilities:

$\phi 0 = E[f(X)]$; $\phi 1 = E[f(X)|X1 = x1] - \phi 0$; $\phi 2 = E[f(X)|X1 = x1, X2 = x2] - \phi 1$; $\phi 3 = E[f(X)|X1 = x1, X2 = x2, X3 = x3] - \phi 2$ and the SHAP values are obtained by averaging the $\phi i$ values over all possible orders.

## Author details

Jacques Bughin[1,2,3]

1 Times[2], SBSEM, Université libre de Bruxelles, Belgium

2 FortinoCapital, Antwerp, Belgium

3 CEO, MachaonAdvisory, Belgium

*Address all correspondence to: bughinjacquesrenejean@gmail.com

## References

[1] Bughin JR, Cincera M, Reykowska D, Ohme R. Big data is decision science: The case of COVID-19 vaccination. In: Handbook of Research on Applied Data Science and Artificial Intelligence in Business and Industry. New York: IGI Global; 2021. pp. 126-150

[2] Gomez-Uribe CA, Hunt N. The Netflix recommender system: Algorithms, business value, and innovation. ACM Transactions on Management Information Systems (TMIS). 2015;**6**(4):1-19

[3] Bughin J. Inside the of successful make up of AI-first organization. Journal of AI, Robotics and Workplace Automation. 2024;**3**(3):1-9

[4] Bughin J. What drives the corporate payoffs of using generative artificial intelligence? Structural Change and Economic Dynamics. 2024;**71**:658-668

[5] Cook TR, Modig ZD, Palmer NM. Explaining Machine Learning by Bootstrapping Partial Marginal Effects and Shapley Values. Kansas City: Federal Bank of Kansas; 2024

[6] Mullainathan S, Spiess J. Machine learning: An applied econometric approach. Journal of Economic Perspectives. 2017;**31**(2):87-106

[7] Baiardi A, Naghi A. The value added of machine learning to causal inference: Evidence from revisited studies. The Econometrics Journal. 2024;**27**:213-234

[8] Bughin J. Resilience and performance: Capturing their synergy for ongoing success. Journal of Business Strategy. 2024c;**45**(2):124-132

[9] Ewertowski T, Güldoğuş BÇ, Kuter S, Akyüz S, Weber GW, Sadłowska-Wrzesińska J, et al. The use of machine learning techniques for assessing the potential of organizational resilience. Central European Journal of Operations Research. 2024;**32**(3):685-710

[10] Uddin MR, Hasan MM, Abadi N. Do intangible assets provide corporate resilience? New evidence from infectious disease pandemics. Economic Modelling. 2022;**110**:105806

[11] Sincorá LA, Oliveira MPVD, Zanquetto-Filho H, Alvarenga MZ. Developing organizational resilience from business process management maturity. Innovation & Management Review. 2023;**20**(2):147-161

[12] Gogas P, Papadimitriou T. Machine learning in economics and finance. Computational Economics. 2021;**57**:1-4

[13] Wang H, Li C, Gu B, Min W. Does AI-based credit scoring improve financial inclusion? Evidence from online payday lending. In: 40th International Conference on Information Systems. ICIS 2019. Munich: Association for Information Systems;

[14] White H. Economic prediction using neural networks: The case of IBM daily stock returns. In: IEEE 1988 International Conference on Neural Networks. Vol. 2. San Diego, CA, USA: IEEE; 1988. pp. 451-458

[15] Varian HR. Big data: New tricks for econometrics. Journal of Economic Perspectives. 2014;**28**(2):3-28

[16] Nosratabadi S, Mosavi A, Duan P, Ghamisi P, Filip F, Band SS, et al. Data science in economics: Comprehensive review of advanced machine learning and deep learning methods. Mathematics. 2020;**8**(10):1799

[17] Çağlayan Akay E, Yılmaz Soydan NT, Kocarık Gacar B. Bibliometric analysis of the published literature on machine learning in economics and econometrics. Social Network Analysis and Mining. 2022;**12**(1):109

[18] Hew JJ, Leong LY, Tan GWH, Ooi KB, Lee VH. The age of mobile social commerce: An artificial neural network analysis on its resistances. Technological Forecasting and Social Change. 2019;**144**:311-324

[19] Sabaitytė J, Davidavičienė V, Straková J, Raudeliūnienė J. Decision tree modelling of E-consumers' preferences for internet marketing communication tools during browsing. Information Management. 2019;**22**:206-221

[20] Agarwal S. Deep learning-based sentiment analysis: Establishing customer dimension as the lifeblood of business management. Global Business Review. 2022;**23**(1):119-136

[21] Chapman JT, Desai A. Macroeconomic predictions using payments data and machine learning. Forecast. 2023;**5**(4):652-683

[22] Kolasa K, Admassu B, Hołownia-Voloskova M, Kędzior KJ, Poirrier JE, Perni S. Systematic reviews of machine learning in healthcare: A literature review. Expert Review of Pharmacoeconomics & Outcomes Research. 2024;**24**(1):63-115

[23] Storm H, Baylis K, Heckelei T. Machine learning in agricultural and applied economics. European Review of Agricultural Economics. 2020;**47**(3):849-892

[24] Dutt P, Tsetlin I. Income distribution and economic development: Insights from machine learning. Economics and Politics. 2021;**33**(1):1-36

[25] Dawson N, Rizoiu MA, Johnston B, Williams MA. Predicting skill shortages in labor markets: A machine learning approach. In: 2020 IEEE International Conference on Big Data (Big Data). Sorrento, Italy: IEEE; 2020. pp. 3052-3061

[26] Pap J, Mako C, Illessy M, Kis N, Mosavi A. Modeling organizational performance with machine learning. Journal of Open Innovation: Technology, Market, and Complexity. 2022;**8**(4):177

[27] Narciso DA, Martins FG. Application of machine learning tools for energy efficiency in industry: A review. Energy Reports. 2020;**6**:1181-1199

[28] Bargagli-Stoffi FJ, Niederreiter J, Riccaboni M. Supervised learning for predicting firm dynamics. In: Data Science for Economics and Finance. Cham: Springer; 2021. pp. 19-41

[29] Corea F, Bertinetti G, Cervellati EM. Hacking the venture industry: An early stage start up investment framework for data-driven investors. Machine Learning with Applications. 2021;**5**:1-13

[30] Meepaganithage A, Rath S, Nicolescu M, Nicolescu M, Sengupta S. Feature selection using the advanced Shapley value. In: 2024 IEEE 14th Annual Computing and Communication Workshop and Conference (CCWC). Las Vegas, US: IEEE; 2024. pp. 207-213

[31] Joseph A. Shapley Regressions: A Framework for Statistical Inference on Machine Learning Models. Vol. 784. London: Bank of England Staff Working Paper; 2019

[32] Jobin A, Ienca M, Vayena E. The global landscape of AI ethics guidelines. Nature Machine. Intelligence. 2019;**1**:389-399

[33] Bughin J. Doing versus saying: Responsible AI among large firms. AI and Society. 2024;**28**(3):1167-1188

[34] Goellner S, Tropmann-Frick M, Brumen B. Responsible artificial intelligence: A structured literature review. arXiv. 2024

[35] Fisher A, Rudin C, Dominici F. All models are wrong, but many are useful: Learning a variable's importance by studying an entire class of prediction models simultaneously. Journal of Machine Learning Research. 2019;**20**(177):1-81

[36] Adadi A, Berrada M. Peeking inside the black-box: A survey on explainable artificial intelligence (xai). IEEE Access. 2018;**6**:52138-52160

[37] Barber R, Candès E, Ramdas A, Ryan RT. Predictive inference with the jackknife+. Annals of Statistics. 2021;**49**:486-507. DOI: 10.1214/20-AOS1965

[38] Breiman L, Friedman J, Stone C, Olshen RA. Classification and Regression Trees. Chapman and Hall ed. New York: CRC Press; 1984

[39] Breiman L. Random forests. Machine Learning. 2001;**45**(1):5-32

[40] Sutera A, Louppe G, Huynh-Thu VA, Wehenkel L, Geurts P. From global to local MDI variable importance for random forests and when they are Shapley values. Advances in Neural Information Processing Systems. 2021;**34**:3533-3543

[41] Shrikumar A, Greenside P, Kundaje A. Learning important features through propagating activation differences. arXiv. 2017

[42] Ribeiro MT, Singh S, Guestrin C. Why should I trust you? Explaining the predictions of any classifier. In: Proceedings of the 22nd ACM SIGKDD International Conference on Knowledge Discovery and Data Mining. 2016. pp. 1135-1144

[43] Lundberg SM, Lee S-I. An unexpected unity among methods for interpreting model predictions. arXiv. 2016

[44] Mazhar K, Dwivedi P. A survey on methods for explainability in deep learning models. In: Dehuri S, Cho SB, Padhy VP, Shanmugam P, Ghosh A, editors. Machine Intelligence, Tools, and Applications. ICMITA 2024. Learning and Analytics in Intelligent Systems. Vol. 40. Cham: Springer; 2024

[45] Shapley LS. A value for n-person games. In: Kuhn HW, Tucker AW, editors. Contributions to the Theory of Games. Annals of Mathematical Studies 28. Princeton, US: Princeton University Press; 1953. pp. 307-317

[46] Chen H, Covert IC, Lundberg SM, Lee SI. Algorithms to estimate Shapley value feature attributions. Nature Machine Intelligence. 2023;**5**(6):590-601

[47] Fokkema H, Heide DR, Erven VT. Attribution-based explanations that provide recourse cannot be robust. Journal of Machine Learning Research. 2022;**24**:1-37. Available from: http://arxiv.org/abs/2205.15834

[48] Bilodeau B, Jaques N, Koh PW, Kim B. Impossibility theorems for feature attribution. Proceedings of the National Academy of Sciences. 2024;**121**(2):e2304406120

[49] Grover A, Leskovec J. node2vec: Scalable feature learning for networks. In: Proceedings of the ACM SIGKDD Conference on Knowledge Discovery and Data Mining (KDD). New York City, NY, USA: ACM Press; 2016. pp. 855-864

[50] Athey S. The impact of machine learning on economics. In: The Economics of Artificial Intelligence: An Agenda. 2018. pp. 507-547

[51] Athey S, Imbens GW, Wager S. Approximate residual balancing: Debiased inference of average treatment effects in high dimensions. Journal of the Royal Statistical Society: Series B (Statistical Methodology). 2018;**80**:597-623

[52] Athey S, Imbens GW. Machine learning methods that economists should know about. Annual Review of Economics. 2019;**11**:685-725

[53] Athey S, Imbens G. Machine learning methods for estimating heterogeneous causal effects. American Economic Review. 2019;**109**(5):2104-2107

[54] Athey S, Wager S. Estimating treatment effects with causal forests: An application. Observational Studies. 2019;**5**:37-51

[55] Chernozhukov V, Chetverikov D, Demirer M, Duflo E, Hansen C, Newey W. Double/debiased/neyman machine learning of treatment effects. American Economic Review. 2017;**107**(5):261-265

[56] Chernozhukov V, Chetverikov D, Demirer M, Duflo E, Hansen C, Newey W, et al. Double/debiased machine learning for treatment and structural parameters. The Econometrics Journal. 2018;**21**:C1-C68

[57] Davis JM, Heller SB. Using causal forests to predict treatment heterogeneity: An application to summer jobs. American Economic Review. 2017;**107**(5):546-550

[58] Nazemi A, Fabozzi FJ. Interpretable machine learning for creditor recovery rates. Journal of Banking & Finance. 2024;**164**:107187

[59] Wager S, Hastie T, Efron B. Confidence intervals for random forests: The jackknife and the infinitesimal jackknife. Journal of Machine Learning Research. 2014;**15**(2014):1625-1651

[60] Mentch L, Hooker G. Quantifying uncertainty in random forests via confidence intervals and hypothesis tests. Journal of Machine Learning Research. 2016;**17**(26):1-41

[61] Coleman T, Peng W, Mentch L. Scalable and efficient hypothesis testing with random forests. Journal of Machine Learning Research. 2022;**23**(170):1-35

[62] Buckmann M, Joseph A, Robertson H. Opening the black box: Machine learning interpretability and inference tools with an application to economic forecasting. In: Data Science for Economics and Finance: Methodologies and Applications. Cham: Springer International Publishing; 2021. pp. 43-63

[63] Yamaguchi K. Feature importance analysis in global manufacturing industry. International Journal of Trade, Economics Finance. 2022;**13**(2):28-35

[64] Zhao Q, Hastie T. Causal interpretations of black-box models. Journal of Business & Economic Statistics. 2019;**39**(1):272-281

[65] Pearl J. Bayesian analysis in expert systems: Comment: Graphical models, causality and intervention. Statistical Science. 1993;**8**(3):266-269

[66] Gulati R. Reorganize for Resilience: Putting Customers at the Center of your Business. Boston, US: Harvard Business Press; 2010

[67] Barney JB. Strategic factor markets: Expectations, luck, and business strategy. Management Science. 1986;**32**(10):1231-1241

[68] Teece DJ, Pisano G, Shuen A. Dynamic capabilities and strategic

management. Strategic Management Journal. 1997;**18**(7):509-533

[69] Buengeler C, Giebels J, Huck-Fries V, Redlbacher F. Advancing the understanding of agility and agile methods in organizations. In: Academy of Management Proceedings. Vol. 2020, no. 1. Briarcliff Manor, NY: Academy of Management; 2020. p. 14365

[70] Hamel G. The why, what, and how of management innovation. Harvard Business Review. 2006;**84**(2):72

[71] Meng T et al. Factors influencing enterprise organizational resilience: Evidence based on machine learning. Managerial and Decision Economics. 2024;**45**(2):578-589

[72] Iftikhar A, Purvis L, Giannoccaro I. A meta-analytical review of antecedents and outcomes of firm resilience. Journal of Business Research. 2021;**135**:408-425

[73] Battisti M, Deakins D. The relationship between dynamic capabilities, the firm's resource base and performance in a post-disaster environment. International Small Business Journal. 2017;**35**(1):78-98

[74] Dyduch W, Chudziński P, Cyfert S, Zastempowski M. Dynamic capabilities, value creation and value capture: Evidence from SMEs under Covid-19 lockdown in Poland. PLoS One. 2021;**16**(6):e0252423

[75] Teece DJ. A capability theory of the firm: An economics and (strategic) management perspective. New Zealand Economic Papers. 2019;**53**(1):1-43

[76] Guo B, Pérez-Castrillo D, Toldrà-Simats A. Firms' innovation strategy under the shadow of analyst coverage. Journal of Financial Economics. 2019;**131**(2):456-483

[77] Mohammad AS. Impact of strategic agility on creating competitive advantage: Evidence from Jordanian insurance companies. International Journal of Business Innovation and Research. 2022;**28**(1):101-118

[78] Woods DD. The strategic agility gap: How organizations are slow and stale to adapt in turbulent worlds. In: Human and Organisational Factors: Practices and Strategies for a Changing World. 2020. pp. 95-104

[79] Adner R. Ecosystem as structure: An actionable construct for strategy. Journal of Management. 2017;**43**(1):39-58

[80] Ameye N, Bughin J, van Zeebroeck N. From experimentation to scaling: What shapes the funnel of AI adoption? Economics of Innovation and New Technology. 2024:1-15

[81] Ellström D, Holtström J, Berg E, Josefsson C. Dynamic capabilities for digital transformation. Journal of Strategy and Management. 2021;**15**(2):272-286

[82] Podsakoff PM, Organ DW. Self-reports in organizational research: Problems and prospects. Journal of Management. 1986;**12**(4):531-544

[83] Barnichon R, Matthes C, Ziegenbein A. The financial crisis at 10: Will we ever recover? FRBSF Economic Letter. 2018;**19**:1-4

[84] Karalashvili N, Viganola D. The evolving effect of COVID-19 on the private sector. World Bank Development Economics-Global Indicators Briefs. 2021;**1**

[85] Bughin J. Are you resilient? Machine learning prediction of corporate rebound out of the Covid-19 pandemic. Managerial and Decision Economics. 2023;**44**(3):1547-1564

[86] Bughin J, Van Zeebroeck N. The best response to digital disruption. MIT Sloan Management Review. 2017;**58**:80-86

[87] Floetgen RJ, Strauss J, Weking J, Hein A, Urmetzer F, Böhm M, et al. Introducing platform ecosystem resilience: Leveraging mobility platforms and their ecosystems for the new normal during COVID-19. European Journal of Information Systems. 2021;**30**(3):304-321

[88] Lingens B, Miehé L, Gassmann O. The ecosystem blueprint: How firms shape the design of an ecosystem according to the surrounding conditions. Long Range Planning. 2021;**54**(2):2021

[89] Hopp C, Antons D, Kaminski J, Salge T. What 40 Years of Research Reveals about the Difference between Disruptive and Radical Innovation. Boston, US: Harvard Business Review; 2018

Chapter 6

# Economic Interdependence and Its Role in the Propagation of Financial Crises: A Theoretical Synthesis

*Raquel Ayestarán Crespo and Ignacio Urrutia Hoyos*


## Abstract

The intensification of global economic interdependence has accelerated the spread of financial crises among nations. Our goal is to identify and categorize the primary channels through which economic interdependence drives financial contagion between countries. To achieve this, we conducted a theoretical review that integrates existing literature on financial and commercial transmission mechanisms. The findings highlight that the most relevant channels are international trade, foreign direct investment, integrated financial markets, global supply chains, and coordinated economic policies, each with varying impacts depending on the economic context. The research highlights that while economic interdependence can foster growth, it simultaneously heightens the vulnerability of economies to financial crises. This study emphasizes the urgency of formulating stronger global economic policies to mitigate these risks and suggests specific areas for future research, such as evaluating the effectiveness of policies in different regions.


**Keywords:** economic interdependence, financial contagion, international financial crises, transmission channels, economic impact

## 1. Introduction

Global economic interdependence is an essential pillar in the structure of the contemporary world economy, enabling the constant and dynamic flow of goods, services, capital, and information among nations. Economic interdependence refers to the mutual reliance between two or more national economies, driven by the exchange of goods, services, capital, and technology across borders. In such a system, economic events in one country can significantly impact others, due to strong commercial and financial ties. Robert Keohane's [1] theory of complex interdependence highlights the interconnectedness of modern economies, emphasizing that states operate within a network of relationships that restricts unilateral actions. This interdependence underscores the necessity for cooperation, as nations are bound by shared economic interests and vulnerabilities in a globalized world.

Global economic interdependence has been key to driving economic growth, fostering technological innovation, and promoting the development of emerging markets, integrating economies into a more cohesive and efficient global network. Global economic interdependence has increased significantly in recent decades, facilitated by globalization and the integration of financial markets. The phenomenon of economic interdependence does not have a specific starting point, but it has evolved throughout history as national economies have become connected and mutually dependent.

However, several historical milestones can be identified that marked the beginning and significant development of this interdependence: the commercial revolution, the industrial revolution, the era of imperialism and colonialism, the Bretton Woods System, Globalization, and Regional Integration.

During the Commercial Revolution (fifteenth and sixteenth centuries), the beginning of global economic interdependence can be traced back to when European powers began exploring and establishing international trade routes. The discovery of new sea routes allowed the exchange of goods, technologies, and resources between continents, creating an incipient global trade network.

In the Industrial Revolution (eighteenth and nineteenth centuries), economic interdependence intensified as production increased and demand for raw materials and markets for manufactured goods grew. Nations began to specialize in different economic sectors, fostering international trade and mutual dependence on the supply of goods and services.

Throughout the era of Imperialism and Colonialism (nineteenth and early twentieth centuries), European powers and other developed nations expanded their colonial territories, establishing dependent economic relationships with the colonies. The colonial economies were oriented to supply raw materials and resources to the metropolises, while the latter exported manufactured goods to the colonies, consolidating an unequal interdependence.

The concept of complex interdependence, proposed by Robert Keohane and Joseph Nye [2], provides a broader understanding of global interactions in the economic context. This theory argues that relations between states and non-state actors are deeply interconnected at multiple levels, reducing the relevance of purely military power relations and highlighting the importance of economic, political, and social connections. In a world characterized by complex interdependence, financial crises spread not only through traditional economic channels such as trade and investment, but also through global networks of political and social institutions.

These networks can exacerbate vulnerabilities, as political and economic decisions in one country impact others more quickly and deeply. This approach highlights the need for internationally coordinated policies, not only to mitigate financial risks, but also to strengthen resilience to external shocks.

The theory of complex interdependence proposed by Keohane and Nye [2] continues to be a fundamental reference for understanding the dynamics of globalized economies in the twenty-first century. This theory has been strengthened by recent research that highlights how economic, technological, and financial interconnection not only increases cooperation between States, but also amplifies the risks of contagion in periods of crisis. Hélène Rey [3], for example, emphasizes that the integrated nature of financial markets allows for rapid transmission of shocks between economies. This reinforces the relevance of international coordination in macroeconomic policies to mitigate the risks inherent to said interdependence [3].

Bretton Woods System (1944): After World War II, the Bretton Woods System was established, creating institutions such as the International Monetary Fund (IMF) and the World Bank. This system promoted international economic cooperation, exchange rate stability, and free trade, thereby strengthening economic interdependence among participating nations.

Globalization (Late twentieth and twenty-first centuries): Globalization has been a key factor in the intensification of economic interdependence. Advances in technology, transportation, and communications have facilitated international trade, foreign direct investment, and the integration of financial markets. As a result, national economies have become highly interconnected, with economic events in one part of the world having global repercussions.

Regional Integration (Examples: European Union, NAFTA/USMCA): The formation of economic blocs and free trade agreements, such as the European Union and the United States-Mexico-Canada Agreement (USMCA), has deepened economic interdependence among member countries. These agreements eliminate trade barriers, harmonize regulations, and foster economic cooperation, thereby increasing mutual dependence for trade and investment.

In *This Time is Different: Eight Centuries of Financial Folly,* Carmen Reinhart and Kenneth Rogoff present a comprehensive comparative analysis of over eight hundred years of financial crises, identifying recurring patterns in global economic history.

Using a rigorous empirical approach, the authors challenge the notion that crises are exceptional phenomena, demonstrating that they are, in fact, cyclical and share common structural characteristics. Financial crises tend to have severe consequences for sovereign debt, weaken economic growth, and exacerbate employment problems in various regions of the world.

Additionally, Reinhart and Rogoff [4] highlight a psychological and behavioral component among economic actors and governments: the propensity to underestimate financial risks during boom periods, operating under the premise that "this time is different", which perpetuates historical mistakes. Their research emphasizes that mismanaged policies, excessive debt accumulation, and institutional complacency are key factors that foster financial bubbles. When these bubbles burst, they severely impact both emerging and developed economies. Reinhart and Rogoff's work serves as an essential frame of reference for preventive policymaking, providing an in-depth understanding of how to avoid the recurrence of financial crises through more prudent and coordinated economic management.

Charles Kindleberger, in his influential work "Manias, Panics, and Crashes: A History of Financial Crises" [5], co-written in later editions with Robert Aliber, provides an essential historical framework for understanding the mechanisms that trigger financial crises and their transmission. Global. Kindleberger and Aliber describe how financial bubbles, fueled by excess speculation and credit, tend to collapse in panics that spread rapidly through interconnected markets. This work highlights that, in an interdependent world, financial imbalances in one region can be amplified and affect other economies through capital flows and investor expectations. Their analysis complements the studies of Reinhart and Rogoff [4], reinforcing the historical understanding of how crises, far from being isolated phenomena, spread with alarming regularity in the global economy.

The fundamental objective of this chapter is to analyze and classify the main transmission channels that allow the spread of financial crises between interdependent economies. The rise of financial globalization and the growing integration of international markets have shaped a deeply interconnected global economic system.

This interconnection, while promoting growth and economic efficiency, has significantly increased the vulnerability of countries to external shocks and systemic crises. Analysis of these channels—such as international trade, foreign direct investment, integrated financial markets, and global supply chains—is essential to understanding the mechanisms through which a financial crisis can escalate and affect multiple regions. Simultaneous.

The key channels that have led to the transmission of financial crises are explored by Joseph Stiglitz [6], who has been instrumental in understanding how international trade and global economic integration shape interdependence among national economies. His analysis highlights that while interdependence can foster growth and cooperation, it can also generate shared vulnerabilities and inequalities that need to be carefully managed through appropriate economic policies. In his work *Globalization and Its Discontents* (2002), Stiglitz critically analyzes how international trade policies, promoted mainly by institutions such as the International Monetary Fund (IMF) and the World Trade Organization (WTO), can contribute to the occurrence of economic crises.

Stiglitz argues that while international trade has the potential to foster growth and economic interdependence, imposed policies often fail to consider country-specific circumstances and needs. These policies, based on a one-size-fits-all approach, frequently call for austerity measures, excessive liberalization, and market opening without adequate support to mitigate adverse social and economic impacts. As a result, vulnerable economies may face macroeconomic imbalances, loss of control over their monetary and fiscal policies, and increased exposure to external shocks. Moreover, the lack of adequate protection and regulatory mechanisms can amplify the vulnerabilities inherent in economic interdependence, facilitating the rapid spread of financial crises globally. In essence, Stiglitz [6] stresses that the design and implementation of international trade policies must be more inclusive and adaptive to prevent economic interdependence from becoming a destabilizing factor during periods of crisis.Thomas Piketty, in his influential work Capital in the Twenty-First Century (2014), offers a comprehensive analysis of the dynamics of inequality in the global economy, providing a crucial perspective for understanding how economic interdependence not only fosters growth and cooperation, but can also exacerbate disparities between nations. Piketty argues that the concentration of capital in the hands of an elite can intensify in the context of globalization, which can be a trigger or amplifier of financial crises. In this sense, their work is relevant to this analysis, as it reinforces the idea that financial transmission channels are not only related to trade and investments, but also to the unequal distribution of wealth, which can generate social tensions. and significant economic benefits in times of crisis [7]. This analysis should be included in the discussion of the long-term impacts of economic interdependence on structural disparities between countries, along with references to Stiglitz and Obstfeld.

Another channel for the transmission of crises is foreign direct investment (FDI) in other countries. According to Barry Eichengreen, foreign investment, by integrating national economies into global financial markets, can increase a country's vulnerability to external and speculative shocks. When FDI flows significantly into a country, they can influence exchange rates and macroeconomic stability. If these flows become volatile or are abruptly withdrawn, they may trigger financial crises by destabilizing the local currency and undermining investor confidence. In his book *Globalizing Capital: A History of the International Monetary System*, Eichengreen provides a comprehensive overview of the evolution of global capital flows, including FDI, and its impact on international economic stability. He analyzes how monetary and fiscal policies, along with capital movements, have contributed to both economic growth and financial crises throughout history.

New studies on FDI, such as those by Van Driel et al. [8], highlight that the flow of capital to emerging economies not only promotes growth, but also introduces significant risks when there are insufficient controls. These flows, in times of crisis, tend to reverse abruptly, creating monetary imbalances and seriously affecting the international reserves of the receiving countries. This underlines the importance of implementing macroprudential policies that regulate such flows to avoid severe financial shocks.

The analysis of global financial integration and the crises that emerge from it would not be complete without reference to the research of Maurice Obstfeld. In his work Global Capital Markets: Integration, Crisis, and Growth (2004), Obstfeld examines how the globalization of financial markets has transformed the economic landscape, making macroeconomic policies essential to mitigate external shocks. Obstfeld argues that the correct implementation of coordinated monetary and fiscal policies can reduce the impact of financial crises, providing countries with tools to better manage volatility and risk in an increasingly interdependent economic environment [9]. His perspective is essential to complement the theories of Hélène Rey and Joseph Stiglitz, since they all emphasize the need for macroprudential policies that strengthen global financial stability and avoid the repetition of systemic crises.

In addition to FDI, Integrated Financial Markets also play a critical role in the transmission of crises. The contributions of Hélène Rey [10], Professor of Economics at the London Business School, are particularly noteworthy in this context. Rey has made significant contributions to understanding how the integration of global financial markets facilitates capital mobility, thereby increasing interdependence between national economies. In her influential article "The Dilemma of the Global Central Bank: Regulation and Stability in Integrated Financial Markets", she argues that the growing connectedness of financial markets allows for rapid capital flows worldwide, heightening the vulnerability of economies to external and speculative shocks. Her analysis shows that while financial integration can promote economic growth and allocative efficiency, it can also amplify the risks of financial contagion, exacerbating mutual dependence among countries. Moreover, Rey stresses the need for international coordination in macroprudential policies to mitigate the adverse effects of this interdependence, proposing regulatory frameworks that balance the benefits of capital mobility with global economic stability. Her work has been instrumental in understanding the complex dynamics of integrated financial markets and their impact on global economic stability.

In his influential work The Globalization Paradox (2012), Dani Rodrik presents a fundamental thesis for understanding how tensions between globalization and national policies can trigger financial instability when not properly managed. Rodrik argues that, in an environment of global economic interdependence, nations face a dilemma between maintaining their autonomy in macroeconomic policies and adapting to the rules imposed by international markets. This tension between the desire for internal stability and the external pressures inherent to globalization can amplify financial crises by weakening national mechanisms for control and response to external shocks. Rodrik's inclusion in this analysis reinforces the need to adopt macroprudential policies that recognize the limitations imposed by economic interdependence, and poses a challenge to policymakers: balance global integration with domestic resilience. In this sense, their work complements previous studies on financial regulation, highlighting how the proper management of these tensions is key to mitigating systemic risks in a globalized world [11].

## 2. Bibliographic analysis

Another factor in economic interdependence is global supply chains, an area explored in depth by Gary Gereffi, Professor of Sociology at the University of North Carolina at Chapel Hill. Gereffi has pioneered the concept of Global Value Chains (GVCs), offering an analytical framework that explains how the fragmentation of production across different countries, aimed at exploiting comparative advantages, enhances economic interdependence on a global scale. In his seminal work, *Global Value Chains and Development: Redefining the Contours of twenty-first Century Capitalism*, Gereffi argues that the geographic dispersion of production stages enables companies to optimize costs and access diverse markets, thereby increasing interconnectedness among national economies.

His analysis reveals that this fragmentation not only promotes efficiency and economic growth but also intensifies mutual dependence between countries, as disruptions in one part of the chain can have cascading effects at the global level. Additionally, Gereffi highlights the importance of public policies and international regulations in managing the risks associated with this interdependence, such as vulnerability to external shocks and inequalities in the distribution of benefits. His work has been instrumental in understanding how global supply chains shape the structure of the world economy, emphasizing both the opportunities and challenges presented by economic interdependence in the context of contemporary globalization.

In the analysis of *Coordinated Economic Policies, Joseph E. Stiglitz*, an American economist and Nobel Prize laureate in Economics (2001), stands out. He has made significant contributions to understanding how cooperation in macroeconomic and regulatory policies among countries reflects and affects a high degree of economic interdependence. In his work "*Globalization and Its Discontents*" (2002), Stiglitz argues that the lack of effective coordination among the world's major economies and international financial institutions can exacerbate economic vulnerabilities and contribute to the outbreak of financial crises. He contends that unilateral economic policies, such as structural adjustment recommendations imposed by the International Monetary Fund (IMF) on developing countries, often ignore local conditions and generate imbalances that have global repercussions due to economic interdependence.

Furthermore, in *The Price of Inequality* (2012), Stiglitz emphasizes the need for greater coordination in fiscal and regulatory policies to mitigate economic inequalities that can destabilize interconnected economies. His analysis highlights that, in a highly interdependent world, international cooperation is essential for designing policies that promote global economic stability, avoid contagion from financial crises, and foster inclusive growth. Stiglitz advocates for the creation of more inclusive and democratic global governance frameworks that facilitate economic policy coordination, thereby reducing the risks associated with interdependence and promoting greater resilience to international financial crises. His work has been essential for understanding the role of coordinated economic policies in a highly interconnected global economy (**Table 1**).

The 2008 subprime mortgage crisis is a paradigmatic example of how a financial crisis can spread globally through various channels of economic interdependence. By analyzing this crisis through the perspectives of key authors—Joseph E. Stiglitz, Barry Eichengreen, Hélène Rey, and Gary Gereffi [12]—we can gain a deeper understanding of the mechanisms that facilitated its global diffusion and the underlying vulnerabilities within the international economic system.

| Factor | Description | Key Author | Key Work |
|---|---|---|---|
| International Trade | The exchange of goods and services between countries fosters growth and interdependence, but inappropriate trade policies can generate macroeconomic imbalances and shared vulnerabilities. | Joseph E. Stiglitz | *Globalization and Its Discontents* (2002) |
| Foreign Direct Investments (FDI) | FDI integrates national economies into global financial markets, increasing vulnerability to external and speculative shocks. Volatility in capital flows can destabilize local economies. | Barry Eichengreen | *Globalizing Capital: A History of the International Monetary System* (1996). |
| Integrated Financial Markets | The integration of global financial markets facilitates capital mobility, increasing interdependence and vulnerability to financial contagion. The lack of coordinated regulation can exacerbate these risks. | Hélène Rey | "Dilemma of the Global Central Bank: Regulation and Stability in Integrated Financial Markets". |
| Global Supply Chains | Fragmentation of production in different countries to exploit comparative advantages strengthens economic interdependence. Disruptions in one part of the chain can have cascading effects worldwide. | Gary Gereffi | *Global Value Chains and Development: Redefining the Contours of 21st Century Capitalism.* |
| Coordinated Economic Policies | Cooperation in macroeconomic and regulatory policies between countries reflects a high degree of interdependence. Lack of coordination can exacerbate economic vulnerabilities and contribute to the outbreak of financial crises. | Joseph E. Stiglitz | *Globalization and Its Discontents* (2002) *The Price of Inequality* (2012) |

**Table 1.**
*Price of inequality.*

## 3. International trade: Joseph E. Stiglitz

According to Joseph E. Stiglitz in *Globalization and Its Discontents*, international trade policies and the recommendations of institutions such as the International Monetary Fund (IMF) can create macroeconomic imbalances that exacerbate economic vulnerabilities during times of crisis. During the 2008 crisis, the contraction of global trade due to reduced demand and disruptions in supply chains intensified the economic recession across multiple countries. Excessive dependence on external markets made interconnected economies more susceptible to the spread of the financial crisis that originated in the United States, where the housing bubble and the collapse of subprime mortgages triggered a decline in global demand for goods and services.

### 3.1 Foreign direct investment (FDI): Barry Eichengreen

According to Barry Eichengreen in *Globalizing Capital*, Foreign Direct Investments (FDI) and other global capital flows increase economic interdependence, which can amplify vulnerability to external shocks [13]. In 2008, the abrupt withdrawal of capital from emerging markets and the freezing of FDI in response to the financial panic in the United States illustrated how highly integrated economies are more prone to contagion. A lack of trust in global financial markets led to a reduction in foreign investments, severely impacting countries that relied on these flows to finance their economic growth and maintain financial stability.

### 3.2 Integrated financial markets: Hélène Rey

Financial globalization has increased the interdependence of markets through capital flows and complex financial products, which has generated greater exposure to systemic risk. von Luckner et al. [14] argue that the increasing interconnection between the banking systems of developed and emerging countries has created an ecosystem where a local financial crisis can quickly become a global crisis. This was evident in previous crises, where exposure to toxic assets caused a cascade of financial bankruptcies in various markets [14].

Hélène Rey, in her article "Dilemma of the Global Central Bank", highlights how the integration of global financial markets facilitates capital mobility, increasing interdependence and vulnerability to financial contagions. The 2008 crisis perfectly illustrated this dynamic, as the collapse of financial markets in the United States quickly spread to other global markets due to the interconnectedness of financial institutions and the globalization of credit markets.

The exposure of banks and financial institutions around the world to toxic assets such as subprime mortgages exacerbated the crisis, demonstrating that financial integration without adequate regulation can amplify systemic risks.

Contemporary theories on global financial risk have evolved significantly, especially with the increasing complexity of global financial systems. Ulrich Beck [15] developed the theory of the "risk society", which argues that globalization and technological advances not only generate growth, but also new forms of structural vulnerability that increase exposure to financial crises. On the other hand, Hélène Rey [3] emphasizes that the integration of global financial markets facilitates capital mobility, but also amplifies the risks of financial contagion when there is no coordinated regulation. In his recent work, Rey examines how deregulated capital flows exacerbate financial crises, as happened during the 2008 global recession. These contributions highlight the need for a more robust global regulatory framework that can mitigate disruptions and improve the resilience of companies. Interconnected Economies forces key points about contemporary theories of financial risk with recent high-impact research.

### 3.3 Global supply chains: Gary Gereffi

In the current context, global supply chains have evolved into even more interdependent and complex systems, making them vulnerable to external crises. Recent research, such as that of Baldwin and Freeman [16], has shown that disruptions in global value chains can amplify economic downturns by affecting not only supply, but also aggregate demand in key sectors such as technology and manufacturing. The interconnection of these chains means that crises in one country have global repercussions, which require more robust resilience policies.

Gary Gereffi, in *Global Value Chains and Development*, explains how the fragmentation of production across different countries strengthens economic interdependence. During the 2008 crisis, disruptions in global supply chains affected multiple industrial sectors. For instance, the decline in demand for automobiles and electronic products in developed markets led to a reduction in production and exports in countries that were integral to these supply chains. This mutual dependence on global

*DOI: http://dx.doi.org/10.5772/intechopen.1008150*

production meant that disruptions in one country quickly translated into negative impacts in others, amplifying the depth and duration of the global recession.

## 4. Coordinated economic policies: Joseph E. Stiglitz

Finally, Joseph E. Stiglitz [17] emphasizes the importance of coordinated economic policies to mitigate the effects of economic interdependence. In 2008, the lack of effective coordination among the world's major economies and international financial institutions initially exacerbated the crisis. Uncoordinated policy responses, characterized by varying speeds and approaches to economic stimulus, generated uncertainty and slowed the global recovery. Stiglitz argues that greater international cooperation in macroeconomic and regulatory policymaking could have facilitated a faster and more effective response to stabilize markets and restore global confidence.

The 2008 subprime mortgage crisis exemplifies how the primary channels of economic interdependence—international trade, foreign direct investment (FDI), integrated financial markets, global supply chains, and coordinated economic policies—can interact and propagate a financial crisis worldwide. This understanding underscores the need for more inclusive, coordinated, and adaptive economic policies to manage economic interdependence and prevent future global financial crises. While economic interdependence can stimulate growth, it also increases the vulnerability of economies to financial crises.

## 5. Conclusion

The central objective of this chapter is to carry out a systematic review of the existing literature on economic interdependence and its role in the propagation of financial crises, in order to consolidate the main theories and approaches developed in this field. Through this review, we seek to offer a comprehensive perspective of the mechanisms through which interconnected economies facilitate the contagion of crises and to critically evaluate the impact of these interactions in diverse economic contexts. This approach allows us not only to organize existing academic knowledge, but also to identify gaps in research that can be addressed in future studies. The relevance of this work lies in its ability to synthesize the most influential theoretical contributions, providing a solid basis for the development of global economic policies that can mitigate the risks associated with financial interdependence. In this way, the article represents a key contribution to the field of international economics, being an essential piece in the evolution of economic theory toward a deeper and more sophisticated understanding of global dynamics.

This study powerfully underlines the imperative of formulating more robust global economic policies to mitigate the risks inherent in economic interdependence. Through a detailed analysis of the various transmission channels—international trade, foreign direct investment, integrated financial markets, global supply chains, and coordinated economic policies—it has become clear how the close interconnectedness of national economies not only promotes growth and cooperation but also significantly increases vulnerability to financial crises. Lessons learned from events such as the 2008 subprime mortgage crisis demonstrate that, without adequate regulation and effective coordination among the world's major economies, the risks of financial contagion are amplified, affecting both emerging and developed countries.

In addition, this study identifies crucial areas for future research, emphasizing the need to evaluate the effectiveness of economic policies implemented in various regions of the world. Understanding regional specificities and how different economic contexts respond to coordinated policies will allow for more adaptive and resilient strategies against potential crises. It is also recommended to explore the impact of new forms of economic interdependence, such as emerging technologies and innovations in digital finance, on global economic stability.

In short, strengthening international economic governance and promoting greater multilateral cooperation are fundamental pillars for building a more secure and equitable global economic system, capable of facing the financial challenges of the future with greater efficiency and solidarity.

The urgency of formulating stronger global economic policies lies not only in preventing future crises but also in creating a framework that fosters inclusive and sustainable economic development. By integrating more inclusive and adaptive approaches into policymaking, the adverse effects of economic interdependence can be effectively mitigated, promoting greater stability and resilience in the global financial system. This study, therefore, not only contributes to a deeper understanding of the mechanisms of financial crisis propagation but also establishes a solid basis for the implementation of preventive policies that respond to the complexities of the contemporary global economy.

## Acknowledgments

The authors acknowledge the use of ChatGPT for language editing in the chapter.

## Author details

Raquel Ayestarán Crespo* and Ignacio Urrutia Hoyos
Universidad Francisco de Vitoria, Spain

*Address all correspondence to: r.ayestaran@ufv.es

## References

[1] Keohane RO. After Hegemony: Cooperation and Discord in the World Political Economy. Princeton University Press; 1979

[2] Keohane R, Nye J. Power and Interdependence: World Politics in Transition. 3rd ed. Boston: Little, Brown; 1998

[3] Rey H. Financial stability as a global public good. Revue d'economie Financiere. 2023;151(3):287-296. Available from: https://shs-cairn-info.acces.bibl.ulaval.ca/journal-revue-d-economie-financiere-2023-3-page-287?lang=en

[4] Reinhart CM, Rogoff KS. Time is Different: Eight Centuries of Financial Folly. Princeton University Press; 2009

[5] Kindleberger CP, Aliber RZ. Manias, Panics, and Crashes: A History of Financial Crises. 6th ed. Palgrave Macmillan; 2011

[6] Stiglitz JE. Globalization and Its Discontents. W.W. Norton C Company; 2002

[7] Piketty T. Capital in the Twenty-First Century. Harvard University Press; 2014. Available from: https://www.degruyter.com/document/doi/10.4159/9780674369542/html

[8] Van Driel M, Biermann F, Vijge MJ, Kim RE. How the World Bank engages with the sustainable development goal on reducing inequalities: A case of organizational Jiu-Jitsu. Global Studies Quarterly. 2023;3(3):ksad035. Available from: https://academic.oup.com/isagsq/article/3/3/ksad035/7223538

[9] Obstfeld M. Global Capital Markets: Integration, Crisis, and Growth. Cambridge University Press; 2004. Available from: https://scholar.google.com.ec/scholar?hl=es&as_sdt=0%2C5&q=Obstfeld%2C+M.+%282004%29.+Global+Capital+Markets%3A+Integration%2C+Crisis%2C+and+Growth.+Cambridge+University+Press.&btnG

[10] Rey H. Dilemma not Trilemma: The Global Financial Cycle and Monetary Policy Independence [Internet]. In: Proceedings of the Economic Policy Symposium – Jackson Hole; 2013 Aug 22-24; Jackson Hole, WY. Kansas City (MO): Federal Reserve Bank of Kansas City; 2013. Available from: https://www.kansascityfed.org/Jackson%20Hole/documents/4575/2013Rey.pdf [cited 2024 OCT 15]

[11] Rodrik D. The Globalization Paradox: Democracy and the Future of the World Economy. W. W. Norton & Company; 2011. Available from: https://www.hks.harvard.edu/publications/globalization-paradox

[12] Gereffi G. Global Value Chains and Development: Redefining the Contours of 21st Century Capitalism. Cambridge University Press; 2018

[13] Eichengreen B. Globalizing Capital: A History of the International Monetary System. Princeton University Press; 1996

[14] von Luckner CG, Reinhart CM, Rogoff K. Decrypting new age international capital flows. Journal of Monetary Economics. 2023;138:104-122. Available from: https://www.sciencedirect.com/science/article/abs/pii/S0304393223000673

[15] Beck U. The Reinvention of Politics: Rethinking Modernity in the Global Social Order. John Wiley & Sons; 2018. Available from: https://books.

google.com.ec/books?hl=es&lr=&id=TwNRDwAAQBAJ&oi=fnd&pg=PP2&dq=Beck,+U.+(2018).+The+reinvention+of+politics:+Rethinking+modernity+in+the+global+social+order.+John+Wiley+%26+Sons.&ots=RKuZ_4L9-j&sig=qw3CRd0tpI40u4GzLZl-BfzI1eA#v=onepage&q=Beck%2C%20U.%20(2018).%20The%20reinvention%20of%20politics%3A%20Rethinking%20modernity%20in%20the%20global%20social%20order.%20John%20Wiley%20%26%20Sons.&f=false

[16] Baldwin R, Freeman R. Risks and global supply chains: What we know and what we need to know. Annual Review of Economics. 2022;14(1):153-180. Available from: https://www.annualreviews.org/content/journals/10.1146/annurev-economics-051420-113737

[17] Stiglitz JE. The Price of Inequality. W.W. Norton C Company; 2012

Chapter 7

# Modeling the Relation between the Price of Oil and the Value of the U.S. Dollar: The Frequency of Observations Matters

*Jaime Marquez and Kelu Ren*


## Abstract

This paper empirically examines the relationship between movements in the price of oil and movements in the dollar's external value. Specifically, to what extent do financial markets arbitrage price differentials among internationally traded assets, such as oil, gold, and foreign exchange? To this end, we use daily data observations from January 1999 to March 2024 to estimate the parameters of vector autoregressive process with six variables and five lags. As it turns out, using a daily frequency carries its own practical complications that do not arise when using either quarterly or monthly observations. One such complication arose on April 20, 2020, when the price for West Texas Intermediate (WTI) closed at *negative* $38 per barrel. A market that can record a negative price cannot be modeled empirically relying on the widely used *logarithmic* formulations. We use this event to motivate the development of an alternative to the logarithmic formulation. There are several results of interest. First, there is one cointegration relation among the prices of these international trade assets; arguably, this finding might be interpreted as suggesting a long-run arbitrage relation. Second, the implied elasticities of the model are far from constant.


**Keywords:** price of oil, price of gold, cointegration, exchange rates, log-linear models, free disposal

## 1. Introduction

> *"Few of us take the pains to study the origin of our cherished convictions; indeed, we have a natural repugnance to so doing. ... The resentment aroused when doubt is cast upon any of our assumptions leads us to seek every manner of excurse for clinging to them. The result is that most of our so-called reasoning consists in finding arguments for going on believing what we already do." [Emphasis added] Joan H. Robinson. Ref. [1]*

This paper empirically examines the relationship between movements in the price of oil and movements in the value of other internationally traded financial assets such as gold and foreign exchange rates. Interest in this relation originated with the work of

Krugman and Golub, who sought to explain the correlation between movements in oil prices and movements in the external value of the dollar. More recently, the increasing relevance of financial considerations for understanding the functioning of the oil market has reignited the interest in this relation. Specifically, one question of interest is to what extent do financial markets arbitrage price differentials among oil, gold, and foreign exchange? We study this question using daily data from January 1999 to March 2024.

Previous research results revealed that there was no consistent conclusion about the relationship between the price of oil and the value of the dollar due to different research methodologies adopted, the sample subjects selected, and the time frames analyzed. Albulescu and Ajmi's studies [2] indicated that there was a bidirectional Granger causal relationship between international oil prices and the real effective exchange rate of the US dollar, which became more pronounced after the financial crisis of 2008 [2]. Amano and Norden [3] proposed a unidirectional impact from oil prices to the exchange rate after the end of the Bretton Woods system and oil prices became a key factor in explaining US macroeconomic situation [3]. Lizardo and Mollick [4] demonstrated that there was a negative relation between the price of oil and the real exchange rate of US dollars, suggesting that the fluctuations of USD value were influenced by changes in the money supply [4]. Likewise, Chen et al. [5] confirmed this negative association between the oil price and the dollar value but proposed that the changes in dollar value were driven by demand factors rather than supply [5]. Conversely, Coudert and Mignon [6] observed a negative relationship between oil prices and the dollar exchange rate across most periods but noted a shift to a positive relation when the dollar value reached extremely high levels [6]. Marquez [7] suggested that the relationship between real price of oil and REER depends on different deflators for oil price and the types of exchange rates (effective & bilateral) [7]. Nandi et al. [8] found that oil price changes have a persistent change on exchange rate volatility, and an increase in oil price will have a larger impact than a decrease in oil price [8]. As far as we know, only the paper by Fratzscher, Schneider and Van Robays deals with daily data.

Indeed, Fratzscher, Schneider, and Van Robays estimate the parameters of their model using daily data from January 2001 until October 2012. Their sample, however, stops before Covid-19, and thus it does not include the *negative* oil price shown in **Figure 1**.

A negative price of oil, even for 1 day, invites us to re-examine one of the most "cherished" assumptions used in this literature—namely, that one can empirically model movements in the price of oil using *logarithmic* formulations.[1] However, that formulation *cannot* be consistent with the workings of an oil market yielding a negative clearing price because, simply put, the logarithm of a negative number does not exist. From a theoretical standpoint, assuming a logarithmic formulation amounts to assuming "free disposal" in the oil market: suppliers can dispose of their excess supplies and avoid *paying* a price to have someone else hold the excess of production.[2]

[1] The following references employ a logarithmic formulation and will be marked with an asterisk (*) in the reference list: [9–45].

[2] Specifically, "On April 20, the price of front-month oil futures contracts for West Texas Intermediate (WTI) closed at negative $38 per barrel. These WTI futures *contracts are settled by physical delivery*; *as worries about the lack of available storage space intensified, prices spiraled downward*. Few contracts were actually traded at these negative prices, and prices recovered in the following days." [*Emphasis added*] Monetary Policy Report June 2020 of the Federal Reserve System. https://www.federalreserve.gov/monetarypolicy/files/20200612_mprfullreport.pdf

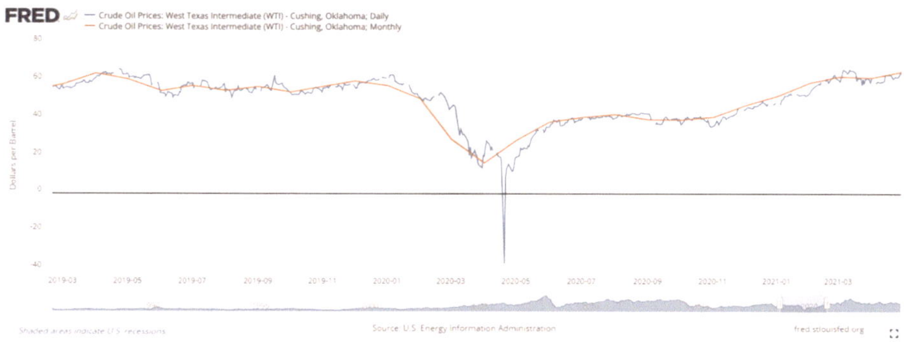


**Figure 1.**
*Daily and monthly prices of West Texas intermediate. The blue line corresponds to the daily price; the red line corresponds to the monthly average of daily prices.*

Effectively, the recorded negative price of oil invalidates the applicability of this assumption and raises the question of what alternative formulations are available to the logarithmic formulation.

One might dismiss the relevancy of a negative oil price for empirical work by arguing that it was just a one-day event and that, by replacing the recorded negative price with a non-negative number while including in the regression a one-off control variable for April 20, 2020, one would restore the feasibility of using logarithmic formulations. An alternative to this patch involves using monthly data, measured as the average of the daily observations. However, as **Figure 1** shows, this alternative induces a loss of information. Specifically, **Figure 1** shows that monthly prices increase just as the daily price declines to become negative.

The analysis begins in Section 2 by developing an empirical alternative to the widely used logarithmic formulation. The strategy is to begin with the established log-linear model and then, through algebraic manipulations and recognition of the limitations of daily data, obtain a linear formulation. Section 3 reports the time-series properties of the daily data used here, followed by the statistical assessment of a vector autoregressive formulation, including its out-of-sample properties. Section 4 examines whether there is a long-run relation among asset prices. Section 5 evaluates one of our most "cherished convictions": that elasticities are constant; Section 6 outlines ideas for expanding and improving this work.

## 2. Empirical modeling

Greatly simplified, the established formulation for characterizing the relation between movements in the real price of oil and movements in the real value of the dollar is

$$ln\left(\frac{Po}{Pus}\right)_t = \alpha + \beta \bullet ln\, REER_t + v_t, \tag{1}$$

where $Po$ is the nominal price of oil; $Pus$ is the U.S. CPI; $REER$ is the real effective value of the dollar (FX/\$), and $v_t$ is a random variable with mean zero and constant variance. The appeal of Eq. (1) is that the elasticity of the price of oil to changes in

REER, $\beta$, is constant. This constancy is especially valuable in evaluating the effects on $\left(\frac{Po}{Pus}\right)_t$ of alternative values for $REER_t$ because the answer is always $\beta$, regardless of the level of the price of oil or the historical period or the magnitude of the change in the exchange rate.

Apart from the oil price taking a negative value, Eq. (1) has several limitations that undermine its applicability to modeling oil prices. First, Eq. (1) uses the U.S. CPI to express the price of oil in real terms. This deflator choice assumes that the consumption basket for the United States is the same for every country. Effectively, this choice of deflator limits the relevancy of Eq. (1) to residents of the United States. To address this limitation, we replace the U.S. CPI with the international price of gold, $P_{g,t}$, which is available on a daily frequency.

Second, empirical analyses rely on measures for *REER* assembled by multilateral organizations and central banks. Specifically, REER is generally measured as a geometric weighted average of price-adjusted bilateral exchange rates:

$$ln\ REER_t = \sum_{i=1}^{n} \omega_{it} \bullet ln \left[ E_{\frac{FX_i}{\$},t} \bullet \left( \frac{P_{us,t}}{P^*_{i,t}} \right)_t \right], \tag{2}$$

where $\omega_{it}$ is a time-varying trade weight; $E_{\frac{FX_i}{\$},t}$ is the nominal price of a dollar in terms of the *ith* currency; $P^*_{i,t}$ is the ith-country's CPI; and $\sum_{i=1}^{n} \omega_{it} = 1$. Substituting Eq. (2) into (1) yields

$$ln\left(\frac{P_{o,t}}{P_{us,t}}\right) = \alpha + \beta \bullet \underbrace{\sum_{i=1}^{n} \omega_{it} \bullet ln \left[ E_{\frac{FX_i}{\$},t} \bullet \left( \frac{P_{us,t}}{P^*_{i,t}} \right) \right]}_{ln\ REER_t} + v_t, \tag{3}$$

which can be rewritten as

$$ln\, P_{o,t} = \alpha + (1+\beta) \bullet ln\, P_{us,t} + \beta \bullet \sum_{i=1}^{n} \omega_{it} \bullet ln\ E_{\frac{FX_i}{\$},t} - \beta \bullet \sum_{i=1}^{n} \omega_{it} \bullet ln\, P^*_{i,t}. \tag{4}$$

Eq. (4) replaces the measure of the dollar's external value from a synthetic construct with market prices of foreign exchange rates.

Third, the assumed constancy of $\beta$ requires that *all* the bilateral exchange rates change in the same proportion and simultaneously. If, instead, only one bilateral currency changes, then the associated exchange-rate elasticity is

$$\frac{\partial\, ln\, P_{o,t}}{\partial\, ln\ E_{\frac{FX_i}{\$},t}} = \beta \bullet \omega_{it}, \tag{5}$$

which is time varying.

Fourth, analysts have to exponentiate the prediction for the logarithm to obtain a prediction for the level of the price of oil. But this exponentiation does not yield the expected value of the level of the oil price because expectations are linear operators. In other words, $\mathrm{E}\ (P_{o,t}) \neq e^{\mathrm{E}\ [\ln(P_{o,t})]}$. Neglecting this observation means that forecasts based on logarithmic formulations generate biased forecasts for the level of the price of oil.

Fourth, there is no official daily data for $P^*_{i,t}$. Thus, we assume that these prices grow over time—that is, $ln\,P^*_{i,t} = \gamma \bullet t$ where $t$ stands for the time trend. With these assumptions we get Eq. (5):

$$ln\,P_{o,t} = \alpha + ln\,P_{g,t} \bullet [1+\beta] + \beta \bullet \sum_{i=1}^{n} \omega_{it} \bullet ln\ E_{\frac{FX_i}{\$},t} - \beta \bullet \gamma \bullet t \underbrace{\sum_{i=1}^{n} \omega_{it}}_{=1} + v_t. \quad (6)$$

Fifth, there is no official daily data on international trade, which means that there is no daily data on $\omega_{it}$. To avoid this complication, we use a formulation in which each bilateral exchange rate has its own, separate coefficient.

With these considerations in mind, the alternative formulation considered here is

$$P_{o,t} = \alpha + \gamma \bullet P_{g,t} + \sum_{i=1}^{n} \mu_i \bullet E_{\frac{FX_i}{\$},t} + \delta \bullet t + u_t, \quad (7)$$

where $u_t$ is a random disturbance with a zero mean and a constant variance. Eq. (7) has the same variables as Eq. (5), so it rests on the same narratives that support Eq. (5). Eq. (7), however, allows parameter estimation with a negative oil price. Note that both Eqs. (5) and (7) assume that the functioning of foreign exchange markets is akin to the functioning of other markets—that is, one uses a fiat medium of exchange to obtain either a service or a product. Exchange rates are, however, the price of one fiat currency for another fiat currency, and as Karaken and Wallace [46] notes, they could be undetermined. Further, the force of Wallace's critique is independent of the negative price of oil, the reliance on logarithmic formulations, and the choice of frequency of observation.

## 3. Empirical work

### 3.1 Data

We use six variables with daily observations from January 4, 1999, to March 1, 2024 (**Figure 2**).

- $P_{o,t}$ Oil price (US$/barrel),
- $E_{\frac{rmb}{\$},t}$ Chinese RMB to US dollar exchange rate,
- $E_{\frac{yen}{\$},t}$ Japanese yen to US dollar exchange rate,
- $P_{g,t}$ Gold price US$/Troy ounce,
- $E_{\frac{euro}{\$},t}$ Euro to US dollar exchange rate,
- $E_{\frac{pound}{\$},t}$ British pounds to US dollar exchange rate.

We selected these exchange rates because the IMF uses them in its Special Drawing Right.

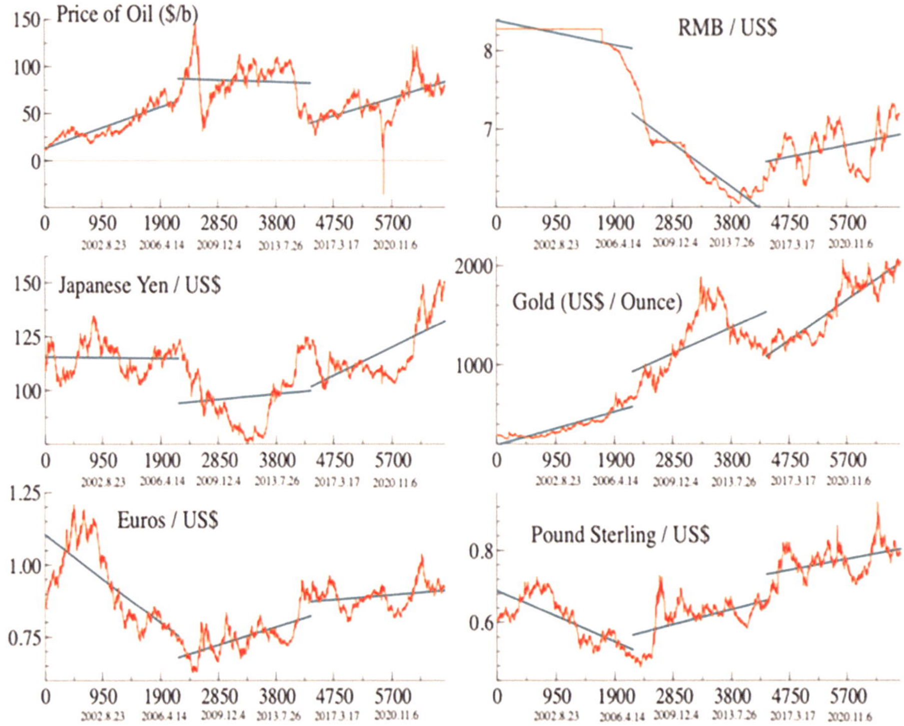


**Figure 2.**
*International market prices for oil, gold, and four foreign currencies: January 4, 1999, to March 1, 2024. The segments in each panel represent the trend associated with the relevant sample.*

To characterize the time-series properties of these variables, we begin by dividing the sample for each variable into three sub-samples of equal length and compute the trend for each sub-sample. We find that only the price of gold shows a positive trend across sub-samples; for the other variables, the sign of the trend changes across sub-samples.

**Figure 3** shows the autocorrelation function for each of these variables using 1200 lags (about 4 years). The results reveal that all of these series exhibit a substantial degree of persistence over an extended period.

In addition, the test results from using the Augmented Dickey Fuller (not shown) indicate that the hypothesis that these series are integrated of order one cannot be rejected.[3] These results suggest that our data are integrated of order 1, which is a necessary condition for the reliability of using (below) Johansen's cointegration method.

Finally, **Figure 4** shows scatterplots between the price of oil (horizontal axis) and the other five variables. The spot price of oil has an unconditional positive correlation with the price of gold and negative (unconditional) correlations with each bilateral exchange rate.

---

[3] The specification of these tests include 28 lags, a constant, and a time trend. As noted by the referee, one could also test for stationarity using Perron's test, which allows testing stationarity while allowing for structural breaks. We choose to use the ADF because of its symmetry with vector error-correction model (Eq. (10)) below); the latter allows testing for the stationarity of the series jointly and not just variable by variable. See Ref. [47].

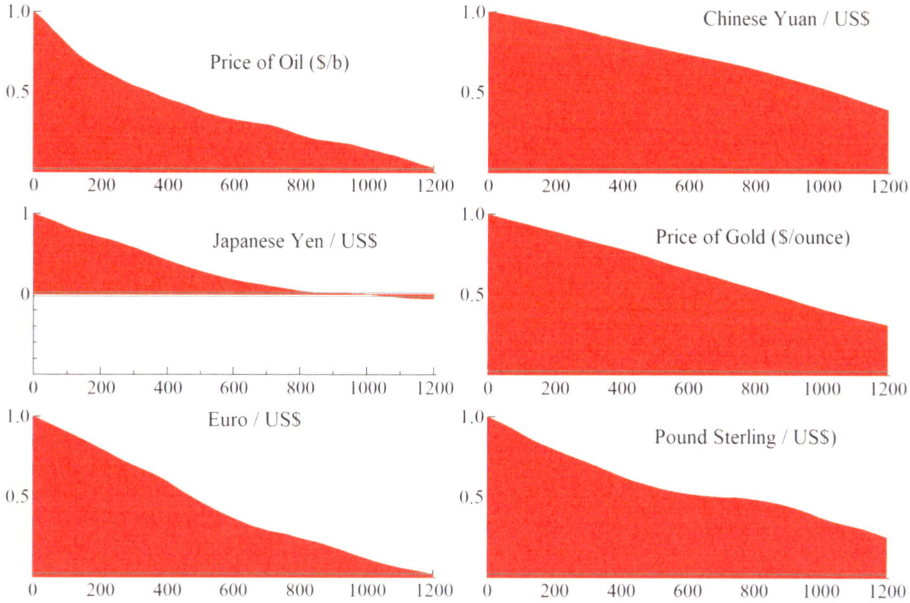


**Figure 3.**
*Results from autocorrelation function using 1200 days as lags. The horizontal green line is the critical value for rejecting the null hypotheses that the autocorrelation coefficient is zero.*

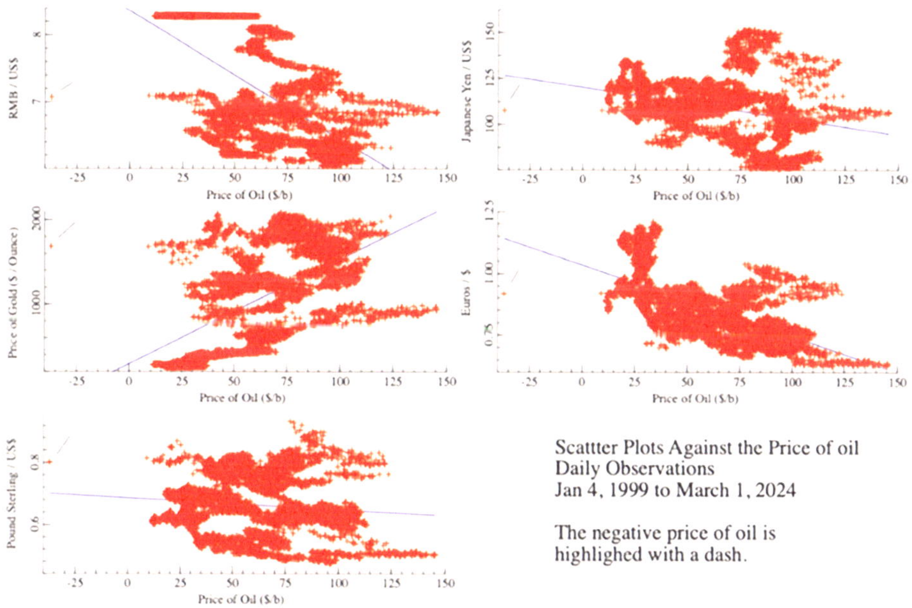


**Figure 4.**
*Scatter plots between the price of oil and gold and foreign exchange rates. The blue line for each frame shows the projection of the bivariate regression line.*

## 3.2 Estimation results

Our empirical work rests on a vector autoregression formulation for all six variables using five lags for each one of them:

$$\underbrace{X_t}_{6\times1} = \underbrace{\aleph}_{6\times1} + \sum_{i=1}^{5} \underbrace{A_i}_{6\times6} * X_{t-i} + \underbrace{\delta}_{6\times1} \bullet t + \underbrace{\boldsymbol{u}_t}_{6\times1} \tag{8}$$

where $X_t{}' = \left(P_{o,t}\ P_{g,t}\ E_{\frac{euro}{\$},t}\ E_{\frac{yen}{\$},t}\ E_{\frac{rmb}{\$},t}\ E_{\frac{pound}{\$},t}\right)$ and $\boldsymbol{u}_t$ is a vector of disturbances with mean zero and a constant variance-covariance matrix; the equations include (not shown) a zero-one control for April 20, 2020. We choose to use a VAR formulation for several reasons. First, it allows all the variables to be endogenous. Second, it is an integral component of the vector error-correction model, now noted explicitly as Eq. (10) along with Johansen method of assessing the extent to which the series are cointegrated. This method begins with a VAR, shown as Eq. (8), and it is one of the reasons we use a VAR. For the derivation details, see Ref. [47]. Another reason is that it enables the derivation of the results to be generated from as impartial a viewpoint as possible: we do not bring our prior beliefs into the generation of results.

For parameter estimation, we use OLS with daily data from January 4, 1999, to March 1, 2024. **Table 1** shows the model's fit for each variable. Column (3) shows the specifications' gain in explanatory power relative to using that variable's sample mean as the sole explanatory variable.

**Figure 5** shows the distributions of the normalized residuals from the model and compares them to a standard normal distribution. We find that the model's estimation residuals are not consistent with the normality assumption, which undermines the strength of the conclusions reached in this paper.

Finally, to assess whether the model is dynamically stable, **Figure 6** reports the model's impulse responses from a one-day unit shock to each of the residuals. The results show that a transitory shock induces transitory responses, and we interpret this result as suggesting that the model is dynamically stable.

### 3.3 Out-of-sample accuracy

To examine the model's out-of-sample predictive performance, we begin by reestimating the parameters after excluding the last 1100 observations from the estimation sample. Then, given the new parameter estimates, we implement 1-step forecasts for all the variables over the 1100 observations excluded from estimation.

| Variable | Units | Gain (%)* | Std. dev | SER | Mean | $R^2$ |
|---|---|---|---|---|---|---|
| (1) | (2) | (3) | (4) | (5) | (6) | (7) |
| $P_{o,t}$ | US$/barrel | 40.76 | 26.64 | 1.57 | 61.49 | 0.997 |
| $E_{\frac{rmb}{\$},t}$ | RMB/US$ | 10.82 | 0.79 | 0.01 | 7.18 | 1.000 |
| $E_{\frac{yen}{\$},t}$ | Yen/US$ | 13.00 | 14.93 | 0.68 | 109.62 | 0.998 |
| $P_{g,t}$ | US$/Ounce | 51.48 | 556.75 | 12.18 | 1057.90 | 1.000 |
| $E_{\frac{euro}{\$},t}$ | Euro/US$ | 13.19 | 0.12 | 0.01 | 0.86 | 0.998 |
| $E_{\frac{pound}{\$},t}$ | Pound/US$ | 13.33 | 0.09 | 0.00 | 0.66 | 0.998 |

**Note: Col (3) = (Col (4) - Col (5))*100 / Col (6).*

**Table 1.**
*Single equation statistics—January 4, 1999: March 1, 2024.*

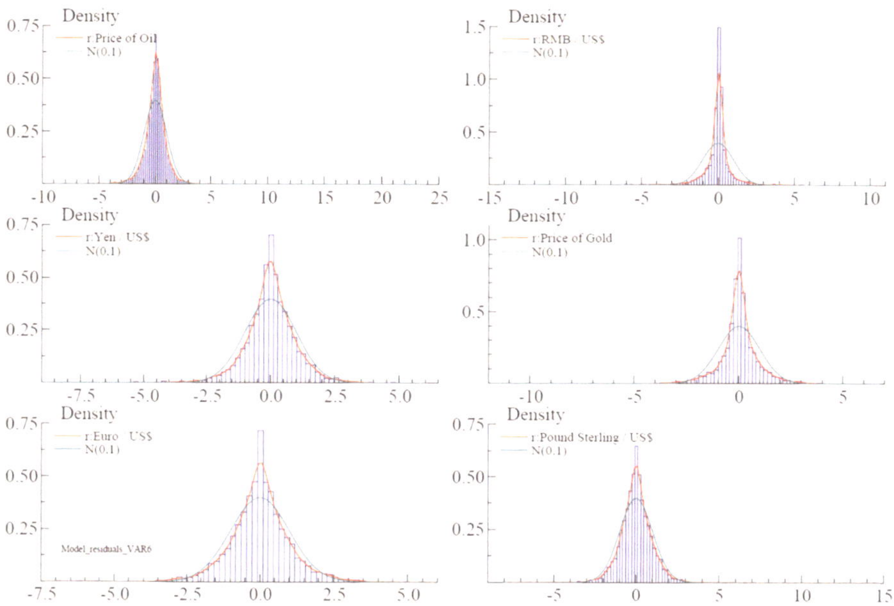

**Figure 5.**
*Empirical distribution of normalized residuals. Each panel in the figure shows the histogram and density of the equations' normalized residuals (i.e., residual / standard error of the regression); the green line shows the density of the standard normal. We also tested for serial correlations of the residuals using their autocorrelation function with 12 lags. The results, not shown, cannot reject serial independence.*

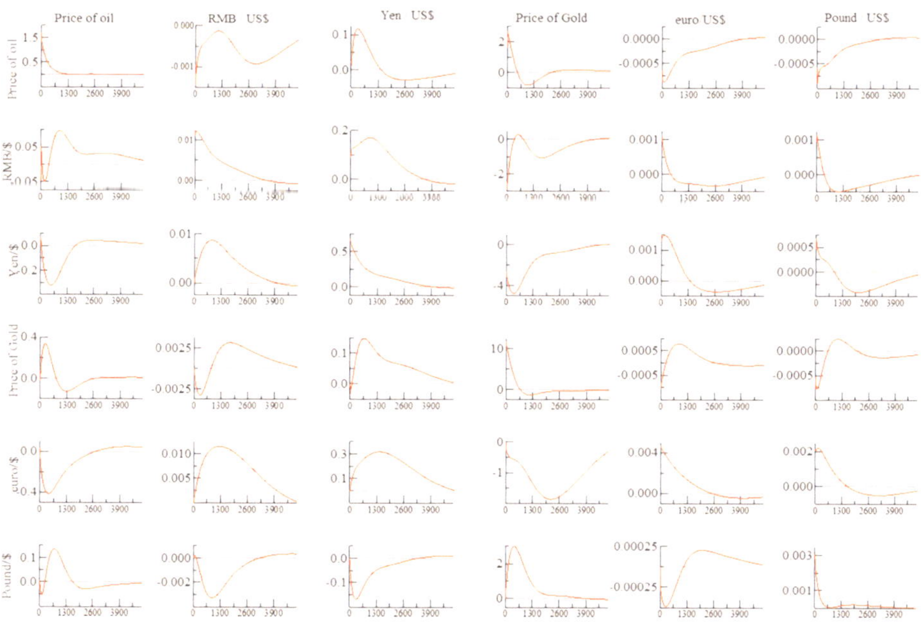

**Figure 6.**
*Impulse response from unit shocks to Eq. (8). Each frame shows the evolution of the response of the variable listed on the top to a unit shoch to a residual to the variable that is listed in on the left:*
*∂variable on top/∂variable on left .*

Arguably, 1-step-ahead forecasts are consistent with professional traders who use historical values as the initial conditions of their extrapolations.

**Figure 7** shows the 95 percent confidence bands for these forecasts. As shown, the model predicts a negative price for oil on April 20, 2020, but not as negative as the price turned out to be on that date. This predictive failure does not affect the model's accuracy for subsequent dates because forecasts' initial conditions are always reset to historical values.

Arguably, a relevant question is what do we gain in terms of forecast accuracy for the price of oil by recognizing its interdependencies with other asset prices. To address this question, we use an autoregressive formulation for the price of oil while excluding the role of gold and foreign exchange. Specifically, we use an autoregressive distributed lag (ADL) model with five lags.

$$P_{o,t} = \alpha + \gamma(L)\bullet P_{o,t-1} + \delta\bullet t + u_t \tag{9}$$

where $\gamma(L)$ is a polynomial of order 5 in the lag operator $L$ and $u_t$ is a random term with a zero mean and constant variance. For parameter estimation, we exclude the last 1100 observations from the estimation sample and then implement 1-step ahead forecasts over these observations; **Figure 8** shows the forecasts associated with the ADL (5) model.

Using the Mean Absolute Percent Error (MAPE) as a summary measure of forecast performance, we find that the MAPE for the VAR formulation is virtually identical to that of the AR(5): 2.9 percent. This result should not be surprising given that the daily price of oil is highly persistent (see **Figure 3**). We view this result as suggesting that if the sole purpose of the model is to deliver daily forecasts of oil prices, then reliance on an AR(5) is just as accurate as the VAR(5). If, however, the goal is to study arbitrage

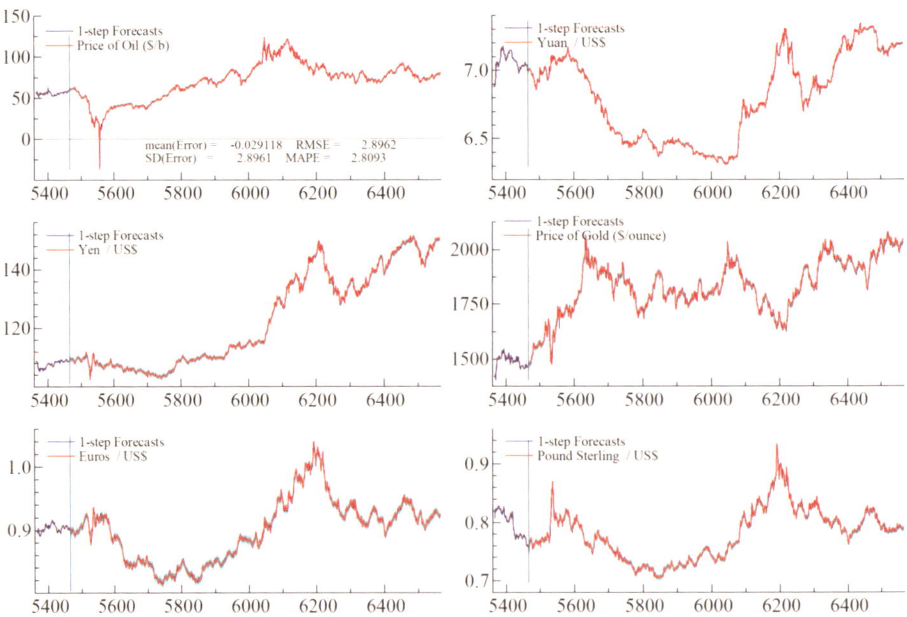


**Figure 7.**
*95 percent confidence bands for 1-step-ahead ex-post forecasts of Eq. (8). The width of these bands recognize two sources of uncertainty: model specification (i.e., residuals) and parameter estimates.*

**Figure 8.**
*Out-of-sample 1-step-ahead forecasts of an ADL(5) for the price of oil. The width of the confidence bands recognize two sources of uncertainty: model specification (i.e., residuals) and parameter estimates.*

opportunities among these assets, then using the VAR involves no loss of accuracy and provides access to a much larger range of interesting questions.

## 4. Cointegration

Central to this investigation is whether the international financial markets (oil, gold, foreign exchange) exhibit a self-correcting equilibrium relationship. To that end, we rewrite Eq. (8) as

$$\underbrace{\Delta X_t}_{6\times 1} = \underbrace{\aleph}_{6\times 1} + \sum_{i=1}^{5} \underbrace{\Gamma_i}_{6\times 6} * \Delta X_{t-i} + \delta\bullet t + \underbrace{\Pi}_{6\times 6} * X_{t-1} + \underbrace{u_t}_{6\times 1}. \tag{10}$$

The question of interest is whether these variables are cointegrated. If they are, then a linear relation among them can be interpreted as their equilibrium relation. The existence and number of cointegration relations among these variables is given by the rank of $\Pi$. We determine the rank of $\Pi$ using two tests: the Maximum Eigenvalue test and the Trace test for the sum of the eigenvalues. The results of **Table 2** reject the hypothesis that the rank of $\Pi$ is 0 and do not reject the hypothesis that the rank is one. In other words, there is just one cointegrating (equilibrium) relationship.

In this case, $\hat{\Pi} = \hat{\alpha}\bullet\hat{\beta}$ where $\hat{\alpha}$ is a $(6 \times 1)$ vector of estimated speeds of adjustment; $\hat{\beta}$ is a $(1 \times 6)$ vector of estimated coefficients associated with the long-run relationship given by $\hat{\beta}\bullet X_{t-1}$. **Figure 9** shows that deviations from the long run are stationary, which is what allows us to interpret $\hat{\beta}\bullet X_{t-1}$ as the arbitrage condition at *t-1* for these three assets.

| Rank | Trace test | [Prob] | Max test | [Prob] | Trace test adj. df | [Prob] | Max test adj. df | [Prob] |
|---|---|---|---|---|---|---|---|---|
| 0 | 121.84 | [0.003] ** | 55.67 | [0.001] ** | 121.28 | [0.004] ** | 55.42 | [0.001] ** |
| 1 | 66.16 | [0.326] | 28.29 | [0.372] | 65.86 | [0.336] | 28.16 | [0.380] |
| 2 | 37.87 | [0.630] | 16.62 | [0.805] | 37.7 | [0.639] | 16.54 | [0.809] |
| 3 | 21.26 | [0.628] | 12.64 | [0.717] | 21.16 | [0.634] | 12.58 | [0.722] |
| 4 | 8.62 | [0.625] | 7.88 | [0.622] | 8.58 | [0.629] | 7.84 | [0.626] |
| 5 | 0.74 | [0.390] | 0.74 | [0.390] | 0.74 | [0.391] | 0.74 | [0.391] |

** *significant at the 1% significant level.*

**Table 2.**
*Johansen Cointegration Test of the rank of Π.*

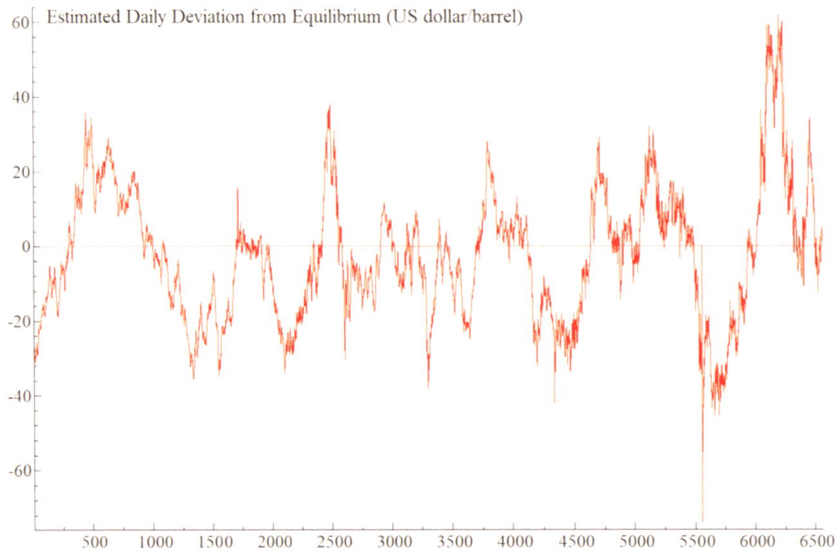


**Figure 9.**
*Daily deviations from equilibrium in asset prices measured in US$/barrel. The estimated daily deviations from equilibrium, in US$ per barrel, are estimated as* $\hat{\beta} \bullet X_{t-1}$.

As an alternative to **Figure 9**, we use out-of-sample dynamic simulations of Eq. (8). By design, dynamic forecasts do not reset the initial conditions to historical values but, instead, use the model's own predictions for the values of those lags. And in doing so, these forecasts incorporate the interdependencies among all the six prices considered here in generating the forecasts for the price of oil. Dynamic forecasts are, in effect, depicting the evolution of these asset prices under ceteris paribus—that is, excluding unforeseen shocks. **Figure 10** shows the 95 percent confidence bands for the dynamic forecasts for the price of oil based on parameter estimates that exclude the last 1100 observations. The blue line in the figure shows that the forecasts for the price of oil steadily rise to about 75$/barrel by April 2024; the red line shows that the actual price of oil fluctuates around the forecast, showing that deviations between forecast and actual prices are transitory.

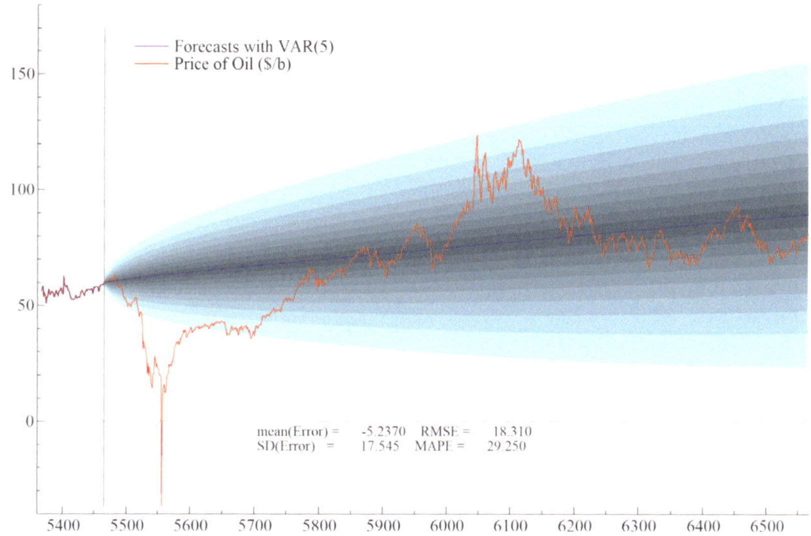


**Figure 10.**
*95 percent confidence bands for S-step ahead oil-price forecast using Eq. (8). The width of the confidence bands recognize two sources of uncertainty: model specification (i.e., residuals) and parameter estimates.*

| | **Coefficient** | | **Coefficient** | |
|---|---|---|---|---|
| Variable | Unrestricted | S.E. | Restricted | S.E. |
| | *(1)* | *(2)* | *(3)* | *(4)* |
| $\beta_{\frac{rmb}{\$}}$ RMB/US$ | 11.036 | 7.4692 | 0.000 | — |
| $\beta_{\frac{yen}{\$}}$ Yen/US$ | −0.007231 | 0.3302 | 0.000 | — |
| $\beta_g$ Price of gold | 0.07266 | 0.0155 | 0.055 | 0.0133 |
| $\beta_{\frac{euro}{\$}}$ Euro/US$ | −101.4 | 55.5110 | −153.660 | 24.5470 |
| $\beta_{\frac{pound}{\$}}$ Pound/US$ | −159.33 | 81.8410 | 0.000 | — |
| Constant | 126.67 | 50.1340 | 177.070 | 23.3910 |
| Trend | −0.007648 | 0.0063 | −0.012 | 0.0038 |
| log-likelihood ratio test | | | 6.0257 | |
| P-level [$Chi^2(3)$] | | | [0.1104] | |

**Table 3.**
*Cointegration vector—Johansen maximum likelihood.*

**Table 3** shows the estimates of $\beta$ along with their standard errors. The estimates indicate that a ceteris paribus increase in the price of gold is directly related to an increase in the price of oil. Further, and with the exception of the RMB/US$ exchange rate, an appreciation of the dollar lowers the price of oil.

Note that several of the exchange-rate coefficients are insignificant when considered individually. To see if they are insignificant when considered jointly, we set them to zero, re-estimate the remaining parameters, and then use a likelihood ratio test to determine whether there is a significant decline in the value of the likelihood function.

The value of the log-likelihood ratio test (last row of **Table 3**) indicates that one cannot reject the null hypothesis that these coefficient estimates are jointly equal to zero. Given this finding, we now examine one of the most cherished assumptions associated with the logarithmic formulation: the constancy of elasticities.

## 5. Oil-price elasticities

Given that the model is linear in the variables, the estimated oil-price elasticities are computed as

$$\varepsilon_{g,\hat{t}day} = \hat{\beta}_g \bullet \left(\frac{P_{g,t}}{P_{o,t}}\right) \tag{11}$$

$$\varepsilon_{euro,\hat{t}day} = \hat{\beta}_{\frac{euro}{\$}} \bullet \left(\frac{E_{\frac{euro}{\$},t}}{P_{o,t}}\right), \tag{12}$$

where $\hat{\beta}_g$ and $\hat{\beta}_{\frac{euro}{\$}}$ are the estimated cointegration coefficients (column 4 of **Table 2**), and the terms in parentheses are the relative prices of gold and of the euro relative to the price of oil. These relative prices change daily, which means that the elasticities are constant only if the recorded movements in relative prices are offset exactly by the (unexplained) movements in the model's parameters, a condition lacking an economic motivation. **Figure 11** shows movements in the estimated elasticities of the oil price with respect to the price of gold (top row) and the euro-dollar exchange rate (bottom row). The elasticities shown in the right column are computed by replacing the daily relative price with its 28-day moving average.

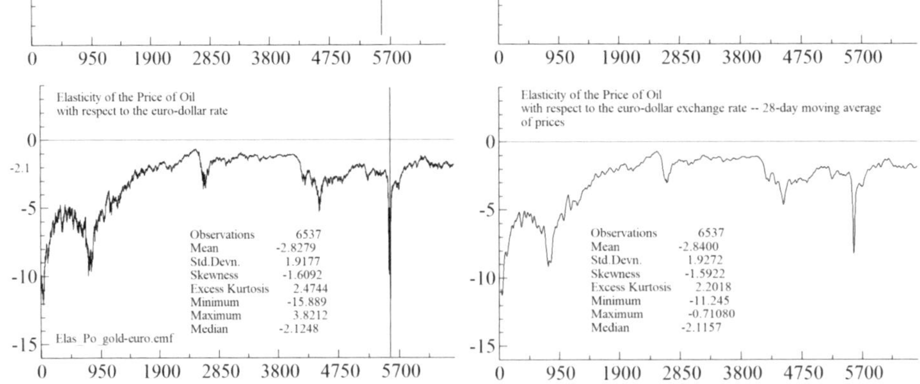


**Figure 11.**
*Estimated elasticities of the price of oil with respect to the price of gold and the euro-dollar exchange rate. Panels on the left use the daily relative price; panels on the right use the ratio of the moving averages of the prices.*

The calculations show that the daily elasticity for the price of gold, $\varepsilon_{g,\hat{t}_{day}}$, ranges from −2.5 to 10.4 with a mean of 0.97 and a median of 0.85, which indicates a significant degree of skewness. Replacing the daily price ratio with the ratio of moving prices yields, as one might expect, a narrower dispersion in the estimated elasticity (from 0.4 to 5.3) with a mean of 0.97 and a median of 0.85, also with a significant degree of skewness. For the euro/US$ exchange rate, the daily elasticity ranges from −15.9 to −2.1 with a median of −2.1, which is comparable to the median of $\varepsilon_{euro,\hat{t}_{mva}}$.

One clear result is that both the volatility and the asymmetry of movements in these elasticities suggest that reliance on constant-elasticity models is accompanied by a potential loss of information.

## 6. Conclusion

The negative price of oil recorded on April 20, 2020, undermines the usefulness of the widely used logarithmic formulation to characterize the relation between the price of oil and the external value of the dollar: the logarithm of a negative number does not exist. Though this difficulty can be avoided by using monthly observations, such an approach carries a loss of information and, effectively, makes the researcher work for the model instead of the model working for the researcher.

The approach used here involves using an econometric formulation that allows negative values. To examine the feasibility of this approach, we use daily data from January 4, 1999, to March 1, 2024, to estimate the parameters of a linear VAR of order 5 for the six asset prices: the price of oil and the prices of both gold and four foreign-exchange rates. The examination involves assessing the properties of the residuals, the stability of the dynamic response of the model, the existence of a cointegration relation for these six prices, and then the accuracy of 1-step-ahead forecasts of this model.

We find that if the goal is to forecast daily oil prices as such, and nothing else, using an ADL(5) of these prices is just as accurate as using the VAR. But if the purpose is to figure out whether there is arbitrage among these six prices, then the VAR offers what we argue is a solid starting point for further work. Specifically, we find a single equilibrium relation among these financial prices.

No doubt, these results have an undeniable tentative nature. Additional testing of other functional forms (i.e., semi-log) and estimation methods (i.e., GARCH) are likely to alter the empirical results reached here. But in doing so, they will reinforce the belief that empirical work assuming constant elasticities is based more on cherished convictions than on empirical evidence. Indeed, a one-day event (the recording of a negative price of oil) led to an alternative formulation showing that one of our most cherished assumptions, constant elasticities, is not consistent with the data that it seeks to explain.

(Entries with a * denote a paper using a logarithmic formulation).

## Author note

Kelu Ren's work was completed as a graduate student at SAIS. We are also grateful to Kubi Johnson's work as a graduate student at SAIS in assembling the daily data. The calculations in this paper are carried out using PcGive 9 (see Ref. [48]). We are very grateful to comments from an anonymous referee and from the editor of this volume.

## Author details

Jaime Marquez and Kelu Ren*
School of Advanced International Studies, Johns Hopkins University, USA

*Address all correspondence to: renlcoco163@gmail.com

## References

[1] Hopkins J. Alumni Magazine Consortium. Johns Hopkins University; 1982. p. VII

[2] *Albulescu CT, Ajmi AN. Oil price and US dollar exchange rate: Change detection of bi-directional causal impact. Energy Economics. 2021;**100**:105385. DOI: 10.1016/j.eneco.2021.105385

[3] *Amano RA, Norden SV. Oil prices and the rise and fall of the US real exchange rate. Journal of International Money and Finance. 1998;**17**(2):299-316. DOI: 10.1016/s0261-5606(98)00004-7

[4] *Lizardo RA, Mollick AV. Oil price fluctuations and U.S. dollar exchange rates. Energy Economics. 2010;**32**(2): 399-408. DOI: 10.1016/j.eneco.2009.10.005

[5] *Chen H, Liu L, Wang Y, Zhu Y. Oil price shocks and U.S. dollar exchange rates. Energy. 2016;**112**:1036-1048. DOI: 10.1016/j.energy.2016.07.012

[6] *Coudert V, Mignon V. Reassessing the empirical relationship between the oil price and the dollar. Energy Policy. 2016;**95**:147-157. DOI: 10.1016/j.enpol.2016.05.002

[7] *Marquez J. Oil prices and exchange rates: Measurement matters. Commodities. 2022;**1**(1):50-64. DOI: 10.3390/commodities1010005

[8] *Nandi BK, Kabir MH, Nandi MK. Crude oil price hikes and exchange rate volatility: A lesson from the Bangladesh economy. Resources Policy. 2024;**91**: 104858-104858. DOI: 10.1016/j.resourpol.2024.104858

[9] *Abubakar AB. Oil price and exchange rate nexus in Nigeria: Are there asymmetries. Central Bank of Nigeria Journal of Applied Statistics. 2019;**10**(1): 1-28. DOI: 10.33429/cjas.10119.1/6

[10] *Adam P, Rosnawintang R, Saidi LO, Tondi L, Sani LOA. The causal relationship between crude oil price, exchange rate and rice price. International Journal of Energy Economics and Policy. 2018;**8**(1):90-94. Available from: https://www.econjournals.com/index.php/ijeep/article/view/5774

[11] *Ajala K, Sakanko MA, Adeniji SO. The asymmetric effect of oil price on the exchange rate and stock price in Nigeria. International Journal of Energy Economics and Policy. 2021;**11**(4):202-208. DOI: 10.32479/ijeep.10977

[12] *Aloui C, Hkiri B, Hammoudeh S, Shahbaz M. A multiple and partial wavelet analysis of the oil price, inflation, exchange rate, and economic growth nexus in Saudi Arabia. Emerging Markets Finance and Trade. 2018;**54**(4): 935-956. DOI: 10.1080/1540496x.2017.1423469

[13] *Asaad Z. Oil price, gold price, exchange rate and stock market in Iraq pre-during COVID-19 outbreak: An ARDL approach. International Journal of Energy Economics and Policy. 2021;**11**(5):562-571. Available from: https://papers.ssrn.com/sol3/papers.cfm?abstract_id=3909143

[14] *Bal DP, Rath BN. Nonlinear causality between crude oil price and exchange rate: A comparative study of China and India. Energy Economics. 2015;**51**:149-156. DOI: 10.1016/j.eneco.2015.06.013

[15] *Basnet HC, Upadhyaya KP. Impact of oil price shocks on output, inflation and the real exchange rate: Evidence

from selected ASEAN countries. Applied Economics. 2015;**47**(29):3078-3091. DOI: 10.1080/00036846.2015.1011322

[16] *Bigerna S. Connectedness analysis of oil price shocks, inflation, and exchange rate for the MENA region countries. Resources Policy. 2024;**88**: 104344-104344. DOI: 10.1016/j.resourpol.2023.104344

[17] *Brayek AB, Sebai S, Naoui K. A study of the interactive relationship between oil prices and exchange rate: A copula approach and a DCC-MGARCH model. The Journal of Economic Asymmetries. 2015;**12**(2):173-189. DOI: 10.1016/j.jeca.2015.09.002

[18] *Breen JD, Hu L. The predictive content of oil price and volatility: New evidence on exchange rate forecasting. Journal of International Financial Markets, Institutions and Money. 2021; **75**:101454. DOI: 10.1016/j.intfin.2021.101454

[19] *Castro C, Jiménez-Rodríguez R. Dynamic interactions between oil price and exchange rate. PLoS One. 2020;**15** (8):e0237172. DOI: 10.1371/journal.pone.0237172

[20] *Chatziantoniou I, Elsayed A, Gabauer D, Gozgor G. Oil price shocks and exchange rate dynamics: Evidence from decomposed and partial connectedness measures for oil importing and exporting economies. Energy Economics. 2023;**120**:106627-106627. DOI: 10.1016/j.eneco.2023.106627

[21] *Chen Y, Xu J, Hu M. Asymmetric volatility spillovers and dynamic correlations between crude oil price, exchange rate and gold price in BRICS. Resources Policy. 2022;**78**: 102857. DOI: 10.1016/j.resourpol.2022.102857

[22] *Chou K-W, Tseng Y-H. Oil prices, exchange rate, and the price asymmetry in the Taiwanese retail gasoline market. Economic Modelling. 2016;**52**:733-741. DOI: 10.1016/j.econmod.2015.10.012

[23] *Chowdhury KB, Garg B. Has COVID-19 intensified the oil price–exchange rate nexus? Economic Analysis and Policy. 2022;**76**:280-298. DOI: 10.1016/j.eap.2022.08.013

[24] *Delgado NAB, Delgado EB, Saucedo E. The relationship between oil prices, the stock market and the exchange rate: Evidence from Mexico. The North American Journal of Economics and Finance. 2018;**45**:266-275. DOI: 10.1016/j.najef.2018.03.006

[25] *Fratzscher M, Schneider D, van Robays I. Oil Prices, Exchange Rates and Asset Prices; ECB Working Paper. Frankfurt, Germany; 2014. p. 1689

[26] *Ghosh T. Oil price, exchange rate and the Indian macroeconomy. In: MPRA Paper. Germany: University Library of Munich; 2016. Available from: https://ideas.repec.org/p/pra/mprapa/90629.html

[27] Golub SS. Oil prices and exchange rates. The Economics Journal. 1983;**93**: 576-593

[28] *Hashmi SM, Chang BH, Huang L, Uche E. Revisiting the relationship between oil prices, exchange rate, and stock prices: An application of quantile ARDL model. Resources Policy. 2022;**75**: 102543. DOI: 10.1016/j.resourpol.2021.102543

[29] *Jain A, Biswal PC. Dynamic linkages among oil price, gold price, exchange rate, and stock market in India. Resources Policy. 2016;**49**:179-185. DOI: 10.1016/j.resourpol.2016.06.001

[30] *Kaushik N, Nag R, Upadhyaya KP. Oil price and real exchange rate: The case of India. International Business & Economics Research Journal (IBER). 2014;**13**(4):809. DOI: 10.19030/iber.v13i4.8688

[31] *Kim J-M, Jung H. Relationship between oil price and exchange rate by FDA and copula. Applied Economics. 2017;**50**(22):2486-2499. DOI: 10.1080/00036846.2017.1400652

[32] *Kocoglu M, Kyophilavong P, Awan A, Lim SY. Time-varying causality between oil price and exchange rate in five ASEAN economies. Economic Change and Restructuring. 2023. DOI: 10.1007/s10644-022-09457-6

[33] *Korley M, Giouvris E. The impact of oil price and oil volatility index (OVX) on the exchange rate in sub-Saharan Africa: Evidence from oil importing/exporting countries. Economies. 2022;**10**(11):272. DOI: 10.3390/economies10110272

[34] *Krugman PR. Oil and the Dollar; NBER Working Paper. Cambridge, MA, USA; 1980

[35] *Kumar S. Asymmetric impact of oil prices on exchange rate and stock prices. The Quarterly Review of Economics and Finance. 2019;**72**:41-51. DOI: 10.1016/j.qref.2018.12.009

[36] *Lin B, Su T. Does oil price have similar effects on the exchange rates of BRICS? International Review of Financial Analysis. 2020;**69**:101461. DOI: 10.1016/j.irfa.2020.101461

[37] *Lv X, Lien D, Chen Q, Yu C. Does exchange rate management affect the causality between exchange rates and oil prices? Evidence from oil-exporting countries. Energy Economics. 2018;**76**:325-343. DOI: 10.1016/j.eneco.2018.10.017

[38] *Nusair SA, Olson D. The effects of oil price shocks on Asian exchange rates: Evidence from quantile regression analysis. Energy Economics. 2019;**78**:44-63. DOI: 10.1016/j.eneco.2018.11.009

[39] *Saidu MT, Naseem NAM, Law SH, Yasmin B. Exploring the asymmetric effect of oil price on exchange rate: Evidence from the top six African net oil importers. Energy Reports. 2021;7:8238-8257. DOI: 10.1016/j.egyr.2021.07.037

[40] *Shahbaz M, Tiwari AK, Tahir MI. Analyzing time–frequency relationship between oil price and exchange rate in Pakistan through wavelets. Journal of Applied Statistics. 2014;**42**(4):690-704. DOI: 10.1080/02664763.2014.980784

[41] *Singhal S, Choudhary S, Biswal PC. Return and volatility linkages among international crude oil price, gold price, exchange rate and stock markets: Evidence from Mexico. Resources Policy. 2019;**60**:255-261. DOI: 10.1016/j.resourpol.2019.01.004

[42] *Wahyudi H, Andriyanto RW, Tresnaningtyas A, Sumanda K, Palupi WA. Analysis of oil price and exchange rate in Indonesia. International Journal of Energy Economics and Policy. 2023;**13**(2):27-33. DOI: 10.32479/ijeep.13925

[43] *Wang J, Niu X, Liu Z, Zhang L. Analysis of the influence of international benchmark oil price on China's real exchange rate forecasting. Engineering Applications of Artificial Intelligence. 2020;**94**:103783. DOI: 10.1016/j.engappai.2020.103783

[44] *Wang P, Liu X, Ho TW, Li Y. The effect of the US dollar exchange rate on oil prices: An oil financialization perspective. International Journal of Finance & Economics. 2022. DOI: 10.1002/ijfe.2736

[45] *Yang L, Cai XJ, Hamori S. Does the crude oil price influence the exchange rates of oil-importing and oil-exporting countries differently ? A wavelet coherence analysis. International Review of Economics & Finance. 2017;**49**:536-547. DOI: 10.1016/j.iref.2017.03.015

[46] Kareken JH, Wallace N. On the Indeterminacy of Equilibrium Exchange Rates. Working Paper 153. Federal Reserve Bank of Minneapolis; 1980

[47] Barrow LJ, Campos NR, Ericsson DF, Hendry HA, Tran, Veloce W. Cointegration. In: Glasner D, editor. Encyclopedia of Business Cycles. New York: Garland Publishing; 1997. pp. 101-106

[48] Doornik J, Hendry D. Empirical Econometric Modelling PcGiveTM 16. U.K: Timberlake; 2022

Chapter 8

# Flexible Error Specification in CAPM

*Hector O. Zapata and Damilola S. Adebayo*


## Abstract

A four-parameter Generalized Lambda Distribution (GLD) quantile regression is applied to a standard capital asset pricing model (CAPM) error specification to jointly estimate moments of the residuals using the daily prices of two farmland Real Estate Investment Trusts (REITs), Nasdaq: LAND and NYSE: FPI as a function of the U.S. S&P 500 from April 2014 to August 2024. The GLD regression also captures the effect of outliers found in the OLS CAPM model, resulting in a closer fit to the theoretical distribution of the GLD residuals. Simulation results revealed symmetrically distributed CAPM coefficients of farmland REITs. The findings suggest that LAND and FPI do not offer portfolio diversification beyond that provided by a market index such as the S&P 500. While the numerical magnitude of the estimated coefficients from the GLD regression is identical to those of least squares, the GLD estimates are more accurate and robust to outliers and more consistent with the distributional properties of daily returns. Future research with this relatively new regression method is briefly discussed.


**Keywords:** capital asset pricing model, least squares, generalized lambda distribution regression, quantile regression, maximum likelihood, farmland REITs

## 1. Introduction

The standard Capital Asset Pricing Model (CAPM), attributed to [1–3] established that the variation in the rate of return of a security is a function of the rate of return on a portfolio of all publicly traded stocks (the market portfolio), adjusted for the opportunity cost of money (the return on a risk-free asset); investors are rewarded with a positive difference (risk premium), or not compensated for taking risks when the risk premium is negative. In time-series applications, this model is a simple linear regression with returns on an asset (the dependent variable), for example, a farmland derivative stock, and returns on a market index (the independent variable), say the U. S. S&P 500.

In the standard CAPM[1], the relationship between risk and return is positive and linear [5]. Its early estimation was based on least squares under the classical

---

[1] A detailed coverage of CAPM and its various forms is found in [4]. The CAPM notation used in this Chapter closely follows CLM.

assumptions that the errors are independent and normally distributed with constant mean and variance. The model's simplicity in representing mean-variance investor behavior under uncertainty may have contributed to its popularity in empirical finance. The penurious record of the simple CAPM in predicting asset returns is highlighted in [6] and efforts to improve its specification and forecasting performance using modern financial econometrics have been extensively documented.

One of the most influential papers, questioning the Gaussian assumption in price changes is [7]; Mandelbrot built on earlier work that challenged this assumption and proposed the stable Paretian model to capture the consistently observed departures from normality. Fama [8] summarizes that before Mandelbrot, the Gaussian hypothesis, that the distribution of price changes is approximately Gaussian or normal, was the prevailing view, and further examined the theoretical and empirical content of Mandelbrot's new model of non-Gaussian distributions with infinite variance. In his conclusions, Fama stressed the need to develop more adequate statistical tools for this new model. The empirical literature on the subject grew exponentially after that, and even to this day, efforts to better approximate the distribution of price changes continue. Frequent reports about skewness, kurtosis, and fat-tails in the distribution of financial returns abound in the literature, an empirical regularity with implications for systematic risk estimation and hypothesis testing in the CAPM model (see [4]).

The Estimation of the CAPM model requires using proxies for expected returns, obtained by averaging realized returns and proxying market returns by an index; this averaging further introduces estimation error and affects empirical tests' power [9], effects which can be present in the model residuals. The sources of specification errors and estimation methods in asset pricing have been a long endeavor in applied financial econometrics. These efforts continue as new statistical tools have introduced more flexible functional forms for the distribution of returns and errors in asset pricing models, and new estimation and hypothesis testing methods [10–14]. A hypothesis can be entertained that the estimation results of the standard CAPM, under least squares and classical econometric assumptions, are not significantly different from those of alternative models that allow for more flexible formation forms on the residuals.

The main purpose of this chapter is to specify a flexible distribution for the error term of the standard CAPM model using parametric regression models based on the generalized lambda distribution (GLD). Section 2 reviews the CAPM, presents the GLD, and provides selected literature of empirical interest. Section 3 contains empirical results for the standard CAPM and compares them to the estimates from a Generalized Lambda Regression Model; this section also describes the data used in the empirical example. Section 4 provides a summary and implications for future research.

## 2. The CAPM

The econometric analysis of the time-series representation of the standard CAPM requires assumptions about the time-series stochastic properties of returns and the residuals of the estimated regression. The classical assumptions are that errors are independent and normally distributed over time.

The econometric specification is given by

$$r_{it} - RF_t = \alpha_i + \beta_i (R_{mt} - RF_t) + \varepsilon_{it}, t = 1, 2, 3, \dots, T. \tag{1}$$

where $i$ denotes the asset and $t$ the period (daily, monthly, annual) of the time series of returns, $r_{it}$ is the individual security returns, $R_{mt}$ denotes the returns of the market portfolio (in practice usually measured by the S&P 500 in the U.S.), $RF_t$ is a risk-free rate of return represented by a Treasury Bill rate, and $\varepsilon_{it}$ is an error term which is assumed *iid*, mean zero, constant variance ($\sigma^2$), and normally distributed for inference purposes (See [4]). The intercept $\alpha_i$ is expected to be zero by financial theory but may deviate from it when estimated with empirical returns data. The $\beta_i$ coefficient, called the *beta* value, is a linear measure of the response in excess returns of a security to changes in the whole market (also named systematic risk), and investors interpret it as follows. When *beta* is greater than 1, the security (stock) is called an "aggressive stock" relative to the market portfolio; when *beta* is less than one, the stock is named "defensive." An investor is practically indifferent to the stock when beta equals 1, a neutral stock.

Note that when expressed as a simple linear regression model, the standard CAPM in (Eq. (1)), can be written as

$$y_t = \alpha + \beta X_t + \varepsilon_t, \tag{2}$$

or in compact matrix form as

$$y = X\boldsymbol{\beta} + \varepsilon. \tag{3}$$

In the compact matrix form, $y$, $X$, $\varepsilon$, and $\beta$ have dimensions $T \times 1$, $T \times 2$, $T \times 1$, and $2 \times 1$, respectively; note that in this notation $\beta$ contains $\alpha$ and $\beta$. The errors are assumed to be independent, and identically distributed following a normal distribution with $\varepsilon \sim N(0,\sigma^2 I_T)$, and $I_T$ is an identity matrix of order $T$.

Over half a century after the introduction of the CAPM in the 1960s, the model is still widely used in applications related to risk assessments of capital projects and financial management. Fama and French [6] point out that the empirical record of the model is poor, and they identify factors that may have contributed to the poor performance, including theoretical failings driven by simplifying assumptions, and difficulties in implementing valid tests of the model. One strand of literature that emerged even before the introduction of the CAPM to the financial literature started with Mandelbrot's observation that extreme tails of empirical distributions of price changes contained higher probability than suggested by the normal distribution and that these departures warranted a new approach to the theory, which Mandelbrot introduced as the L-stable hypothesis [7, 8]. Essentially, the hypothesis proposed that variances of empirical distributions of price changes behaved as if they were infinite and conformed better to non-Gaussian members of this new family of distributions. A rich literature emerged from this hypothesis and one implication of relevance to the purposes of this chapter is that if variances are infinite then estimation methods such as least squares regression, the standard CAPM with the assumption of a constant and finite variance (Eq. (1)) may give very misleading answers. The literature on how to improve the estimation of parameters and moments of the distribution of prices beyond that of a Gaussian (normal) distribution grew exponentially and continues to be of research interest today. For readers interested in the progression of the thinking about tail behavior, modeling, estimation, and testing (see [13]). A salient theme arising from some of these works, and briefly mentioned in [6], is the need for better statistical tools to estimate empirical distribution functions and regression models that add flexibility to the specification of the residual distribution beyond the Gaussian distribution and over the past two decades these new methods permit the estimation of higher moments of empirical distributions and have been generalized to allow joint estimation of higher moments. One such distribution is the Generalized Lambda Distribution (GLD), which represents a family of distributions (see [10, 11, 15, 16].

### 2.1 The generalized lambda distribution regression analysis

The Generalized Lambda Distribution (GLD) is a family of distributions with parameters $\lambda_1, \lambda_2, \lambda_3, \lambda_4$, represented as GLD$(\lambda_1, \lambda_2, \lambda_3, \lambda_4)$; it has been used as a flexible representation of the behavior of security returns with extreme (fat) tails [17]. The GLD is commonly given as [12].

$$F^{-1}(u; \lambda_1, \lambda_2, \lambda_3, \lambda_4) = \lambda_1 + \frac{u^{\lambda_3} - (1-u)^{\lambda_4}}{\lambda_2} \tag{4}$$

where the variable $u$ represents probabilities and thus falls in the range $0 \leq u \leq 1$. A good way to think about this is by reviewing the concepts of distribution function (d. f.), probability density function (p.d.f.), and percentile function (p.f.) which is also called the inverse distribution function. The p.f. is the function used to generate the GLD. A good review of these concepts applicable to the GLD is found in [12]. Eq. (4) is the RS parameterization of the GLD [18][2]. The GLD $(\lambda_1, \lambda_2, \lambda_3, \lambda_4)$ specifies a valid distribution if and only if [12],

$$\frac{\lambda 2}{\lambda_3 u^{\lambda_3 - 1} + \lambda_4 (1-u)^{\lambda_4 - 1}} \geq 0 \, for \; all \; u \in [0, 1]. \tag{5}$$

The first thing to note is that Eq. (5) does not involve $\lambda_1$ making it an unrestricted parameter (a location parameter). If one forces this distribution to have zero location, that is GLD $(0, \lambda_2, \lambda_3, \lambda_4)$, then the random variable $X + \lambda_1$ is distributed as GLD $(\lambda_2, \lambda_3, \lambda_4)$. The proof of this result is given in [12]. It can also be shown that under special conditions, the GLD $(\lambda_1, \lambda_2, \lambda_3, \lambda_4)$ can be written as a function of the shape parameters $(\lambda_3, \lambda_4)$.

A second form to represent the GLD is the FKML GLD due to [19] which introduced a parameterization to relax the constraints in the RS specification. The FKML GLD is given by

$$F^{-1}(u; \lambda_1; \lambda_2; \lambda_3; \lambda_4) = \lambda_1 + \frac{1}{\lambda_2}\left(\frac{u^{\lambda_3} - 1)}{\lambda_3} - \frac{(1-u)^{\lambda_4} - 1)}{\lambda_4}\right. \tag{6}$$

where $0 \leq u \leq 1$; $\lambda_1$ is the location parameter, $\lambda_2$ is the scale parameter, and $\lambda_3$ and $\lambda_4$ are related to skewness and kurtosis, respectively; the only constraint added by this distribution is that $\lambda_2$ must be positive.

The two forms to represent the GLD function; RS and FKML (also known as FMKL) are used in applications and the only difference is the restrictions imposed on the parameters of the GLD. The FMKL representation is preferred due to its simplicity. It is well-defined for all parameter values, with the only requirement being that

[2] A primer on the specification and estimation of GLDs using discretized and maximum likelihood methods is [11].

$\lambda_2 > 0$ and for a finite kth moment, the condition $\min(\lambda_3, \lambda_4) > -1/k$ must be satisfied[3]. Both representations, RS and FMKL, are used in applied work, and the FMKL GLD will be used in the empirical application below. Depending on the range of values for the parameters, the FMKL GLD can be classified into five categories [13]. There are several estimation methods for the GLD [17], and the maximum likelihood method (MLE) of the GLDEX package in R [11] is used in this Chapter. A recent application supporting the superior performance of MLE when compared to Moment Matching (MM) in high-frequency data is [20][4].

The Kolmogorov-Smirnov (KS) and Anderson-Darling (AD) goodness-of-fit tests are often used to test for differences between the estimated GLD and a theoretical distribution. Corlu et al. [13] conducted a comprehensive numerical analysis comparing the overall suitability of five alternative distributions to evaluate the behavior of daily equity index returns of twenty countries over the period 1979–2014, concluding that, using KS and AD, the GLD had superior performance relative to the skewed Student-t, the Johnson system, the normal inverse Gaussian, and the g-and-h distributions, with normality rejected for all sub-periods and markets[5]. The KS test will be used in the empirical example below.

Empirical literature in financial econometric models often reports the existence of non-normality, skewness, and kurtosis. Higher moments are found at all levels of aggregation, and non-normality is often reported in daily data (e.g., [4, 7, 8, 13]). The assumption that stock price changes follow a normal, or more generally, stable distribution, was standard practice in asset and option pricing models. More recently this assumption has been the subject of much theoretical and empirical research. The assumption is critical in several applied contexts. For example, accurate estimates of Value-at-Risk (VaR) depend entirely on fitting the best statistical distribution to stock price changes and VaR estimates that are sub-optimal lead to sub-optimal investment decisions. As a result, the quest for fitting the best empirical statistical distribution is pervasive and continual. For financial data, [13] reviews the vast literature on this quest and addresses the question of best fit for daily equity index returns data using several popular distributions. The dominant conclusion from a VaR assessment is that the GLD performed best in all markets and periods

---

[3] Karian et al. [12] provide illustrations of the basic shapes of the GLD (unimodal, U-shape, monotone, and S-shape), and support regions for the RS and FKML parameters. It must be noted that Eq. (4) is not always a well-defined distribution. A condition is needed so it integrates to 1; thus, restrictions must be imposed on the parameters and u must be in the range [0,1].

[4] There is growing literature on using the GLD to model financial returns for univariate and multivariate distributions. A discussion with extensive graphical illustrations for the simplest case of a multivariate distribution, the bivariate GLD, is found in [12]. Alternative estimation methods for finding optimal parameter values for the GLD include moment-matching, percentile methods, maximum likelihood, and many others. The shapes of the FKML GLD distributions and regions of valid parameter spaces have led to various categories referred to as Class I, Class II, Class III, Class IV, and Class V to represent, unimodal, U-shaped, J-shaped, and monotone probability density functions, which can be symmetric or asymmetric. Also, within these classes, regions of finite or infinite support can exist. An application of the GLD to nonstandard regression models such as the proportional hazard model is [16].

[5] A history of the progress on the application of the GLD to the U.S. and other international market returns is available in [13] they give details on distribution performance, as well as a summary table of papers on the subject with differing and conflicting results; additionally, they have a nice description of the above distributions in Section 3).

considered in their analysis. In CAPM, stock returns are the dependent variable, given that the GLD distribution is reported to be a good fit for empirical returns, it seems natural to model the CAPM residuals using the GLD, rather than the standard assumptions of normality.

## 2.2 The GLD regression model

The standard linear regression can be re-specified using a GLD distribution for the errors [21]. This specification produces a GLD regression line that is less influenced by (more robust to) outliers. The statistical model is formulated with a robust, zero mean, residual reference line, from which a quantile regression is estimated. A rich set of statistical models can be generated with restrictions on the model parameters, and these models can be fit parametrically and nonparametrically. As indicated earlier, the MLE method is used in this chapter to estimate the parametric model in (Eq. (4)). This flexible parametric model is estimated with the GLDreg package in R [22].

Consider the regression model given in Eq. (3) above. We want to estimate the two coefficients in $\beta$, $\alpha$ and $\beta$, under the assumption that the errors follow a GLD distribution, that is $\varepsilon \sim$ GLD $(\lambda_1, \lambda_2, \lambda_3, \lambda_4)$, with $\varepsilon$ having a zero mean. The zero mean condition shifts the GLDs to have zero mean by calculating the first coefficient after the other three parameters have been calculated. This can be done by modeling the residuals with MLE or some other method such as L-moment matching. The algorithm for estimating the regression model and the final quantile function is based on the following steps [22].

1. Estimate β in (Eq. (3)) by least squares to obtain $\hat{\beta}$ and $\hat{\varepsilon}$;

2. Estimate the distribution of the residuals $\hat{\varepsilon}$ using FKML GLD (or RS GLD); the goal in this step is to obtain initial values for the optimization.

3. Estimate the log-likelihood of the model for FKML GLD (or RS GLD);

4. Use an optimization algorithm to find the maximum value of the log-likelihood (the Nelder-Mead algorithm is used by default);[6]

5. Adjust the intercept in step 4 so that the residuals in the final regression sum to zero;

6. Use simulation to obtain the distribution properties of the regression coefficients, say in 1000 replications, and generate consistent estimates between the simulation and the expected model.

---

[6] To fit the GLD regression model, The Nelder-Mead simplex algorithm is used to find the maximum value of the log-likelihood function conditional on previous estimates of the GLD conditional on zero first moments and zero mean residuals for both, the RS GLD and FKML GLD. Currently, this algorithm is considered the most general and stable method for optimization and estimation under GLD [22].

### *2.2.1 Empirical example*

U.S. Farmland is a main input in food production and has attracted investment interest from the non-farm sector. Berkshire Hathaway, for example, has included farmland investments in Berkshire's diverse portfolio for years. Historically, stories abound of how technological advances and farmland economics have made it a successful investment. One important reason behind the interest in farmland as an investment is the everlasting need to feed a growing world population. One of the first applications of financial econometrics to pricing farmland is found in Ref. [23], who framed the research question as the level of risk an investor can expect to incur given the rate of return in farmland investments in a well-diversified market portfolio, sort of how Berkshire thought about portfolio diversification. A recent survey examining farmland and prices is [24]. In financial markets, farmland is considered an illiquid asset that fits long-term investors' view of the markets. But for investors who feel attracted by returns farmland offers, alternatives have been developed, these are called farmland derivative stocks, a type of Real Estate Investment Trust (REITs). Examples of REITs include Gladstone Land (Nasdaq ticker symbol: LAND) and Farmland Partners (NYSE ticker symbol: FPI) which are used in this chapter to illustrate the econometric methodology.

The CAPM models regress LAND and FPI returns on a market portfolio of stocks, such as the U.S. S&P 500. Plots of the S&P 500, LAND, and FPI prices and returns are shown in **Figures 1–3**; the top panel of each graph shows prices, and the bottom panel shows the log returns (i.e., $r_t = \ln\left(\frac{p_t}{p_{t-1}}\right) * 100$). Daily and monthly prices for the three series were downloaded from Yahoo Finance (finance.yahoo.com) from April 11, 2014, to August 31, 2024. The daily S&P 500 prices in **Figure 1** experienced a steady uptrend with high-price fluctuations around COVID-19 (early 2020s) and 2022; this

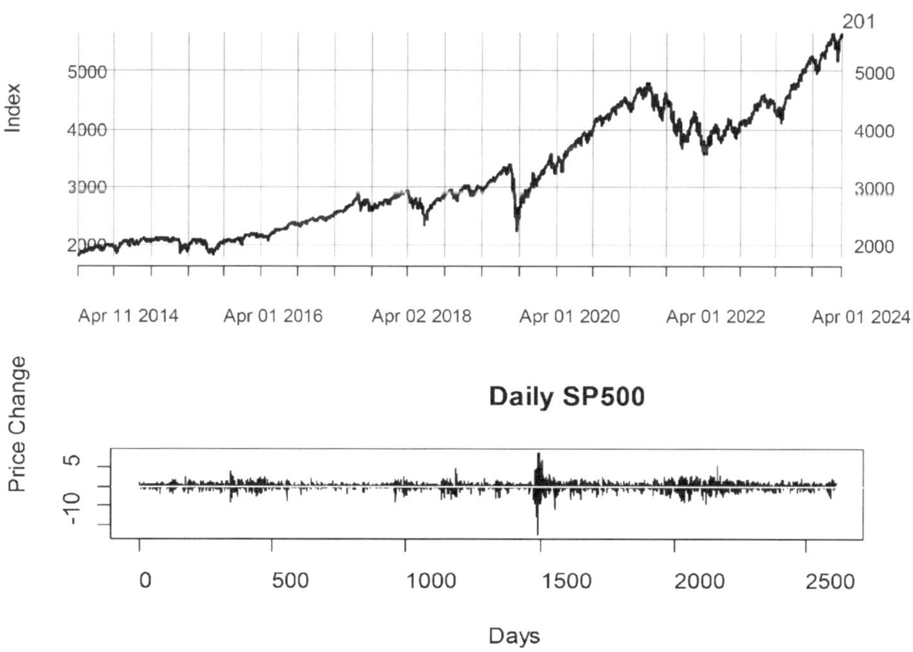


**Figure 1.**
*U.S. S&P 500 daily prices and returns, April 2014 to August 2024.*

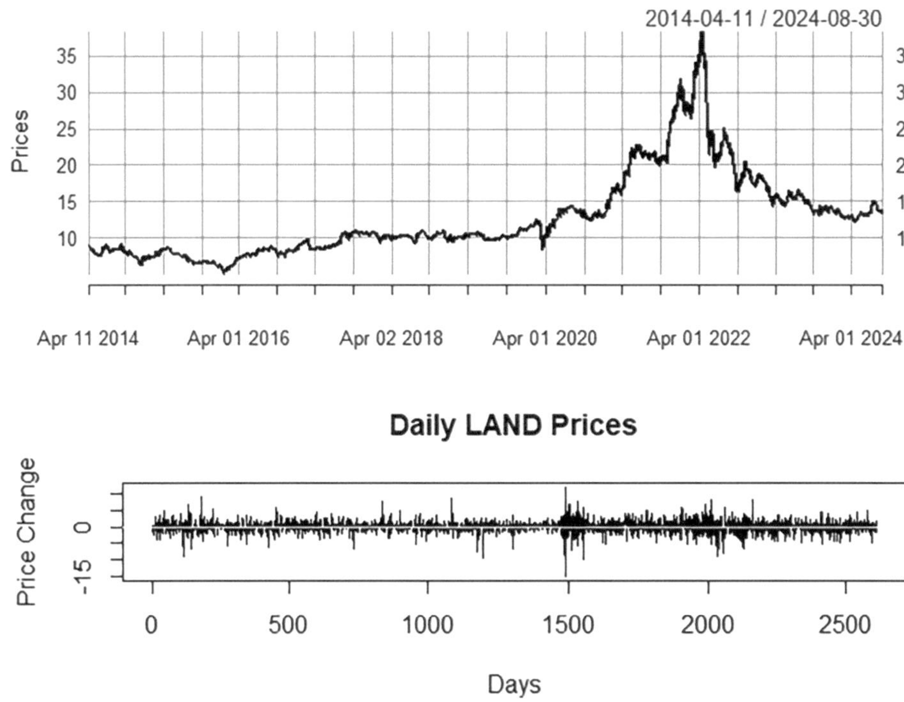


**Figure 2.**
*Gladstone land REIT (LAND) daily prices and returns, April 2014 to August 2024.*

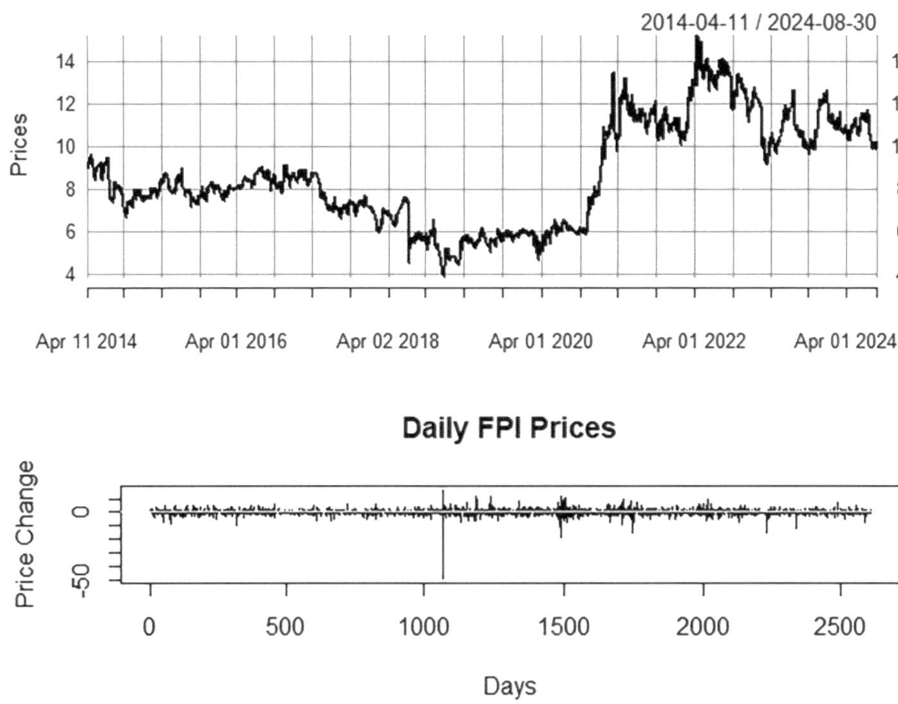


**Figure 3.**
*Farmland partners REIT (FPI) daily prices and returns, April 2014 to August 2024.*

clearly shows up in the bottom panel where extreme daily fluctuations in returns were observed. Based on the values in **Table 1**, the mean daily return for the S&P 500 was 0.0443%, a standard deviation of 1.1106%, with fluctuations ranging from −12.76% to 8.97%; also note that skewness was close to −1% and high kurtosis (29.0415). Overall, price changes in the S&P 500 seem not to follow a normal distribution, and this is confirmed by the Jarque-Bera test of normality with very high values, and p-values much lower than a critical level of 0.01. Statistics for monthly prices and returns are shown in Panel B of **Table 1**; the conclusion is that a normal distribution of monthly returns is rejected. **Table 1** shows descriptive statistics for other market indexes for comparison purposes only.

Concerning farmland REITs (**Figures 2** and **3**), LAND experienced exponential price growth until the middle of 2022, and prices have been declining ever since; the price pattern in FPI shows an uptrend to the middle of 2022 but has declined since. LAND has generated higher average daily returns (0.41%) than FPI (0.04%), with very similar standard deviations (8.66 vs. 8.43%), and minimum and maximum values. The normality of returns in LAND and FPI is strongly rejected by the Jarque-Bera test at any significance level.

In the remainder of this chapter, the analysis will proceed with daily returns, using LAND, FPI, and the S&P 500, consistent with findings in existing literature (see [4]) that normality is often found in daily data. In this empirical application, Eq. (1) for LAND and FPI becomes

$$r_{LANDt} - TBILL_t = \alpha_{FPI} + \beta_{LAND}(r_{SPt} - TBILL_t) + \varepsilon_{LANDt}, \quad (7)$$

$$r_{FPIt} - TBILL_t = \alpha_{FPI} + \beta_{FPI}(r_{SPt} - TBILL_t) + \varepsilon_{FPI}. \quad (8)$$

| Security | Mean | S.D. | Skew. | Kurt. | Min. | Max. |
|---|---|---|---|---|---|---|
| **Panel A: Daily Returns** | | | | | | |
| S&P 500 | 0.044 | 1.111 | −0.955 | 29.042 | −12.765 | 8.9683 |
| DOW 30 | 0.038 | 1.093 | −1.127 | 37.390 | −13.149 | 10.7643 |
| NASDAQ | 0.057 | 1.325 | −1.199 | 34.789 | −13.149 | 8.9347 |
| Russel 2 K | 0.026 | 1.431 | −2.471 | 60.350 | −15.399 | 8.9763 |
| LAND | 0.016 | 1.888 | −2.612 | 111.842 | −15.2375 | 12.1686 |
| FPI | 0.006 | 2.321 | −47.577 | 2535.158 | −49.3633 | 16.7054 |
| **Panel B: Monthly Returns** | | | | | | |
| S&P 500 | 0.886 | 4.352 | 5.428 | 1242.590 | −13.3668 | 11.9421 |
| DOW 30 | 0.741 | 4.319 | 12.837 | 1429.847 | −14.7848 | 13.0597 |
| NASDAQ | 1.177 | 5.163 | 33.850 | 2281.684 | −14.2270 | 14.3640 |
| Russ. 2 K | 0.546 | 5.917 | −66.026 | 5778.753 | −24.7170 | 16.7940 |
| LAND | 0.407 | 8.662 | −32.971 | 24393.60 | −30.2808 | 25.6566 |
| FPI | 0.043 | 8.427 | −16.479 | 22884.66 | −30.0621 | 22.6849 |

*The summary statistics for daily and monthly returns are in percent. Skew. and Kurt, represent skewness and kurtosis, respectively. The Jarque/Bera (JB) strongly rejected normality in all series at any significance level, except for monthly NASDAQ, with JB (4.8493, 0.10) Chi-square and p values, respectively.*

**Table 1.**
*Financial market and farmland derivatives returns, 2014–2024.*

where $t = 1,2,3, \ldots ,T$, $r$ represents returns as before, and TBILL is the daily 3-month U.S. Treasury Bill rate.

Least Squares estimates of (Eq. (7) and Eq. (8)) produced the following results

$$\begin{gathered}\hat{LAND} = 0.0002 + 1.0003 * X \\ (0.0005)\ (0.0002) \\ R^2 = 0.9999, \mathrm{SSE} = 0.0174\end{gathered} \tag{9}$$

$$\begin{gathered}\hat{FPI} = -0.00005 + 1.0000 * X \\ (0.0006)\ (0.0002) \\ R^2 = 0.9998, \mathrm{SSE} = 0.0223,\end{gathered} \tag{10}$$

where $\hat{LAND}$ *and* $\hat{FPI}$ represent the predicted excess returns for LAND and FPI, and $X$ is the excess returns to the market portfolio (see (Eq. (1) and Eq. (3)). The intercept in both equations is negative but insignificant; the beta coefficient is positive and significant. The residuals have outliers in both LAND and FPI, and both histograms appear symmetrical but with longer tails in FPI (**Figure 4**). However, the Jarque-Bera tests and p-values for LAND and FPI regression results were (2128.6,0.0000) and (899,020,0.0000), respectively, resoundingly rejecting the normality of residuals for both least squares regressions. These results are consistent with previous empirical findings in the cited literature and lead us to estimate the CAPM under alternative flexible error specifications, the GLD discussed earlier.

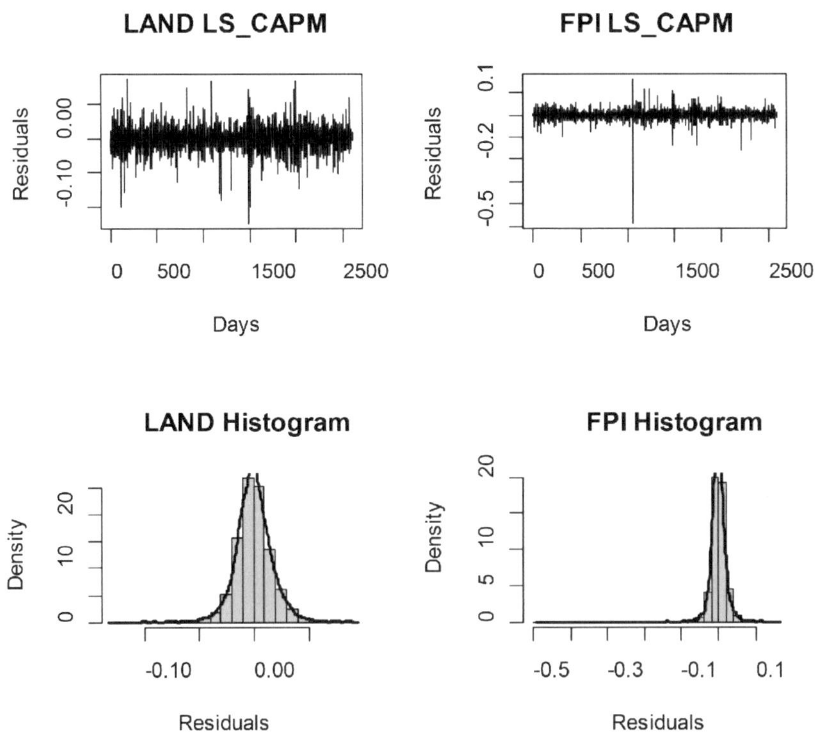


**Figure 4.**
*Time plots (top panel) and histograms of daily residuals from least squares of the CAPM linear regression for LAND and FPI, April 2014–August 2024.*

Specifying a GLD error structure of the CAPM, the model was estimated under the FKML using maximum likelihood with the GLDreg package in *R* [22]; the Nelder-Mead algorithm converged and produced the following results

$$\begin{gathered} \hat{LAND} = -0.0004 + 1.0002 * X \\ GLD(-0.0002, 131.6135, -0.1122, -0.1307) \end{gathered} \tag{11}$$

$$\text{KS p} - \text{value} = 0.6548; \text{R} - \text{KS Test} > 0.05 = 89.1\%.$$

The KS p-value = 0.65 is much larger than 0.05 and the Resample KS test =90.6% gives a range of 0.65 to 0.09 for the p-value, suggesting that the GLD specification is a good fit to the data. The QQ plot of the residuals is shown in **Figure 5**. The CAPM GLD residuals closely follow the theoretical GLD distribution for the estimated values in (Eq. (9′)) and (Eq. (10')). Estimates of the CAPM for FPI using the GLD specification of the residuals under the FKML form and maximum likelihood generated the following results at convergence

$$\begin{gathered} (10')\ \hat{FPI} = -0.00004 + 1.0000 * X \\ GLD(-0.0002, 132 - 0.1122, -0.0131) \end{gathered} \tag{12}$$

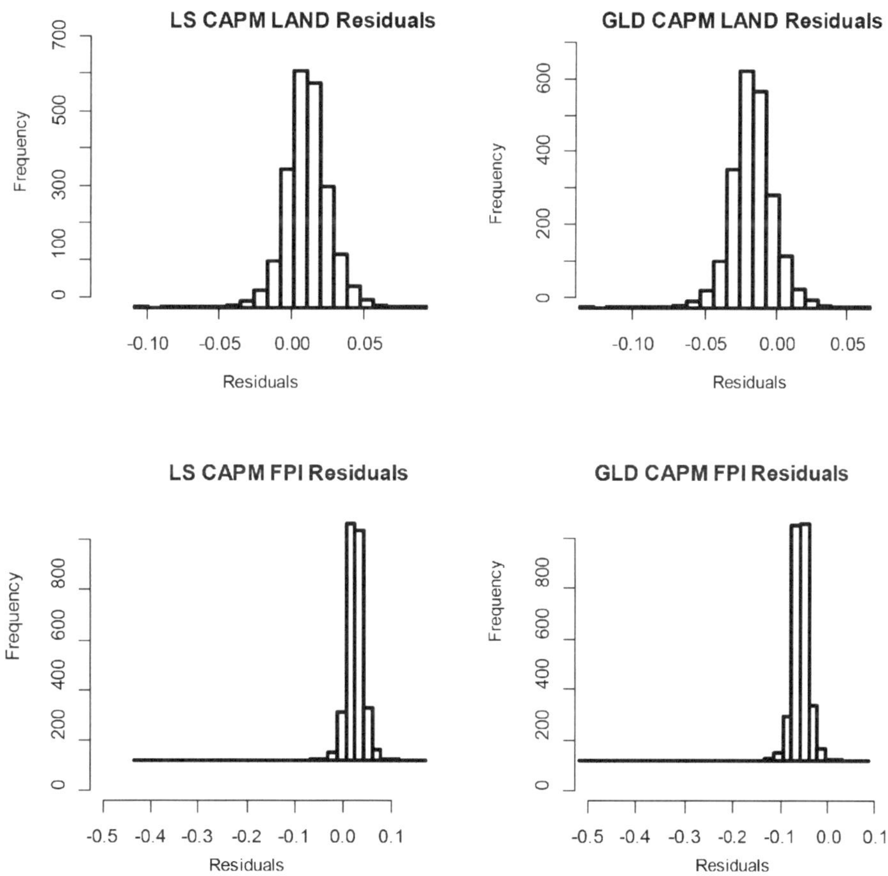


**Figure 5.**
*Residual histograms for LAND and FPI regressions, least squares (left column), and GLD regression (right column), April 2014–August 2024.*

$$\text{KS p} - \text{values} = 0.6585; \text{R} - \text{KS Test} > 0.05 = 89.9\%.$$

These results were generated by simulating the GLD regression 1000 times using the *GLD.lm.full* function in R. While not reported here, the QQplots of the residuals were undistinguishable from the theoretical distribution, indicating a very good and robust fit to the CAPM. The parameter estimates for the $\alpha$ and $\beta$ showed a symmetric distribution; however, the asymptotic distribution of these coefficients is yet unavailable. The 95% confidence intervals for these coefficients were narrow (−0.0008, 0.0009) for alpha and 1,1 for beta, also suggesting reliable estimates of the parameters of the CAPM between LAND excess returns and the excess returns in the market portfolio.

A comparison of the LAND and FPI residual plots from least squares (LS) and GLD regressions is given in **Figure 5**.[7] While the general impression given by these graphs is one of symmetry and normal, as previously noted, the Jarque-Bera test strongly rejected normality in the residuals of both LSU equations. Given the skewness and kurtosis in the LS residuals, the GLD regression in the right column of **Figure 5** generated more robust (less susceptible to outliers) regression results. While the estimated coefficients of the GLD CAPM model were symmetrical in the histograms from the simulation analysis at 1000 replications, statistical tests of such coefficients are not currently possible.

## 3. Conclusions

This chapter presents a flexible model specification for the capital asset pricing model using GLD quantile regression that specifies the error structure as a four-parameter GLD function. The analysis used prices of farmland REITs, namely Gladstone Land (LAND) and Farmland Partners (FPI), and the U.S. S&P 500 index to represent the market portfolio. A statistical analysis of returns revealed the presence of extreme values, skewness, and kurtosis. The Jarque-Bera test for normality was highly significant for all daily returns from April 2014 to August 2024. The CAPM model was estimated using least squares and this analysis further confirmed the presence of higher moments in the residuals. Therefore, the analysis re-specified the errors of the regression CAPM using a more flexible GLD distribution. The flexibility of shapes offered with the GLD and since outliers were present in the residual plots from least squares, a more robust GLD regression was estimated. The results suggested that LAND and FPI do not offer portfolio diversification beyond that provided by a market index such as the U.S. S&P 500. While the numerical magnitude of the estimated coefficients is identical to the least squares results, the GLD estimates are more accurate and robust to outliers and more consistent with the distributional properties of returns. Nonetheless, further theoretical developments on the distribution of the estimated coefficients of the GLD regression are needed for inference with

[7] Residual diagnostics for the GLD CAPM model were based on the analysis of the sample autocorrelation function (SACF) of the residuals, the Ljung-Box test of residual correlations, the Breusch-Pagan test for heteroskedasticity, and, as reported above, the QQ-plots of the residuals. The Ljung-Box and the BP tests show autocorrelation and GARCH effects in the GLD regression residuals, which requires further exploration as done in robust GARCH models [25].

the time series CAPM. Also, additional testing is required using a broader set of assets and portfolios as in [6] and the works cited there.[8]

The literature recognizes that GLD is a highly flexible statistical distribution that allows a wide range of shapes and approximates a wide range of distributions (normal, exponential, logistic, Weibull, etc.). This distribution is often called a "family of distributions" due to the multiple distributions it can encompass. This flexibility is appealing in applied work since it permits the errors of a parametric model to be specified in a manner consistent with empirical regularities. If the researcher feels it is best to define a flexible error structure rather than arbitrarily assume normality, then GLD regressions offer a modeling option. There is a caveat, however, because the probability theory of linear models under this type of flexible specification is a work in progress, whereas assuming error normality, the standard practice, has a well-established asymptotic theory. The ongoing progress consists of deriving parameter distributions using Bootstrap methods and some of these results are included here. Also, classical models can be compared to more robust alternatives [15]. The regression results reported here, however, have important properties, including the estimation of a reference line with robustness to outliers, a quantile regression model from the reference line with smooth regression coefficients across quantiles, and goodness-of-fit tests (QQ plots and Kolmogorov–Smirnov test), providing a more complete picture of the model structure for the problem at hand when compared to an average regression line.

## Acknowledgements

This research was supported in part by the USDA National Institute of Food and Agriculture, Hatch Project LAB94491, accession number 1023839.

[8] Future research may also explore Generalized Autoregressive Conditional Heteroskedasticity (GARM) type models. A reviewer suggested to explore this further. We use the Ljung-Box statistic for serial dependence in the squared residuals and the Breusch-Pagan test for GARCH effects. Both tests were significant at the 1% level suggesting that this may be an additional area of further exploration.

## Author details

Hector O. Zapata[1*] and Damilola S. Adebayo[2]

1 LSU AgCenter, Louisiana State University, Baton Rouge, USA

2 Louisiana State University, Baton Rouge, Louisiana, USA

*Address all correspondence to: hzapata@lsu.edu

## References

[1] Sharpe WF. Risk-aversion in the stock market: Some empirical evidence. The Journal of Finance. 1965;**20**(3):416-422. DOI: 10.2307/2977991

[2] Lintner J. The valuation of risk assets and the selection of risky investments in stock portfolios and capital budgets. The Review of Economics and Statistics. 1965;**47**(1):13-37. DOI: 10.2307/1926735

[3] Mossin J. Equilibrium in a capital asset market. Econometrica. 1966;**34**: 768-783. DOI: 10.2307/1910098

[4] Campbell J, Lo A, Mackinlay C. The Econometrics of Financial Markets. Princeton: Princeton University Press; 1997. DOI: 10.1515/9781400830213-004

[5] Poncet P, Portait R. Chapter 22. In: Capital Market Finance. Cergy-Pontoise, France: Springer Texts in Business and Economics; 2022. pp. 929-962. DOI: 10.1007/978-3-030-84600-8_22

[6] Fama EF, French KR. The capital asset pricing model: Theory and evidence. Journal of Economic Perspectives. 2004;**18**(3):25-46. DOI: 10.1257/0895330042162430

[7] Mandelbrot B. The variation of certain speculative prices. Journal of Business. 1963;**36**(4):394-419. DOI: 10.1086/294632

[8] Fama EF. Mandelbrot and the stable paretian hypothesis. The Journal of Business. 1963;**36**(4):420-429. DOI: 10.1086/294633

[9] Guermat C. Yes, the CAPM is testable. Journal of Banking & Finance. 2014;**46**:31-42. DOI: 10.1016/j.jbankfin.2014.05.001

[10] Su S. A discretized approach to flexibly fit generalized lambda distributions to data. Journal of Modern Applied Statistical Methods. 2005;**4**(2):7. DOI: 10.22237/jmasm/1130803560

[11] Su S. Numerical maximum log likelihood estimation for generalized lambda distributions. Computational Statistics & Data Analysis. 2007;**51**(8): 3983-3998. DOI: 10.1016/j.csda.2006.06.008

[12] Karian ZA, Dudewicz EJ. Fitting Statistical Distributions: The Generalized Lambda Distribution and Generalized Bootstrap Methods. New York: Chapman and Hall/CRC; 2000. DOI: 10.1201/9781420038040

[13] Corlu CG, Meterelliyoz M, Tinic M. Empirical distributions of daily equity index returns: A comparison. Expert Systems With Applications. 2016;**54**: 170-192. DOI: 10.1016/j.eswa.2015.12.048

[14] Aldeni M, Lee C, Famoye F. Families of distributions arising from the quantile of generalized lambda distribution. Journal of Statistical Distributions and Applications. 2017;**4**:1-8. DOI: 10.1186/s40488-017-0081-4

[15] Su S. Flexible modelling of survival curves for censored data. Journal of Statistical Distributions and Applications. 2016;**3**:1-20. DOI: 10.1186/s40488-016-0045-0

[16] Su S. Flexible parametric accelerated failure time model. Journal of Biopharmaceutical Statistics. 2021;**31**(5): 650-667. DOI: 10.1080/10543406.2021.1934854

[17] Corlu CG, Meterelliyoz M. Estimating the parameters of the generalized lambda distribution: Which

method performs best? Communications in Statistics - Simulation and Computation. 2015;**45**(7):2276-2296. DOI: 10.1080/03610918.2014.901355

[18] Ramberg JS, Schmeiser BW. An approximate method for generating asymmetric random variables. Communications of the ACM. 1974; **17**(2):78-82. DOI: 10.1145/360827.360840

[19] Freimer M, Kollia G, Mudholkar GS, Lin CT. A study of the generalized Tukey lambda family. Communications in Statistics-Theory and Methods. 1988; **17**(10):3547-3567. DOI: 10.1080/03610928808829820

[20] Junior PO, Jeyasreedharan N, Alagidede I. On the goodness-of-fits of the generalized lambda distribution on high-frequency stock index returns. Cogent Economics & Finance. 2022;**10**: 1-20. DOI: 10.1080/23322039.2022.2095764

[21] Su S. Flexible parametric quantile regression model. Statistics and Computing. 2015;**25**:635-650. DOI: 10.1007/s11222-014-9457-1

[22] Su S. Fitting flexible parametric regression models with GLDreg in R. Journal of Modern Applied Statistical Methods. 2016;**15**(2):46. DOI: 10.22237/jmasm/1478004240

[23] Barry PJ. Capital asset pricing and farm real estate. American Journal of Agricultural Economics. 1980;**62**(3): 549-553. DOI: 10.2307/1240213

[24] Deaton BJ, Lawley C. A survey of literature examining farmland prices: A Canadian focus. Canadian Journal of Agricultural Economics/Revue canadienne d'agroeconomie. 2022;**70**(2): 95-121. DOI: 10.1111/cjag.12307

[25] Muler N, Yohai VJ. Robust estimates for GARCH models. Journal of Statistical Planning and Inference. 2008;**138**(10): 2918-2940. DOI: 10.1016/j.jspi.2007.11.003

Chapter 9

# Does Local Media Convey a Different Impression in Stock Markets?

*Linda Pettersson and Taylan Mavruk*

**Abstract**

We examine how local media influences trading activity in local stocks by separating the effects of national news from local news and local printed press news from local web page news. Our results show that information provided by local web pages induces investors to become net buyers. The results are particularly strong in rural districts known as relatively poor information environments. Local media garners more attention from local investors than national media. These results have implications for information efficiency in the stock markets. As local information induces investors to become net buyers, it decreases investors' information search costs that tend to be greater for stock purchases than stock sales. Thus, information asymmetry between local and remote investors may decrease by paying more attention to local news. Finally, local journalists influence investor beliefs, indicating that their actions and incentives directly affect prices and allocations.

**Keywords:** individual investors, buy-sell imbalance, local news, national news, urban areas, rural areas

## 1. Introduction

This study examines the local and national media news about firms and how it affects individual investors' trading. Likely, the news in local media is also published in national media. However, there is a possibility of a media slant [1, 2]. In other words, although the stories about local firms are based on the same underlying event, the journalists' choice of words in local media may convey a different impression of the event than what is presented by national media.

Local media may present the news differently because local media may serve as watchdogs [3–5]. This is because local media is more likely to obtain information from employees and local suppliers and may publish news that a firm has not yet disclosed. Thus, local media may utilize its proximity to the local firms and any potential asymmetric disclosure provided by the insiders [6]. This advantage may not only cause local media to publish stories before national newspapers but also allow them to interpret and publish the news differently from the national newspapers. The proximity to the local firms may also allow local media to act as cheerleaders, referred to as hype [2].

Hype in local media may influence the choice of language, quotes, and the framing of events by journalists, whose text forms and reshapes cultural memories, thereby influencing our perspectives on the past, present, and future [7]. The choice of words by local journalists may also be influenced by historical events that enter journalists' memory agendas, which can be long and varied. The size of the past events, their perceived cultural and geographical proximity, and the distance in time between an event and its memory are all important determinants of journalists' memory agendas. Studies examining the heterogeneity in the writing styles of journalists suggest that sentence structure, complexity, article length, and even pessimism or optimism about market conditions influence market outcomes and investor behavior [8, 9].

Overall, if local media convey different information about the same underlying event than national media, it could affect trading activity in local and remote trades differently. We test this hypothesis by examining individual investors' trading activity measured as buy-sell imbalance [10, 11], which indicates the change in individuals' trade position. In efficient markets, stock prices should incorporate all available value-relevant information instantaneously. However, we know from earlier studies [12] that investors only follow and process a subset of information on some firms. We add to this knowledge in the previous studies by providing evidence on the differences in the local vs. national news published in the urban vs. local areas and their effects on individual trading activity.

Using the news dataset from Retriever through the University of Gothenburg's library, we obtained the number of news articles covered in the national, local, and foreign printed press and web pages about the listed firms between 2006 and 2014. To measure individual investors' buy-sell imbalances, we use investor data from Euroclear Sweden that covers quarterly holdings of all the investments in firms listed on Swedish stock markets between 2006 and 2014. This provides us with 36 waves of panel data, covering about 1.8 million individual investors and their 30 million trades of which 16.29% are local trades and 83.71% remote trades.

We show that local news found on web pages serves as a proxy for local investor sentiment and trading. One additional local (national) news article increases individual investors' buy-sell imbalances by 4.1 percentage points (5.4 pp.) from the mean. Our results show that most local news effects can be attributed to the web page news from local media sources. This effect is significantly stronger for local trades and more pronounced in rural areas. Interestingly, the local newspapers (printed press news) do not appear to significantly impact local investor trading. This is consistent with the previous evidence examining only the information contained in earnings announcements or in printed national newspapers [13, 14]. One reason for this result could be that individuals have already read the same or similar news online. Our study has some implications on whether the local news induces, amplifies, or reflects investors' attention to the local stock performance.

## 2. Literature review

This study examines whether investors buy stocks based on their familiarity to the firms [12]. More specifically, the study tests the hypothesis that investors buy attention-grabbing stocks on the news [10]. In theory, there should be no difference in the signals that informed investors observe when buying and selling stocks. This means informed investors are equally likely to buy stocks with positive news than sell stocks with negative news. Uninformed investors, on the other hand, are equally likely to make random buys and sells. While, in theory, the decision to buy or sell should not differ, the previous research [10] documented that real-life investors trade differently. Particularly, individual investors did not buy all the stocks that garnered their attention and were more likely to buy attention-grabbing stocks than to sell them. The suggested reason was that investors cannot process all available information, meaning their choice set is limited. For example, in Ref. [15] investors limited their choice to those stocks that recently garnered attention. Investors' risk preferences determined which attention-grabbing stocks they bought.

While many studies have examined these theories, empirical evidence is consistent with the pattern of investor behavior that individual investors hold a few stocks in their portfolios and they do not sell short, meaning that they only sell the stocks they already own. The evidence shows that momentum investors chase past winners, but contrarian investors buy stocks based on attention. Rational investors tend to sell their past losers, delaying tax payments, while investors who trade based on behavioral reasons sell past winners, postponing the feeling of regret concerning potential losses [16]. Recent empirical studies have showed an ambiguous effect of local trading activity and asset prices.[1]

We add to this literature by examining the differences in local and national news, which could improve the earlier evidence on the effects of news on trading activity and hence enhance informational efficiency in local markets. Some remote investors may not be aware that local investors have already obtained information from local media and traded on that news. This may induce remote investors to behave differently, perhaps showing some biases such as overreaction [31] when the news becomes more widespread.

Although media slant may substantially influence asset prices [2, 32], previous results were mixed. Some studies showed no relationship between earnings announcements and stock prices [13, 14]. The post-earnings announcement drift does not seem to relate to individual investor trades. In contrast, other studies have shown a strong relationship between news coverage and asset prices. Evidence of a significant relationship exists between individual trading in local markets and local newspaper coverage of earnings announcements [33]. Trading volume and return volatility increased with communication activity measured by messages in internet chat rooms [34]. Although unrelated to the returns, the ambient noise level in a futures pit seems to move trading volume, volatility, and depth [35].

Our contribution to this more general evidence on trade behavior is our analysis of a more extensive database of local news to examine the differences in the media appearance of local firms. Unlike previous studies, which mostly covered local newspapers, our media data contain a richer information set as it covers local newspapers and web pages (even social media) provided by local media sources. This distinction might be important as web page news and social media have become significant information channels with the development of the internet. Examining the news on the web page covered by local media will enrich our understanding of the attention hypothesis.

Our results may contribute to the literature by allowing us to infer information asymmetry between local and remote investors. The local news appears to affect liquidity in local markets. More importantly, local news induces individual investors

---

[1] See Refs. [17–25] for evidence from institutional investors and see Refs. [11, 26–30] for evidence from individual investors.

to become net buyers. This means that local news could reduce investors' information search costs, which tends to be greater for purchases than sales. Thus, local news can help reduce the information asymmetry between local and remote investors.

In sum, investors' decision to buy or sell differs. Individual investors tend to focus on future returns of the purchased stocks but consider the past returns of the stocks they sell. Institutional investors, on the other hand, show a different pattern. They have a search problem when they sell as they own more stocks than individual investors. Institutional investors tend to sell short, devote more time to their trades, manage larger amounts of capital, and may have more information about the stocks [10].

## 3. Data and method

### 3.1 Data

We collected news articles about firms from Retriever ("Mediaarkivet") through the University of Gothenburg's library. Our media data cover news articles about firms that appeared in all media sources between January 1, 2006, and December 31, 2014. News sources include Swedish or foreign printed press (newspapers) and Swedish and foreign web pages. In Retriever, we were able to separate these sources further to determine whether news appeared in national media sources (e.g., national newspapers) or local media sources.

To collect the news articles, we followed three steps. First, we limited our search to a maximum of 10,000 news articles because of downloading restrictions in Retriever.[2] Second, Retriever also allowed us to analyze the news articles in their database to separate them between national news and local news. More importantly, Retriever presents news articles coming from media firms headquartered in each district. Thus, we could locate local news (both printed press and web pages) from local media sources headquartered in each district. Finally, we could identify media outlets headquartered in urban and local areas.

Our investor data comes from Euroclear Sweden, which covers the quarterly holdings of all the shareholders of firms listed in Sweden's stock markets and spans over 36 periods between March 2006 and December 2014. The firms in the data are listed mainly on the OMX (large, mid, and small cap) exchange, but some firms are listed on the alternative minor stock markets. Following Barber et al. [10], we removed all the passive positions of investors as we are interested in examining the active trades, not the holdings.[3] Thus, the sample includes only buy-and-sell transactions. We also removed the trades of individuals older than 85 and younger than 18 as it is unlikely that these individuals make active trading decisions themselves.

---

[2] For instance, our search word is Volvo to begin with. If Volvo has more than 10,000 articles, then we first restrict our search word to Volvo AB (AB stands for public company). If word Volvo AB still hits more than 10,000 news articles in printed press or web pages, we mark this firm for the next step.

[3] Including the holdings (passive positions), the observations will exceed 240 million in the data. We, therefore, use several subgroups to examine the differences between the role of local media and these benchmarks in investor trading.

## 4. Method

One important challenge with examining the attention hypothesis in local bias studies has been to separate whether the observed results are based on superior information or familiarity with the firms. Familiarity has several definitions, such as interpretation advantage of the given public information [12], feeling connection to the local firms, optimism, or overconfidence toward the local firms [36], and indisputable preferences toward local firms [28]. We attempted to tackle this challenge by following three approaches in our setting.

First, to examine whether local information affects local trading activity, we created two groups of trades. In our first (treatment) group, the local trades of individual investors are assumed to be informed by local media sources. In our second (control) group, the remote trades of individual investors are assumed to be either uninformed or informed by remote media sources.[4] This setting allowed us to estimate the effects of attention on local trades relative to a control group of remote trades of individual investors. If local information induces the local investors to become net buyers of the local stocks, our attention hypothesis about local media and trades would hold. If, on the other hand, local information induces local investors to become net sellers, it is unlikely that the attention hypothesis can explain the results. Local investors' stock purchases are more likely motivated by attention to local information. In contrast, their sales may be driven by multiple motivations, for example, diversification and personal liquidity shocks.

Second, we examined the effects of local printed press news and local web page news separately, as some investors may have read the same or similar news on local web pages or other local media channels before the printed press published it. This could be one reason why investors do not pay attention to printed news [13, 14]. Third, we examined and compared the effects of local and national news on individual trading activity in urban and rural areas separately. Previous research suggests that firms headquartered in rural areas are characterized as illiquid firms, firms with high idiosyncratic volatility, and informationally opaque [37]. Thus, rural areas are expected to be relatively poor information areas. If the attention hypothesis holds, the effects of local information on local trades could be more pronounced in rural areas than in urban areas.

### 4.1 Model specification

Our first analysis is more descriptive, aiming to show differences in media appearance in local vs. national outlets in urban vs. rural areas. We presented our data over time and provided mean difference tests. We then examined how national and local news influence investors' trading activity measured as investors' buy-sell imbalances on stock $j$ at time $t$ [10]. Eq. (1) presents our firm-level measure of buy-sell imbalances. We used both the number of shares bought/sold and the value of the bought/sold shares, but we present the version that used the number of shares in the equation. For the value regression, we replaced the number of shares with the value of the shares in Eq. 1.

---

[4] The remote investments can be seen either as investments by local investors or investments in local firms made by remote investors. As our unit of analysis is the trades or investments, the interpretation of the results in either way should be interesting. Henceforth, if the individual makes a local trade, we will name her/him a local investor, and if she/he makes a remote trade, we will name her/him a remote investor.

$$BSI_{j,t} = \frac{\sum_{j=i}^{n} NB_{j,t} - \sum_{j=i}^{n} NS_{j,t}}{\sum_{j=i}^{n} NB_{j,t} + \sum_{j=i}^{n} NS_{j,t}}, \qquad (1)$$

where $BSI_{j,t}$ is the firm-level buy-sell imbalance, the number of bought $NB_{j,t}$, and the sold shares $NS_{j,t}$ are aggregated to the firm level. The denominator shows the aggregated level of both bought and sold trades on the firm stock.

In the regression analysis, the independent variables are the news variables and the number of articles that appeared in the media, which measure the attention effect. The news variables are separated as national news and local news. A media type is 1 for printed news and 0 for web news, which is dropped from the model due to collinearity, but the interaction effects remain. Firm urban dummy is assigned 1 if the firm is headquartered in either the Stockholm, Gothenburg or Malmo area, else it is 0. We also controlled for the overall news sentiment in the market, represented by the dummy variable that equals 1 if the number of media appearances is greater than the median number of media appearances in the dataset. Locally biased (LB) investor is the intensity of locally biased investors in the firm, measured as the capital invested in the firm coming from local owners normalized by the firm's market value.

Various interaction effects are included. Eq. 2 presents our main model more formally:

$$BSI_{j,t} = \mu_t + \beta News_{j,t} + \rho Type_{j,t} + \partial News_{j,t} * Type_{j,t} + \gamma X_{it} + \varepsilon_{it}, \qquad (2)$$

where the dependent variable is the buy-sell imbalance $BSI_{j,t}$ in stock $j$ based on either the value of the trades or the number of shares traded at time $t$. $News_{j,t}$ is the number of published articles, either local or national, about the firm. $Type_{j,t}$ is a dummy variable taking the value of 1 if the news is a printed press, else it is a web page news. More specifically, we examined the frequency distribution of the printed news vs. web page news about the firm. If the printed news appears more than 50% for the firm, then $Type_{j,t}$ is assigned as 1, else 0. $News_{j,t} * Type_{j,t}$ is the interaction term between the type of media and the number of news, and $X_{it}$ represents the control variables that are discussed above.

## 4.2 Fama-Macbeth approach

Fama-Macbeth [38] regressions are run with Newey-West [39] serial correlation consistent standard errors. The original Fama-Macbeth [38] model examined the relationship between risk and return for New York Stock Exchange common stocks. One reason for choosing the Fama-Macbeth approach in this study was that it considers that the betas change over time. Examining time-varying betas is not possible in cross-sectional regressions. However, suppose the betas are constant over time. In that case, the estimates from the Fama-Macbeth regressions will be the same as those obtained from the cross-sectional regressions. Another reason for choosing the Fama-Macbeth approach in this study was that we have a large investor dataset and investors' decisions, and hence, the errors may be correlated with each other. If the errors are uncorrelated across investors over time, we could just as well run OLS regressions. The betas from the OLS estimates would be consistent, but the standard errors would be incorrect. We could cluster standard errors on some groups and still apply OLS, but this approach will not consider time-varying betas. The Fama-Macbeth approach is one way of correcting standard errors while allowing time-varying betas.

Following the Fama-Macbeth approach, a two-step method, we first ran the following time series regressions to obtain the betas.

$$BSI_t = \mu_j + \beta_j News_t + \rho_j Type_t + \partial_j News_t * Type_t + \gamma_j X_t + e_t, t = 1, 2, \dots T \text{ for each } j. \quad (3)$$

In the second step, we performed a cross-sectional regression for each time period:

$$BSI_{j,t} = b_{0t} + b_{1t}\beta_j' + b_{2t}\rho_j' + b_{3t}\partial_j' + b_{4t}\gamma_j' + e_{j,t}, j = 1, 2, \dots N \text{ for each } t, \quad (4)$$

where the estimated coefficients $\beta_j'$, $\rho_j'$, $\partial_j'$, and $\gamma_j'$ from Eq. 3 are now used as independent variables in Eq. 4. As a final step, the Fama-Macbeth coefficients are computed as the averages across time:

$$\hat{b}_0 = \frac{1}{T}\sum_{t=1}^{T} b_{0t}, \hat{b}_1 = \frac{1}{T}\sum_{t=1}^{T} b_{1t}, \hat{b}_2 = \frac{1}{T}\sum_{t=1}^{T} b_{2t}, \hat{b}_3 = \frac{1}{T}\sum_{t=1}^{T} b_{3t}, \hat{b}_4 = \frac{1}{T}\sum_{t=1}^{T} b_{4t}, \quad (5)$$

In the original regressions, the standard errors are assumed uncorrelated over time and thus the variance, for example, of $\hat{b}_4$ is computed as:

$$\sigma^2\left(\hat{b}_4\right) = \frac{1}{T} var(b_{4t}) = \frac{1}{T^2}\sum_{t=1}^{T}\left(b_{4t} - \hat{b}_4\right)^2, \quad (6)$$

and the covariance of the standard errors is given as:

$$cov(\hat{e}) = \frac{1}{T} cov(\hat{e}_t) = \frac{1}{T^2}\sum_{t=1}^{T}(\hat{e}_{jt} - \hat{e}_j)(\hat{e}_{it} - \hat{e}_i). \quad (7)$$

However, to adjust for both heteroskedasticity and autocorrelation (HAC) in the standard errors, the Newey-West variance estimator is used. We chose autocorrelation up to a lag of 4, considering our quarterly data and serial correlation up to 1 year. Implementing Newey-West standard errors with automatic bandwidth selection did not alter the results qualitatively. Using the Newey-West estimator, the variance of $\hat{b}_4$ can be written as:

$$\sigma^2\left(\hat{b}_4\right) = \left[\frac{1}{T}\frac{\sigma_e^2}{\left(\sigma_\gamma^2\right)^2}\right] \times f_T, \quad (8)$$

where $f_T$ is estimated as:

$$\hat{f}_T = 1 + 2\sum_{k=1}^{m-1}\left(\frac{m-k}{m}\right)\tilde{\rho}_k, \quad (9)$$

where $m$ is the truncation parameter and $\rho$ is the autocorrelation coefficient. If $\rho$ is 0 then $\hat{f}_T = 1$, yielding the conventional OLS standard error formula.

## 5. Results

### 5.1 Analysis of media data

**Table 1** presents descriptive statistics on the number of media appearances (regardless of media type) over time. The media data are divided into national, local, and foreign media.

The table shows that the average number of news articles is 8.20, covering an average of 466 firms during our study period. News articles increased by about 190% between 2006 and 2014. Local news articles increased about 54%, national news articles increased about 82%, and foreign news articles increased about 300%. Thus, most of the increase in the total number of articles can be attributed to foreign news articles, except for the increase in the number of local news articles in 2010. This deviation can perhaps be explained by the post-effects of the financial crisis; the stock market in Sweden started rising after late 2009. This is also one reason why the average number of local news articles is about 1% higher than the average number of national news articles.

**Table 2** presents descriptive statistics on the number of news articles by media type in urban vs. rural districts. The number of printed press and web page news covering 489 firms in urban districts is similar (95,324 vs. 97,486). The number of web page news covering 110 firms in rural districts is about 95% more than printed press news in rural firms. The distribution of printed press news and web page news from local media is similar. The number of printed press articles in urban (rural) districts is 94,817 (253,559), and the number of web page news in urban (rural) districts is 95,032 (227,690).

The local media in rural districts is more pronounced. The number of printed press and web page news in rural districts is about 2.5 times more than in urban districts. The number of nationally printed press news outlets in urban districts is less than the number of web page news outlets in urban districts (507 vs. 2454). In rural districts, national web page news is about 3.4 times more than national printed press news. Again, the national media sources in rural districts provided more news articles than those in urban districts in our data. The local media types from urban and rural districts seem to provide more news articles than national media types (an average of 7.43 vs. 3.6 news articles). The number of printed press and web page news from foreign sources is higher than that of national media sources.

### 5.2 Individual trading activity and media

**Table 3** shows how national and local media influence individual investors' buy-sell imbalances. The effects are clearer when the buy-sell imbalance is measured by the number of shares traded, unlike the measure based on the value of the trades. The reason could be that the trade value may change depending on many other factors and isolating these factors in a regression is more difficult. We interpreted our results based on the buy-sell imbalance measure, using the number of shares traded.

**Table 3** shows that local and national news increases investors' net trade. One additional local (national) news article increased buy-sell imbalances by

| | | Total | | | | Local | | | | National | | | | Foreign | | | |
|---|---|---|---|---|---|---|---|---|---|---|---|---|---|---|---|---|---|
| **Year** | **No. Firms** | **N** | **Mean** | **Max** | **Std.** | **N** | **Mean** | **Max** | **Std.** | **N** | **Mean** | **Max** | **Std.** | **N** | **Mean** | **Max** | **Std.** |
| 2006 | 340 | 183,100 | 6.41 | 2179 | 17.28 | 36,432 | 5.95 | 434 | 12.88 | 51,730 | 7.38 | 443 | 17.82 | 94,938 | 6.06 | 2179 | 18.39 |
| 2007 | 393 | 251,314 | 7.01 | 1639 | 21.29 | 38,666 | 6.22 | 443 | 13.39 | 54,662 | 6.18 | 540 | 15.76 | 157,986 | 7.49 | 1639 | 24.30 |
| 2008 | 408 | 301,285 | 8.70 | 4939 | 39.24 | 56,598 | 9.19 | 461 | 14.00 | 60,543 | 5.99 | 813 | 17.77 | 184,144 | 9.44 | 4939 | 48.50 |
| 2009 | 425 | 357,279 | 10.48 | 8284 | 53.91 | 83,592 | 12.65 | 804 | 15.93 | 70,182 | 7.37 | 932 | 25.04 | 203,505 | 10.66 | 8284 | 69.11 |
| 2010 | 448 | 412,007 | 10.17 | 15,421 | 50.43 | 104,264 | 14.74 | 779 | 16.89 | 76,346 | 6.16 | 619 | 16.06 | 231,397 | 9.44 | 15,421 | 65.57 |
| 2011 | 470 | 395,742 | 8.03 | 7616 | 54.25 | 71,131 | 7.45 | 579 | 12.92 | 73,977 | 5.81 | 556 | 15.03 | 250,634 | 8.85 | 7616 | 67.31 |
| 2012 | 492 | 469,505 | 8.13 | 13,379 | 83.72 | 55,867 | 4.31 | 606 | 10.99 | 73,930 | 6.26 | 670 | 18.22 | 339,708 | 9.17 | 13,379 | 97.93 |
| 2013 | 525 | 511,001 | 8.21 | 20,519 | 100.80 | 55,012 | 3.98 | 618 | 10.59 | 78,193 | 6.24 | 667 | 19.29 | 377,796 | 9.23 | 20,519 | 116.82 |
| 2014 | 563 | 540,586 | 7.44 | 19,631 | 110.99 | 58,782 | 4.16 | 627 | 10.97 | 80,462 | 4.72 | 596 | 14.23 | 401,342 | 8.47 | 19,631 | 128.57 |
| 2015 | 596 | 533,435 | 7.40 | 12,209 | 90.77 | 56,156 | 4.44 | 621 | 11.29 | 94,316 | 5.95 | 2119 | 20.68 | 382,963 | 8.19 | 12,209 | 106.53 |
| Average | 466 | 395,525 | 8.20 | | | 61,650 | 7.31 | | | 71,434 | 6.21 | | | 262,441 | 8.70 | | |

*The table presents statistics on the number of media appearances for listed firms (regardless of media type) in local, national, and foreign media. The second column represents the number of firms exist with media information in each year in the data. The media data is obtained from Retriever ("Mediaarkivet") through the University of Gothenburg's library.*

**Table 1.**
*Summary statistics on the number of media appearances over time.*

| | | | Total | | | | Local | | | | National | | | |
|---|---|---|---|---|---|---|---|---|---|---|---|---|---|---|
| | | No. Firms | N | Mean | Max | Std. | N | Mean | Max | Std. | N | Mean | Max | Std. |
| Urban | Printed Press | 489 | 95,324 | 7.57 | 804 | 21.66 | 94,817 | 7.60 | 804 | 21.70 | 507 | 1.97 | 147 | 7.04 |
| | Webb | | 97,486 | 5.32 | 513 | 16.12 | 95,032 | 5.42 | 513 | 16.31 | 2454 | 1.42 | 62 | 2.10 |
| Rural | Printed Press | 110 | 433,036 | 8.70 | 296 | 11.66 | 253,559 | 11.99 | 296 | 12.59 | 179,477 | 4.06 | 210 | 8.20 |
| | Webb | | 844,497 | 6.34 | 2119 | 18.37 | 227,690 | 4.71 | 203 | 8.32 | 616,807 | 6.94 | 2119 | 20.86 |
| Foreign | Printed Press | | 498,790 | 11.62 | 1185 | 30.46 | | | | | | | | |
| | Webb | | 2,564,297 | 7.97 | 20,519 | 97.79 | | | | | | | | |
| Average | | | 755,572 | 7.92 | | | 167,775 | 7.43 | | | 199,811 | 3.60 | | |

*The table presents statistics on the number of media appearances for listed firms in local, national, and foreign media by media type and in urban vs. rural areas. The third column represents the number of firms exist with media information in urban vs. rural districts in the data. The postal zip code information on the firm headquarters is obtained from ORBIS through the University of Gothenburg's library.*

**Table 2.**
*Summary statistics on the number of media appearances by media type in urban vs. rural areas.*

| | (1) | (2) |
|---|---|---|
| **Variables** | **No. Imbalance** | **Value Imbalance** |
| Intercept No news | 0.489*** | 0.029*** |
| | (53.17) | (3.66) |
| Local News | 0.041*** | 0.013 |
| | (2.46) | (0.78) |
| National News | 0.054*** | 0.011 |
| | (2.83) | (0.50) |
| Local News*Media Type | −0.073*** | −0.076*** |
| | (−2.82) | (−3.17) |
| National News*Media Type | −0.005 | −0.030 |
| | (−0.10) | (−0.55) |
| Firm Urban | −0.017*** | −0.003 |
| | (−2.50) | (−0.41) |
| No. Media app. = > Median | 0.011 | 0.025*** |
| | (1.41) | (2.63) |
| Local News*No. Media app. | 0.053*** | 0.047 |
| | (2.52) | (1.54) |
| National News*No. Media app. | 0.073*** | 0.046 |
| | (3.29) | (1.24) |
| LB Investor | 0.035*** | 0.158*** |
| | (3.21) | (18.21) |

*The t-values are presented right under the coefficients and stars ***, **, * indicate the significant coefficients at the 1%, 5%, and 10% levels, respectively.*
*The table shows results from Barber and Odean [10] analyses of buy-sell imbalance, which is the dependent variable. No. imbalance represents the number of trades made while value imbalance is the value of the trades. The news variables are separated as national news and local news. Media type is 1 for printed news and 0 for web news, it is dropped from the model due to collinearity, but the interaction effects remain. Firm urban dummy is assigned 1 if the firm is headquartered in either Stockholm or Gothenburg or Malmö area, else it is 0. The dummy number of media appearances greater than the 75th percentile in the data represents the overall news sentiment in the market. LB investor is the intensity of locally biased investors in the firm. The interaction effects are included. Fama-Macbeth regressions are run with Newey-West serial correlation consistent standard errors. Approximative t-values are presented within the parentheses. The bold mark coefficients are statistically significant at 5% or lower levels.*

**Table 3.**
*Firm-level buy-sell imbalances.*

4.1 pp. (5.4 pp.) from the mean. Expectedly, national news had more effect on net trade than local news, and it is also possible that some of the national news will be republished in local news. However, these analyses aim to convey that national and local news affect individual investors' buy-sell imbalances differently. This was also evident when we interacted with the news with the type, printed vs. web page news. Printed (web page news) local news seemed to decrease (increase) net trade, while there was no difference in the effects of printed national news or web page national news. Regarding the control variables, firms that were local in urban areas seemed to have fewer buy-sell imbalances than firms located in rural areas. The attention effect of local and national media improved when overall news sentiment was high in the markets. Finally, buy-sell imbalances increased with more locally biased investors in the firm.

Our results imply that local news induces local investors to become net buyers of the stock, and local investors in rural districts are more net buyers than any other group. Hirshleifer et al. [14] documented the result that individual investors are net buyers. Our analyses add to this knowledge by showing that local individuals are also net buyers, and this result is particularly pronounced in rural districts. The results are consistent with those found in Refs. [2, 9, 31, 33, 40] in suggesting that local trading activity increases with local news.

These results can be interpreted as attention induces local investors to become net buyers. This interpretation is consistent with Refs. [10, 41], arguing that investors may consider stocks that first catch their attention. For instance, stocks in the news or stocks with large price moves greatly influence individual investor decisions. This can be explained by the fact that investors face information search costs when choosing stocks to buy [12], and rather than searching systematically, they may buy stocks that catch their attention. Our results that the investors are more net buyers of these attention-grabbing stocks are also consistent with the view that selling poses less information search costs and, therefore, would be less sensitive to the attention-grabbing stocks.[5]

## 6. Conclusions and implications

We examined whether local information influences local trading activity. We found that local information provided by local web pages increased local trading activity and, in particular, induced investors to become net buyers. The effects were stronger in rural districts, which are known as relatively poor information environments, home to illiquid firms, firms with high idiosyncratic volatility, and informationally opaque firms [37]. The result suggests that local investors have a higher ability to process information for local news because of familiarity. Local media garners local investors' attention more than national media. When new information arrives about local firms, local investors process the information quicker and more accurately. In contrast to results from local web page news, we did not find significant effects of local printed press news on local trading activity.

Our results have some implications for investors in stock markets. First, to understand any potential local information advantage caused by attention to local media coverage and its effects on local trading, one needs to examine local information sources much deeper. Previous literature (with a few exceptions) on local bias seems to lack this important information channel of local media effects. Second, local information sources should be isolated from national information sources separating the information hypothesis from the familiarity hypothesis. Third, the internet and web page news have become significant information channels in our daily lives and have almost replaced printed press news. Even if we would like to hold the book or the article in a printed version, reading the news on a web page appears more convenient and cheaper. This makes intuitively the printed news become old news.

---

[5] The news variables are collected using the software Python. All the data management and model estimations are done in STATA software.

Fourth, trading liquidity increased by local investors may affect market efficiency. Our result is that local information induces individual investors to become net buyers, which has implications for overall information efficiency in the markets. Our interpretation of this result is that individuals face more information search costs when choosing stocks to buy rather than when choosing stocks to sell. If local web page news increases local investors' purchases, it must be that local web page news decreases information search costs. This result also holds for remote investors, albeit to a lesser extent. Thus, paying more attention to local information may increase overall information efficiency as information asymmetry between local and remote investors decreases.

Finally, our results indicated significant differences between the appearance of local and national news and how they influenced individual trading behavior. This implies that journalists should carefully consider their words and how they present them when writing about firm events. Further research could focus on this channel by examining how journalists choose their words, the heterogeneity in their presentation, and their writing style to convey news about firm-specific events.

## Additional information

**JEL classification:** G11, G14

## Author details

Linda Pettersson[1] and Taylan Mavruk[2]*

1 Independent Researcher, Kristinehamn, Sweden

2 University of Gothenburg, Gothenburg, Sweden

*Address all correspondence to: taylan.mavruk@handels.gu.se

## References

[1] Gentzkow M, Shapiro JM. Media bias and reputation. Journal of Political Economy. 2006;**114**:280-316

[2] Gurun UG, Butler AW. Don't believe the hype: Local media slant, local advertising, and firm value. Journal of Finance. 2012;**67**:561-598

[3] Dyck A, Volchkova N, Zingales L. The corporate governance role of the media: Evidence from Russia. Journal of Finance. 2008;**63**:1093-1135

[4] Dyck A, Morse A, Zingales L. Who blows the whistle on corporate fraud? Journal of Finance. 2010;**65**:2213-2253

[5] Miller GS. The press as a watchdog for accounting fraud. Journal of Accounting Research. 2006;**44**:1001-1033

[6] Kothari SP, Shu S, Wysocki PD. Do managers withhold bad news? Journal of Accounting Research. 2009;**47**:241-276

[7] Trumper S, Broer IGB. Non-commemorative Memory in News Production: Discovering Underlying Motivations for Journalists' Memory Work2019. DOI: 10.1177/1750698019863158

[8] Dougal C, Engelberg J, Garcıa D, Parsons CA. Journalists and the stock market. Review of Financial Studies. 2012;**25**:639-679

[9] Tetlock PC. Giving content to investor sentiment: The role of media in the stock market. Journal of Finance. 2007;**62**:1139-1168

[10] Barber BM, Odean T. All that glitters: The effect of attention on the buying behavior of individual and institutional investors. Review of Financial Studies. 2008;**21**:785-818

[11] Ning Z. The Local Bias of Individual Investors (October 2002). Yale ICF Working Paper No. 02-30. Available at SSRN: https://ssrn.com/abstract=302620 or DOI: 10.2139/ssrn.302620

[12] Merton RC. A simple model of capital market equilibrium with incomplete information. Journal of Finance. 1987;**42**:483-510

[13] Cutler DM, Poterba JM, Summers LH. What moves stock prices? Journal of Portfolio Management. 1989; **15**:4-12

[14] Hirshleifer D, James N, Myers L, Myers A, Teoh SH. Do individual investors drive post-earnings announcement drift? Direct Evidence from Personal Trades, Accounting Review. 2008;**83**:1521-1150

[15] Odean T. Do investors trade too much? American Economic Review. 1999;**89**(5):1279-1298

[16] Shefrin H, Statman M. The disposition to sell winners too early and ride losers too long: Theory and evidence. Journal of Finance. 1985;**40**: 777-790

[17] Baik B, Kang J-K, Kim J-M. Local institutional investors, information asymmetries, and equity returns. Journal of Financial Economics. 2010;**97**:81-106

[18] Cooper I, Sercu P, Vanpée R. The equity home bias: Survey and synthesis. Foundations and Trends in Finance. 2013;7:289-416

[19] Coval JD, Moskowitz TJ. Home bias at home: Local equity preference in domestic portfolios. Journal of Finance. 1999;**54**:2045-2073

[20] French KR, Poterba JM. Investor diversification and international equity markets. American Economic Review. 1991;**81**:222-226

[21] Hamberg M, Mavruk T, Sjögren S. Investment allocation decisions, home bias and the mandatory IFRS adoption. Journal of International Money and Finance. 2013;**36**:107-130

[22] Hau H. Location matters: An examination of trading profits. Journal of Finance. 2001;**56**:1959-1983

[23] Kang J-K, Stulz RM. Why is there a home bias? An analysis of foreign portfolio equity ownership in Japan. Journal of Financial Economics. 1997;**46**:3-28

[24] Lewis KK. Trying to explain home bias in equities and consumption. Journal of Economic Literature. 1999;**37**:571-608

[25] Tesar LL, Werner IM. Home bias and high turnover. Journal of International Money and Finance. 1995;**14**:467-492

[26] Bodnaruk A. Proximity always matters: Local bias when the set of local companies changes. Review of Finance. 2009;**13**:629-656

[27] Grinblatt M, Keloharju M. How distance, language, and culture influence stockholdings and trades. Journal of Finance. 2001;**56**:549-578

[28] Ted L, Taylan M, Stefan S. East or West, Home is Best: The Birthplace Bias of Individual Investors. Journal of Banking and Finance. 2018;**92**: 323-339

[29] Massa M, Simonov A. Hedging, familiarity, and portfolio choice. Review of Financial Studies. 2006;**19**: 633-685

[30] Seasholes MS, Zhu N. Individual investors and local bias. Journal of Finance. 2010;**65**:1987-2010

[31] Tetlock PC. All the news that's fit to reprint: Do investors react to stale information? Review of Financial Studies. 2011;**24**:1481-1512

[32] Groseclose T, Milyo J. A measure of media bias. Quarterly Journal of Economics. 2005;**120**:1191-1237

[33] Engelberg J, Parsons CA. The causal impact of media in financial markets. Journal of Finance. 2011;**66**:67-97

[34] Antweiler W, Frank MZ. Is all that talk just noise? The information content of internet stock message boards. Journal of Finance. 2004;**59**:1259-1293

[35] Coval JD, Shumway T. Is sound just noise? Journal of Finance. 2001;**56**: 1887-1910

[36] Pool VK, Stoffman N, Yonker SE. No place like home: Familiarity in mutual fund manager portfolio choice. Review of Financial Studies. 2012;**25**:2563-2599

[37] Hong H, Kubik J, Stein J. The only game in town: Stock-price consequences of local bias. Journal of Financial Economics. 2008;**90**:20-37

[38] Fama EF, MacBeth JD. Risk, return, and equilibrium: Empirical tests. Journal of Political Economy. 1973;**81**:607-636

[39] Newey WK, West KD. A simple, positive semi-definite, heteroskedasticity and autocorrelation consistent covariance matrix. Econometrica. 1987;**55**:703-708

[40] Gurun UG. Good news is endogenous [Working paper]. Dallas: University of Texas; 2010

[41] Seasholes MS, Guojun W. Predictable behavior, profits, and attention. Journal of Empirical Finance. 2007;**15**:590-610

Chapter 10

# Strategic Flexibility, Firm Performance, and Firm Value

*Xinyuan Zhang and Chee-Heong Quah*

## Abstract

This paper introduces ambidextrous innovation into the linkage between strategic flexibility and firm performance. It aims to theoretically reveal the strategic flexibility mechanism that affects firm performance and expands the theoretical perspective of ambidextrous innovation. From the perspective of resource orchestration theory, the moderating role of resource orchestration is considered. This study analyzes the influence of strategic flexibility, ambidextrous innovation, and resource orchestration on firm performance, to supplement and improve the existing research deficiencies. This work also explores the scientificity and rationality of firm value as a standard of firm performance.

**Keywords:** strategic flexibility, ambidextrous innovation, resource orchestration, firm performance, firm value

## 1. Introduction

For the purpose of maintaining competitive advantages and achieving sustainable development in a dynamic and complex environment, continuous innovation has become a top priority of enterprises. Governments around the world have provided great support for innovation, for which scholars and researchers have attached much importance to the topic that how enterprises improve their performance through innovation [1].

Enterprises regard innovation as their "food" and "lifeline", and their performance on innovation directly affects a country's ability to support structural reform, high-quality development, and scientific and technological power, which is related to the overall development of the country's scientific and technological innovation in the field. However, relevant research is scarce on a number of key questions, such as what is the innovation performance of enterprises, what are the main factors affecting the innovation performance of enterprises and what are the influencing mechanisms? Why are these questions worth further exploring?

Enterprises have different resource strengths at different stages of development, facing various internal and external factors, which have a significant impact on the process of enterprise innovation and the choice of innovation mode, thus affecting the enterprises' performance [2]. An enterprise that has been operating in a certain mode for a long time, tends to develop certain organizational inertia and will face more pressure and resistance in innovation [3]. Moreover, due to the existence of resource rigidity, enterprises may "excessively" focus on the existing business with only the development activities of the existing products, ignoring the exploratory innovation, in addition to which, the operational rigidity leads the enterprise to fall into a repetitive response mode, which makes the organization fail to develop new capabilities.

The solution to these problems requires the introduction of strategic flexibility. It is urgent for enterprises to improve their adaptability to the changing environment and enhance their creativity to guarantee their capability of coping with the uncertainty and complexity of the environment to realize a healthy and sustainable development of enterprises. Two professional concepts of strategic flexibility and innovation are used by scholars to describe the solution, which means that enterprises can combine strategic flexibility with enterprise innovation to address their problems in enterprise performance. From the perspective of strategic flexibility, enterprises can transform their performance through innovation, improve their value, and achieve healthy and sustainable development [4].

The two dimensions of ambidextrous innovation are explorative innovation and exploitative innovation. Both of these two kinds of innovation represent the development direction of the enterprise, but they will plunder the scarce resources of the enterprise and follow completely different operation modes. The two dimensions of strategic flexibility, namely resource flexibility and coordination flexibility, can well coordinate the contradiction between the two kinds of innovation in ambidextrous innovation.

In short, strategic flexibility influences firm performance through influencing ambidextrous innovation. At the same time, ambidextrous innovation can better play the role of strategic flexibility, so as to affect the performance of enterprises.

Therefore, this study will explore the relationship between strategic flexibility, ambidextrous innovation, and firm performance, in an attempt to theoretically reveal the mechanism by which strategic flexibility affects firm performance.

For enterprises with similar resources in the industry, their performance also varies. This refers to the heterogeneity of dynamic management ability of different enterprises' resources, that is, the heterogeneity of resource arrangement ability, which is the source of the competitive advantage of enterprises and explains how the strategic flexibility of enterprises changes with the change of resource arrangement ability.

This study believes that the transformation process of strategic flexibility to innovation behavior depends on the level of resource orchestration of enterprises because the practice of enterprises has proved that only strategic flexibility cannot be completely transformed into innovative activities, which is still insufficient for the decision-making and implementation of innovation strategy. Enterprises must also have a strong strategic flexible transformation and utilization of resources orchestration level [5]. Enterprise resource orchestration level is the enterprise's strategic flexibility potential is the key to the development and utilization, is the enterprise strategy flexibility to the transformation of innovation activities, is an enterprise integrating strategic flexible classification management of core competence, and enterprises to transform strategic flexibility for innovation activities to carry out an important factor of the resources needed to.

Therefore, this study explores the moderating role of different resource orchestration in the impact of strategic flexibility on ambidextrous innovation, enriches the research contents of resource-based theory and firm capability theory, and provides the theoretical basis for the sustainable development of firms from the perspective of resources and capabilities.

In management, the management which aims at enhancing firm value is defined as firm value management. From the perspective of financial management, firm value has many different forms of expression—book value, market value, appraisal value, liquidation value, auction value and so on. Objectively speaking, each kind of value form has its rationality and applicability. In this study, firm value is taken as the scientific standard of firm performance evaluation.

## 2. Theoretical underpinning

### 2.1 Resource-based view

This research draws on the resource-based view proposed by Wemerfelt [6] in the growth stage of resource-based theory as the theoretical basis, which advocates that resources are the competitive strength of enterprises, meaning that for the purpose of achieving a high level of performance, enterprises should attach importance to the development and utilization of resources, especially the rare, valuable, unique resources that are difficult to imitate and replace [6].

Moreover, the framework of "resource—strategic—performance" proposed by Ansoff [7], which is one of the core ideas and frameworks of resource-based view research, is adopted in this research to analyze the influence of strategic flexibility as the enterprise's internal resource and ability on the enterprise strategic choice, and further explore the logic of influence on enterprise performance and competitive strength [7].

### 2.2 Organization ambidexterity theory

The word "Ambidextrous", derived from "Ambidexter", refers to the ability to do two different things at the same time, which is a concept first proposed by Duncan [8]. With its novel content and unique perspective, the ambidextrous theory has attracted much attention both in the domestic and international academia and has also become one of the mainstream paradigms of future management research [8, 9]. In 2006 and 2009, the Academy of Management Journal and Organization Science, the top journals in the field of management, launched ambidextrous research columns respectively, which show the important role of ambidextrous theory in the study of management science.

Therefore, ambidextrous innovation refers to the ability to pursue two kinds of innovation at the same time (**Figure 1**).

In this study, the perspectives of resource-based view and inter-organizational relationship (including social networks) were selected to study the application of this theory in the field of technological innovation and explore its impact on enterprise performance.

### 2.3 Resource orchestration theory

According to the resource orchestration theory, resource orchestration is the result of diversification of resources by enterprises through effective construction of resource combination, stripping of nonproductive resources to gather and combine resources, and improving the efficiency of conversion and utilization of existing resources. Resource orchestration means that enterprises construct resource

**Figure 1.**
*Organization ambidexterity theory comprehensive model.*

combination, assemble resources, transform and utilize resources, and dynamically manage the strategic flexibility of enterprises [10]. The development of enterprises is facing a significant strategic opportunity brought by the rise of new paradigms. How to construct and adjust the strategic flexibility of enterprises dynamically to enhance the ambidextrous innovation and improve the performance of enterprises has become the focus of the theoretical and practical circles [11].

### 2.4 The fusion application of the three theories in this study

Starting from the resource-based view, this study regards strategic flexibility as a managerial resource and a heterogeneous strategic resource, exploring the direct and indirect effect mechanisms of strategic flexibility on firm performance. With regard to the indirect effect mechanism, this study takes the theory of ambidextrous organization as the theoretical basis to explore the effect mechanism of ambidextrous innovation strategy. Based on the resource-based view, explorative innovation refers to the creation of new resource bundles, while exploitative innovation refers to the improvement and perfection of the existing resources.

Based on the resource-based theory and dynamic capability theory, Sirmon et al. [12] proposed the resource orchestration theory. The resource orchestration theory emphasizes the dynamic management of resources, which is actually an expansion of the existing resource-based theory. It pays more attention to the full utilization of resources by enterprise management and emphasizes the scientific combination of resources and capabilities, which is an important source of value creation for enterprises.

## 3. Variables and dimensions

### 3.1 Strategic flexibility

This study summarizes previous literature and redefines strategic flexibility as the regulator between environment volatility and enterprise flexibility, the ability of an enterprise to respond to the various demands resulting from the dynamic competition environment, the ability to seize the development opportunity to gain a competitive strength from coping with the change of conditions and environment, as well as a kind of valuable strategic resource [13].

Based on the theory of Sanchez [14], this study divides strategic flexibility into two dimensions: resource flexibility and coordination flexibility [14]. Resource flexibility refers to the ability to accumulate flexible resources for a variety of purposes, which reflects the efficiency and cost issues of the development, manufacturing, as well as selling of different types of products with the internal resources of an enterprise. Coordination flexibility refers to the ability to create new resource portfolios through internal coordination processes, which emphasizes the flexibility of an enterprise to use these resources from the aspects of strategy formulation, strategy implementation, operational allocation, etc.

### 3.2 Ambidextrous innovation

Drawing on previous studies on ambidextrous innovation, this study defines ambidextrous innovation as the simultaneous pursuit and integration of explorative innovation and exploitative innovation [15].

Based on the research methods of scholars, this study divides ambidextrous innovation into two dimensions of explorative innovation and exploitative innovation. Based on the resource-based view, explorative innovation refers to the creation of new resource bundles, while exploitative innovation refers to the improvement and perfection of existing resources.

### 3.3 Resource orchestration

Components of the resource management model include structuring the resource portfolio, bundling resources to build capabilities, and leveraging capabilities to provide value to customers, gain a competitive advantage, and create wealth for owners. Structuring the resource portfolio mainly refers to the reconfiguration and combination of existing resources or potential resources. Bundling resources refers to an enterprise separating nonproductive resources from different departments for reconfiguration and combination through the integration of internally dispersed resources to give full play to the potential of resources. Leveraging capabilities refers to that enterprises coordinate the work of various departments and business units and share newly acquired resources through resource reconfiguration to realize the value of resource reconfiguration combination [10, 16, 17].

Based on the above analysis, this study believes that the level of enterprise resource orchestration can play a moderating role in the influence process of strategic flexibility and ambidextrous innovation. The resource orchestration is divided into three dimensions, namely structuring the resource portfolio, bundling resources, and leveraging capabilities, as the moderating variables in this study.

### 3.4 Firm value and firm performance

There are many standards for evaluating the performance of a company, but none of them are as comprehensive and scientific as the firm value standard.

#### *3.4.1 While other criteria can be short-term, values must be long-term*

Earnings per share, profit, and return on investment indexes reflects basically is the enterprise has already occurred, if the enterprise managers use these indexes as evaluation standards, often leads to short-term behavior, to make them to focus on the management of the income statement, and ignore the actual number of cash flow and the timing, to grasp the future potential of the enterprise [18].

#### *3.4.2 Take firm value as the evaluation standard to make the tradeoff process more transparent*

No matter what kind of system, what kind of social background, enterprises in the distribution of benefits should be among the interests of the balance, so as to make a more appropriate decision. Taking the firm value as the standard can make the request of any interested party be evaluated, make the process of tradeoff more transparent, and make all interested parties get the satisfactory result [19].

#### *3.4.3 The firm value standard makes the best use of all kinds of information*

In order to judge the value a company is creating, it is necessary to deal with all cash flows on the income statement and balance sheet and understand how to compare cash flows from period to period on a risk-adjusted basis. You cannot make a value judgment without complete information, which is not required for any other performance measurement.

When measuring firm performance, this research mainly considers firm value standard from the perspective of management research. From multiple dimensions, comprehensively consider the enterprise's profitability (net profit, return on investment, etc.), growth (revenue growth rate, sales growth rate, etc.) and liquidity (net cash flow). At the same time, the subjective and objective performance measurement standards are combined. The objective indicators are helpful for the evaluation from the absolute perspective, while the subjective indicators (such as the realization of corporate goals, performance satisfaction, etc.) can improve the accuracy of the objective indicators [20].

## 4. Theoretical framework and hypotheses development

### 4.1 Theoretical framework

The model and hypothesis of this study mainly include the following two parts:

Firstly, based on the resource-based view and organizational ambidexterity theory, this paper analyzes the influence of strategic flexibility (resource flexibility and coordination flexibility) on firm performance, and then further analyzes the mediating role of ambidextrous innovation (explorative innovation and exploitative innovation) in the relationship between strategic flexibility and firm performance.

Secondly, the resource orchestration theory is used as the auxiliary theory to supplement the resource-based view and enrich the theoretical framework. The moderating effect of resource orchestration (structuring the resource portfolio, bundling resources and leveraging capabilities) on strategic flexibility and ambidextrous innovation strategy is analyzed.

Based on the above analysis, the theoretical model and hypothesis are proposed (**Figure 2**):

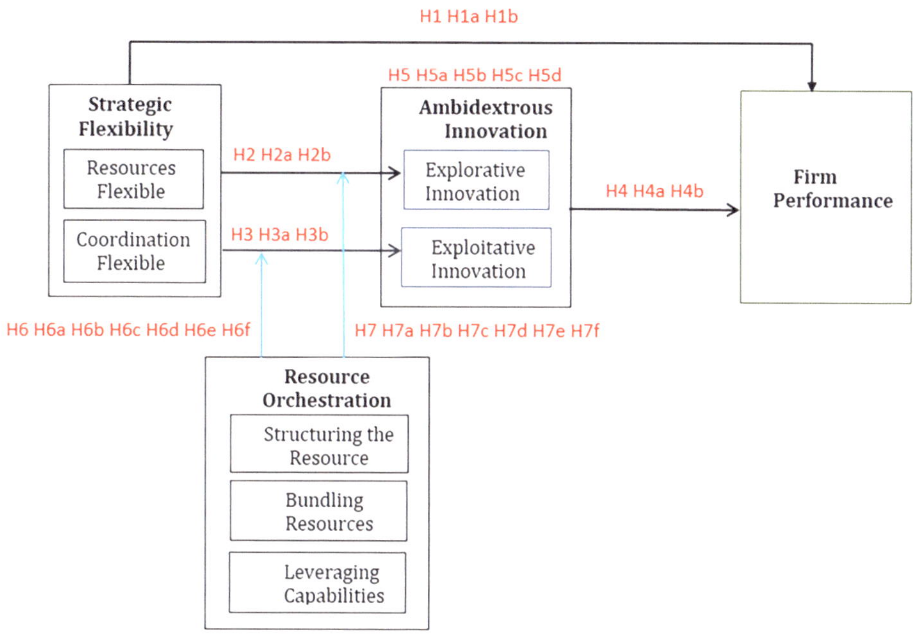


**Figure 2.**
*The theoretical framework and hypothesis of this study.*

## 4.2 Hypotheses development

### *4.2.1 Strategic flexibility and firm performance*

Previous studies reveal that enterprises with strategic flexibility are often able to respond flexibly to changes in the external environment and can reach commanding heights in the competitive environment. As strategic flexibility effectively mitigates the adverse impacts of organizational inertia and is widely recognized as enhancing firm performance.

It is found in the relevant literature that the independent variable (strategic flexibility) and the dependent variable (firm performance) in this study have a relatively stable positive relationship [21, 22].

To sum up, the following hypotheses are proposed in this study:

H1: There is a positive relationship between strategic flexibility and firm performance.

H1a: There is a positive relationship between resource flexibility and firm performance.

H1b: There is a positive relationship between coordination flexibility and firm performance.

### *4.2.2 Strategic flexibility and ambidextrous innovation strategy*

Research results show that resource flexibility is beneficial to the innovation process. Meanwhile, enterprises with coordination flexibility can make reasonable use of the resources they have to improve the innovation conversion rate, and further enhance their performance.

H2: There is a positive relationship between strategic flexibility and explorative innovation.

H2a: There is a positive relationship between resource flexibility and explorative innovation.

H2b: There is a positive relationship between coordination flexibility and explorative innovation.

H3: There is a positive relationship between strategic flexibility and exploitative innovation.

H3a: There is a positive relationship between resource flexibility and exploitative innovation.

H3b: There is a positive relationship between coordination flexibility and exploitative innovation.

### *4.2.3 Ambidextrous innovation and firm performance*

The relationship between mediating variable (ambidextrous innovation) and the dependent variable (firm performance) shows multiple conclusions, including positive correlation, negative correlation, and nonlinear relation [23].

H4: There is a positive relationship between ambidextrous innovation strategic and firm performance.

H4a: There is a positive relationship between explorative innovation and firm performance.

H4b: There is a positive relationship between exploitative innovation and firm performance.

### *4.2.4 role of ambidextrous innovation strategy in strategic flexibility—Firm performance relationship*

From previous studies and the above review, it can be found the relationship between strategic flexibility, ambidextrous innovation, and firm performance all showed a relatively-significant correlation.

Abidextrous innovation can better explain how strategic flexibility affects firm performance.

H5: Ambidextrous innovation strategy mediates the relationship between strategic flexibility and firm performance.

H5a: Explorative innovation mediates the relationship between resource flexibility and firm performance.

H5b: Explorative innovation mediates the relationship between coordination flexibility and firm performance.

H5c: Exploitative innovation mediates the relationship between resource flexibility and firm performance.

H5d: Exploitative innovation mediates the relationship between resource flexibility and firm performance.

### *4.2.5 Moderating effect of resource orchestration on strategic flexibility—Firm performance relationship*

Compared with resource management, there is little research on resource orchestration, and the research on resource orchestration mainly includes the structuring the researches on resource management and asset arrangement. Resource orchestration includes three processes: structuring the resource portfolio, bundling resources, and leveraging capabilities.

The transformation process of strategic flexibility to innovation behavior depends on the level of resource orchestration of enterprises because the practice of enterprises has proved that only strategic flexibility cannot be completely transformed into innovative activities, which is still insufficient for the decision-making and implementation of innovation strategy. Enterprises must also have a strong strategic flexibility transformation and utilization of resources arrangement, the level of enterprise resources orchestration is the key to the development and utilization of strategic flexibility potential, is an important factor for enterprises to transform strategic flexibility into innovative activities, is the core ability of enterprises to classify and integrate the management of strategic flexibility. At the same time, it is also an important factor for enterprises to transform strategic flexibility into the resources needed to carry out innovation activities.

H6: Resource orchestration has a positive moderating effect on the relationship between strategic flexibility and exploitative innovation.

H6a: Structuring the resource portfolio has a positive moderating effect on the relationship between resource flexibility and exploitative innovation.

H6b: Structuring the resource portfolio has a positive moderating effect on the relationship between coordination flexibility and exploitative innovation.

H6c: Bundling resources has a positive moderating effect on the relationship between resource flexibility and exploitative innovation.

H6d: Bundling resources has a positive moderating effect on the relationship between coordination flexibility and exploitative innovation.

H6e: Leveraging capabilities has a positive moderating effect on the relationship between resource flexibility and exploitative innovation.

H6f: Leveraging capabilities has a positive moderating effect on the relationship between coordination flexibility and exploitative innovation.

H7: Resource orchestration has a positive moderating effect on the relationship between strategic flexibility and explorative innovation.

H7a: Structuring the resource portfolio has a positive moderating effect on the relationship between resource flexibility and explorative innovation.

H7b: Structuring the resource portfolio has a positive moderating effect on the relationship between coordination flexibility and explorative innovation.

H7c: Bundling resources has a positive moderating effect on the relationship between resource flexibility and explorative innovation.

H7d: Bundling resources has a positive moderating effect on the relationship between coordination flexibility and explorative innovation.

H7e: Leveraging capabilities has a positive moderating effect on the relationship between resource flexibility and explorative innovation.

H7f: Leveraging capabilities has a positive moderating effect on the relationship between coordination flexibility and explorative innovation.

## 5. Research design and methodology

### 5.1 Research design

In this research, a nonexperimental quantitative research method was used to ensure the objectivity, universality, and reliability. And questionnaire survey method was used to collect the data. Questionnaire survey is one of the most commonly used methods for quantitative research in the field of management.

(Advantage: Fast, effective, cost saving, less interference by respondents, strong operability)

In positivist research, a statement of relationships between the observed phenomena (hypothesis) is first formulated, and a rigorous statistical method is applied to analyze quantitative data. Based on the positivist approach, quantitative research was conducted according to this process.

The steps of the investigation are as follows:

1. Determine the population, sample framework, and respondents.
2. Design an investigation tool. (the investigation tool in this research is a questionnaire survey).
3. Preliminary research to test the questionnaire.
4. Collect data through questionnaire survey.
5. Data analysis.
6. Hypothesis testing.

## 5.2 Data collection

This survey mainly selects the regions with high active innovation activities in mainland China and selects four regions in China: Beijing, Tianjin, Shenzhen, and Shanghai for research.

The selected companies are concentrated in the following eight high-tech fields, including electronic information, biology, and new medicine, aviation and aerospace, new materials, high-tech services, new energy and energy conservation, resources, and environment, as well as advanced manufacturing and automation. The survey was conducted by managers familiar with the operations of the company, such as CEOs or key department heads.

Data for this study were obtained from two sources:

The first channel is to distribute and collect questionnaires through the author's existing social relations. Such as obtaining the assistance of the MBA center and EMBA center of several universities in the research area, as well as the help of relevant government departments, such as the National Bureau of Statistics, National Development and Reform Commission, and other departments.

The second channel is to issue and collect questionnaires through a professional consulting company in Beijing. The consulting company's business scope includes providing business consulting and investigation. Through the consulting company, it issues and collects questionnaires in these four regions on a large scale, and carries out follow-up and screening to ensure the source and quality of questionnaires.

## 5.3 The measurement and variables

The variable scale for this research was derived from the scales used in the research published in top journals in this field. The content of the foreign scales was modified in accordance with the language habits of the interviewed companies in China, while maintaining the original meaning of the foreign scales. These scales have been empirically tested and recognized by research scholars in the same field, thus these indicator scales have relatively high validity and reliability, which is conducive to the smooth progress of our empirical test. Likert-5 scale was used for measurement. The scoring standards are: (1) means completely inconsistent, (2) means relatively inconsistent, (3) means fair, (4) means fairly consistent, and (5) means very consistent.

### *5.3.1 Independent variables*

Based on previous references, the measurement scale for independent variable strategic flexibility in this study is as follows (**Table 1**):

| Variable | Dimension | Numbers and test items |
|---|---|---|
| Strategic Flexibility | Resource Flexibility | A1. Your company's resources can be transformed into more products and services.<br>A2. The cost of transforming your company's resources into corresponding products and services is relatively small.<br>A3. The time required for your company's resources to be converted into corresponding products and services is relatively short.<br>A4. The production resources your company has are more flexible for competitors |
| | Coordination Flexibility | B1. Your company is more adaptable to the environment and can discover and identify future opportunities better than the competitors.<br>B2. Your company can obtain new resources more quickly at a lower cost than competitors.<br>B3. Your company can expand to new markets faster than competitors.<br>B4. Your company is more advantageous in solving the issue of resource utilization efficiency. |

*Source: Organized by the author [14, 24, 25].*

**Table 1.**
*Measurement scale for strategic flexibility.*

| Variable | Dimension | Numbers and test items |
|---|---|---|
| Ambidextrous Innovation Strategy | Explorative innovation | C1. Your company always accepts demand beyond existing products and services<br>C2. Your company always develops new products and services<br>C3 Your company often tests new products and services in the market<br>C4. Your company will commercialize completely novel products and services<br>C5. Your company often explores new opportunities in new markets<br>C6. Your company often uses new distribution channels<br>C7. Your company continues to develop creative channels to meet the needs of customers |
| | Exploitative innovation | D1. Your company often improves existing products and services<br>D2. Your company regularly makes small-scale adjustments to existing products and services<br>D3. Your company often introduces improved products and services to the market<br>D4. Your company has improved the efficiency of products and services<br>D5. Your company has increased the economic scale of the existing market<br>D6. Your company has expanded the scope of services for existing customers |

*Source: Organized by the author.*

**Table 2.**
*Measurement scale for ambidextrous innovation.*

### 5.3.2 Meditating variables

Based on previous references Bachmann et al. [26], the measurement scale for meditating variable ambidextrous innovation strategy in this study is as follows (**Table 2**):

### 5.3.3 Moderating variables

Based on a comprehensive review and analysis of previous literature, the resource orchestration scale used as the moderating variable in this study is presented below (**Table 3**).

### 5.3.4 Dependent variables

See **Table 4**.

| dimension | Numbers and test items |
|---|---|
| Structuring the resource portfolio | E1 Your company will be through external recruitment and merger and reorganization, reserve technical personnel<br>E2 Your company will complete industrial chain expansion and market layout through joint ventures and mergers<br>E3 Your company will form alliances with upstream and downstream core industry chain members to share resources and strengthen their relationship commitment<br>E4 Your company to establish a technology development center as a channel to promote the localization of services<br>E5 Your company can reasonably allocate the existing resources and construct a diversified and flexible resource combination mode according to the requirements to meet the needs of Your company |
| Bundling Resources | F1 Your company can dynamically control the size of the organization, promote flat organization for product innovation, and quickly adjust the jobs according to the requirements of the work<br>F2 Your company specially set up a customer service center and product service department to provide more resources and technical support<br>F3 Your company can adopt some temporary and task-oriented team structures to replace some fixed and formal organizational structures, which is convenient and flexible<br>F3 Your company will conduct subdivision management for customers and provide appropriate products and service solutions<br>F4 Your company establishes a learning organization to create a culture and system to promote the creation of new knowledge, as well as the collection, transmission and transformation of knowledge |
| Leveraging Capabilities | G1 Your company can use technology to quickly turn information into business action, so they can always stay one step ahead of competitors<br>G2 Your company's products are highly professional, and can use the existing technical advantages, to provide customers with more perfect products and services<br>G3 Your company will organize employees to attend innovation conferences, learn further, accumulate market information, and improve the advantages of products and services<br>G4 Your company can systematically improve products according to customer needs to meet market demands and consolidate the market position of products<br>G5 Your company can rely on the research and development platform, and effectively use the advantages of enterprise resources to create product integration solutions |

*Source: Organized by the author [10, 16, 17].*

**Table 3.**
*Measurement scale for resource orchestration.*

| Variable | Numbers and test items |
|---|---|
| Firm Performance | H1. Compared with the main competitors, your company has a higher yield<br>H2. Compared with the main competitors, your company has a higher rate of return on investment<br>H3. Compared with the main competitors, your company has a higher level of market share<br>H4. Compared with the main competitors, your company has faster growth of market share<br>H5. Compared with the main competitors, your company has faster growth in sales<br>H6. Compared with the main competitors, your company has faster growth in the number of new employees<br>H7. Compared with the main competitors, your company develops new products or new services faster |

*Source: Organized by the author [23].*

**Table 4.**
*Measurement scale for performance.*

### *5.3.5 Control variables*

Based on the existing research results and the research context, the age of the company, the size of the company, and the industry to which the company belongs were selected as the control variables.

#### *5.3.5.1 Age of the company*

There are three options in the questionnaire: 5–8 years, 8–10 years, and more than 10 years.

#### *5.3.5.2 Size of the company*

In this study, the size of the company is measured by the number of employees. There are five options for this item in the questionnaire, namely, 10 people, 11–30 people, 31–50 people, 51–100 people, and more than 100 people.

#### *5.3.5.3 Industry*

There are two options for this item. The respondent directly chooses whether the company is a high-tech company or a traditional company.

## **5.4 Data analysis**

This study mainly conducts data analysis through the following steps:
Step 1 Descriptive statistical analysis.
(descriptive statistics of the basic information of the company and questionnaire respondents)
Step 2 Sample feature analysis, reliability and validity analysis of each variable.
Step 3 Test the hypothesis in these ways: Partial Least Squares Structural Equation Modeling (PLS-SEM).

In this study, Partial Least Squares Structural Equation Modeling (PLS-SEM) was used in data analysis.

1. Models that include both mediating and moderating variables typically involve complex relationships and multiple pathways. When researchers encounter difficulties like small sample sizes or non-normally distributed data, CB-SEM might not be viable. In these instances, PLS-SEM provides a powerful alternative, offering dependable results despite these limitations.

2. PLS-SEM exhibits a strong capability to handle complex interconnections among latent variables, allowing each latent construct to be evaluated through several observable indicators. In mediating variable models, PLS-SEM enables accurate estimation of indirect effects, providing a clearer and more rigorous understanding of the mediating mechanisms. When applied to moderator models, PLS-SEM adeptly supports intricate analyses of interaction effects, even in situations where both interaction and main effects are present simultaneously [27, 28].

## 6. Conclusion

By analyzing the impact of strategic flexibility on firm performance, explorative innovation, and exploitative innovation are identified as mediating variables respectively, and resource orchestration is identified as the moderating variable between strategic flexibility and ambidextrous innovation, so as to determine the measurement of each variable and the relationship between each variable. Building upon this foundation, the study formulates the research hypothesis, constructs a detailed theoretical model, and performs an empirical analysis using questionnaire data collected from China's enterprises. Partial Least Squares Structural Equation Modeling (PLS-SEM) is employed as the analytical method.

The main theoretical contributions of this study are as follows: First, from the perspective of ambidextrous innovation, the black box between strategic flexibility and firm performance is opened, and the internal mechanism between strategic flexibility and firm performance is explored. Through theoretical and empirical analysis, it is proposed that the impact of strategic flexibility on firm performance is achieved through the mediating role of ambidextrous innovation. Secondly, based on the perspective of resource orchestration, this study researches the influence of heterogeneity of enterprise resource management on performance and its influence on the transformation of strategic flexibility into enterprise innovation. Moreover, this study also has practical significance and provides guidance for managers to deal with the coordination relationship between strategic flexibility and ambidextrous innovation. It also enables enterprise managers to realize the impact of differences in resource management levels on innovation and performance, so that enterprises can achieve higher resource management levels and innovation efficiency, and then enhance enterprise value.

## Acknowledgements

We are grateful for the comments provided by my supervisors, Quah Chee Heong and Mohammad Nazri Bin Mohd Nor on previous drafts of this paper. We also appreciate the cooperation of the authors from whom we requested additional data.

## Conflict of interest

The authors declare no conflict of interest.

## Author details

Xinyuan Zhang and Chee-Heong Quah*
Faculty of Business and Economics, Universiti Malaya, Kuala Lumpur, Malaysia

*Address all correspondence to: quahch@um.edu.my

## References

[1] Sijabat EA, Nimran U, Utami HN, Prasetya A. Ambidextrous innovation in mediating entrepreneurial creativity on firm performance and competitive advantage. The Journal of Asian Finance, Economics, and Business. 2020;**7**(11):737-746

[2] Wang T, Thornhill S, De Castro JO. Entrepreneurial orientation, legitimation, and new venture performance. Strategic Entrepreneurship Journal. 2017;**11**(4):373-392

[3] Bamel UK, Bamel N. Organizational resources, KM process capability and strategic flexibility: A dynamic resource-capability perspective. Journal of Knowledge Management. 4 Sep 2018;**22**(7):1555-1572

[4] Khan M. A retrospective analysis of organizational change: A case study of octaware technologies. International Journal of Business Strategies. 2021;**6**(1):1-1

[5] Zhao Y, Wang X. Organisational unlearning, relearning and strategic flexibility: From the perspective of updating routines and knowledge. Technology Analysis and Strategic Management. 2020;**32**(11):1251-1263

[6] Wernerfelt B. A resource-based view of the firm. Strategic Management Journal. Apr 1984;**5**(2):171-180

[7] Ansoff HI. The emerging paradigm of strategic behavior. Strategic Management Journal. 1987;**8**(6):501-515

[8] Duncan RB. The ambidextrous organization: Designing dual structures for innovation. The Management of Organization. 1976;**1**(1):167-188

[9] Raisch S, Birkinshaw J, Probst G, Tushman ML. Organizational ambidexterity: Balancing exploitation and exploration for sustained performance. Organization Science. 2009;**20**(4):685-695

[10] Sirmon DG, Hitt MA, Ireland RD, Gilbert BA. Resource orchestration to create competitive advantage: Breadth, depth, and life cycle effects. Journal of Management. 2011;**37**(5):1390-1412

[11] Chirico F, Sirmon DG, Sciascia S, Mazzola P. Resource orchestration in family firms: Investigating how entrepreneurial orientation, generational involvement, and participative strategy affect performance. Strategic Entrepreneurship Journal. 2011;**5**(4):307-326

[12] Sirmon DG, Hitt MA, Ireland RD. Managing firm resources in dynamic environments to create value: Looking inside the black box. Academy of Management Review. 1 Jan 2007;**32**(1):273-292

[13] Harrigan KR. Strategic flexibility and competitive advantage. In: Oxford Research Encyclopedia of Business and Management. 29 Mar 2017

[14] Sanchez R. Strategic flexibility in product competition. Strategic Management Journal. 1995;**16**(S1):135-159

[15] Lin C, Chang CC. A patent-based study of the relationships among technological portfolio, ambidextrous innovation, and firm performance. Technology Analysis and Strategic Management. 2015;**27**(10):1193-1211

[16] Hitt MA, Ireland RD, Sirmon DG, Trahms CA. Strategic entrepreneurship: Creating value for individuals, organizations, and society. Academy of Management Perspectives. 2011;**25**(2):57-75

[17] Ma W, Zhang Q, Samal SK, Wang F, Gao B, Pan H, et al. Core–sheath structured electrospun nanofibrous membranes for oil–water separation. RSC Advances. 2016;**6**(48):41861-41870

[18] Berger PG, Ofek E. Diversification's effect on firm value. Journal of Financial Economics. 1995;**37**(1):39-65

[19] Carter DA, Simkins BJ, Simpson WG. Corporate governance, board diversity, and firm value. Financial Review. 2003;**38**(1):33-53

[20] Buchanan B, Cao CX, Chen C. Corporate social responsibility, firm value, and influential institutional ownership. Journal of Corporate Finance. 2018;**52**:73-95

[21] Brozović M, Benner LA, McMichael JG, Giorgini JD, Pravec P, Scheirich P, et al. Goldstone and Arecibo radar observations of (99942) Apophis in 2012-2013. Icarus. 2018;**300**:115-128

[22] Anwar J. Strategic consistency, flexibility and reactors: A comparative analysis. Pakistan Business Review. 2019;**20**(3):600-611

[23] Hou B, Hong J, Zhu R. Exploration/exploitation innovation and firm performance: The mediation of entrepreneurial orientation and moderation of competitive intensity. Journal of Asia Business Studies. 7 Oct 2019;**13**(4):489-506

[24] Saffer DM, Wallace LM, Barnes PM, Pecher IA, Petronotis KE, LeVay LJ, et al. Expedition 372B/375 summary. Proceedings of the International Ocean Discovery Program. 2019;**372**:1-35

[25] Li L, Liu Y, Wu P, Peng Z, Wang X, Chen T, et al. Influenza-associated excess respiratory mortality in China, 2010-15: A population-based study. The Lancet Public Health. 2019;**4**(9):e473-e481

[26] Bachmann JT, Ohlies I, Flatten T. Effects of entrepreneurial marketing on new ventures' exploitative and exploratory innovation: The moderating role of competitive intensity and firm size. Industrial Marketing Management. 1 Jan 2021;**92**:87-100

[27] Baron RM, Kenny DA. The moderator–mediator variable distinction in social psychological research: Conceptual, strategic, and statistical considerations. Journal of Personality and Social Psychology. Dec 1986;**51**(6):1173

[28] Hayes AF, Scharkow M. The relative trustworthiness of inferential tests of the indirect effect in statistical mediation analysis: Does method really matter? Psychological Science. Oct 2013;**24**(10):1918-1927

Chapter 11

# Adam Smith's Modeling of Agents: Roots versus Consequences of Action

*Vernon L. Smith and Sabiou M. Inoua*

## Abstract

Adam Smith founded his investigations of economic and social exchanges on the roots of human action (sympathy, need, self-interest), unlike the utilitarians (Hume and the neoclassical economists), who centered theirs on the consequences of human action (pleasure, utility of outcome). This distinction is key to understanding the contrast between the two schools of thought, as we emphasize in this chapter.

**Keywords:** Adam Smith, classical economics, neoclassical economics, value theory, humanomics

## 1. Introduction

Samuel Alexander, in his book *Beauty and Other Forms of Value,* revealed, in a brief commentary on Adam Smith and David Hume, his own insight into the deep insight that Smith brought to the task of understanding human conduct:

> *"Like the utilitarians who came after him, he [Hume] looked ultimately to the effects of action in the way of giving pleasure or pain. Adam Smith, with a surer eye, declared the sympathy which determines our approbation or disapprobation, not so much to be directed towards the effects of action as to the impulses from which action proceeds. He considered our actions in their origin rather than in their outcome."* ([1], p. 249)

Alexander is referring to *The Theory of Moral Sentiments*, and the roots of human sociality, because this is where Adam Smith introduced his key distinction between modeling agents in terms of the origins, versus the consequences, of their actions. This perspective, however, carries over into Smith's examination of market price formation.

Generally, Alexander is addressing alternative ways of thinking about observations and the meaning we associate with them—the larger topic of this paper, as it relates to social and economic action. He refers to neoclassical analysis in which an individual's utility function represents agent choice and links the individual's private "outcome," in the form of internal pleasure or pain, to the "external outcome" of choice as in a social or economic exchange. Thus, a person has utility $U(x)$, where $U$

is a measure of the individual's preference for (or pleasure or pain from) $x$, and $x$ is the external "thing" or object of choice. Utility welds the internal consequence for the individual with the external outcome. In this manner, individual rationality is envisioned as the cause or source of socio-economic rationality rather than interactive social and market collectives.

We have identified classical economics with Adam Smith's way of thinking and modeling action that contrasts classical with neoclassical (marginal utilitarian) economics, wherein important insights of classical economics were lost in the 1870s revolution. We have argued that economics, under the developmental program of the marginal revolution, displaced rather than built upon the accomplishments of its predecessor [2–6]. Herein, we identify Cournot as defining the key turning point in economic thinking and modeling.

We begin with Smith's treatment of this distinction in his first published book, showing how he develops the roots of human action for social exchange. Referring to his second book, we explicate his parallel discussion of action by traders in a market. Then, we introduce Cournot as the turning point at which neoclassical theory focused on modeling the outcomes of agent action.

Here is how the "surer eye" of Adam Smith introduces the study of sentiments and human social conduct: "The sentiment or affection of the heart from which any action proceeds, and upon which its whole virtue or vice must ultimately depend, may be considered under two different aspects, or in two different relations; first, in relation to the cause which excites it, or the motive which gives occasion to it; and secondly, in relation to the end which it proposes, or the effect which it tends to produce" ([7], 1853, vol. I, p. 93).

## 2. Social exchange

Adam Smith's model of human sociability led to propositions that apply naturally to our everyday interactions. Thus, your waste management service emptied your trash barrel on schedule, but you neglected to bring your barrel in from the street, and your neighbor brought it in for you. This illustrates Smith's concept of beneficence, one of the two pillars of society, the other being justice. Beneficence governs our conduct according to the proposition: "Actions of a beneficent tendency, which proceed from proper motives, seem alone to require reward; because such alone are the approved objects of gratitude, or excite the sympathetic gratitude of the spectator" ([7], 1853, vol. 1, p. 112).

As Smith explains, this proposition, "proper motives" means intentional. Your neighbor deliberately brought in your barrel. She did not have to do it, but chose nevertheless to do it, and indeed, you feel a warm sense of gratitude (Any third party "spectator", like another neighbor, would entirely concur and approve of what is transpiring between you and this neighbor). So, you thank her, and—somewhat compellingly—givc her three avocados freshly picked off your tree.

Adam Smith models conduct among strictly self-interested actors that generates and predicts such other-regarding actions of good neighborliness that always arise from, depend on, and reflect their context-specific circumstances ([8], pp. 81–94). Such rule-following conduct is what gives content to our particular forms of sociality (norms). It not only springs from among self-interested people, but it also depends on common knowledge that all locally prefer more, and disprefer less, of a good thing. That is how you knew, without a thought, that your neighbor's action was personally costly to her. In addition, you know that she benefits from three avocados. She knows her action benefited you and that it was costly for you to give up the avocados. Without knowledge that we are all self-interested, we cannot implement Smith's beneficence rule, enabling us to live in harmony with our neighbors.

## 3. Economic exchange

Smith's insightful way of thinking about social exchange, however, carries over without qualification in principle to his second book on economic exchange, where, again, actors are all self-interested, except that their actions, usually, but not necessarily, are directly intended to satisfy that self-interest.

We first note that Smith distinguished value in use from value in exchange:

> *"The word VALUE, it is to be observed, has two different meanings, and sometimes expresses the utility of some particular object, and sometimes the power of purchasing other goods which the possession of that object conveys. The one may be called "value in use;" the other, "value in exchange." ([9], 1853, vol. I, p. 30)*

Value in use corresponds to willingness to pay for a desired quantity of a good or service in view of its usefulness—a quantity given mightily by needs and habit [2–4, 6]. Value in exchange is the market price, where the "natural" price is a supply price that covers all costs, including the profit necessary to bring it to market.

Smith begins his narrative of price formation by describing the experience of producer-suppliers who, knowing their cost, bring corresponding quantities to market:

> *"When the quantity of any commodity which is brought to market falls short of the effectual demand, all those who are willing to pay the whole value of the rent, wages and profit, which must be paid in order to bring it thither, cannot be supplied with the quantity which they want. Rather than want it altogether, some of them will be willing to give more. A competition will immediately begin among them, and the market price will rise more or less above the natural price, according as either the greatness of the deficiency, or the...eagerness of the competition." ([9], 1904, vol. 1, p. 58)*

From Smith's careful choice of words, he is describing the interactive experience of sellers and buyers, and their responses in their shared context of interaction. Sellers know the "whole value" of their goods necessary to recover their costs. Buyers, whose wants are not all satisfied at that whole value price, are willing to pay more rather than want for it. Competition among the buyers will raise the price depending on the extent of the deficiency and their eagerness. Smith's language describes the experiences and actions of the actors in the market, as he observes, thinks about, and models them. He describes what a modern economist would say is excess demand, reading off the supply curve and the demand curve as the economist visualizes them in governing the Walrasian movement of prices in response to excess demand. Smith does not use this modern language because it is not part of the knowledge and experience of the actors. He describes behavior in its origins. For Smith, there are indeed external outcome consequences for the people in markets and for society—no less than the causes of the wealth of nations!—*but none of that is part of people's experience or intentions.* Smith's thought process keeps separate these distinct effects.

Similarly, and contrastingly to the above,

*"When the quantity brought to market exceeds the effectual demand, it cannot be all sold to those who are willing to pay the whole value of the rent, wages and profit, which must be paid in order to bring it thither. Some part must be sold to those who are willing to pay less, and the low price which they give for it must reduce the price of the whole. The market price will sink more or less below the natural price, according as the greatness of the excess increases more or less the competition of the sellers, or according as it happens to be more or less important to them to get immediately rid of the commodity." ([9], 1904, vol. 1, p. 59)*

Following the thought pattern in Smith's first book on social psychology, the words describe the experience and response of the economic actors—buyers and sellers—not the formal model of efficiency-producing outcomes by the modern economist. The writings of the classical economists continued in this thought-vein.

## 4. Hume versus Smith: A prophetic disagreement

Concerning the distinction between origins and outcomes, Smith reported a significant disagreement with his good friend David Hume, a disagreement prophetic of neoclassical things to come ([7], 1976, pp. 179–188). Smith discovered the mainsprings of human sociality, systematically modeled them in terms of the "Sentiment of Approbation" (or disapprobation), and characterized them as an emergent social order of rules. Though founded on self-interested actors, no part of the model was utilitarian. People came to other-regarding action *via* self-command in their adherence to general rules arising voluntarily in a collective process of mutual simultaneous discipline. Fellow-feeling was the gravity that shaped and bound.

Hume also recognized that sympathy is the sole ultimate source of our happiness. "We can form no wish, which has not a reference to society.... Every pleasure languishes when enjoy'd a-part from company, and every pain becomes crueller and more intolerable... Let all the powers and elements of nature conspire to serve and obey one man... He will still be miserable, till you give him some one person at least, with whom he may share his happiness, and whose esteem and friendship he may enjoy." But for Hume, in all such orderly systems "their beauty is chiefly deriv'd from their utility, and from their fitness for that purpose, to which they are destin'd." ([10], pp. 363–364).

For Smith, however, it was the other way around; what is wanted, "it seems, was not so much this conveniency, as that arrangement of things which promotes it... and bestows upon it the whole of its propriety and beauty." And in this context: "These affections, that harmony, this commerce, are felt...to be of more importance to happiness than all the little services which could be expected to flow from them." ([7], 1853, p. 258, 53). The "little services" were utilitarian, but the larger pattern of conduct is what made them possible. In Smith's view, it is your relationship with your neighbor that led to the trash barrel incident.

In a similar vein, Hume elsewhere refers to the emergence of property (justice) as having its origin in efficiency:

*"Nor is the rule concerning the stability of possession the less deriv'd from human conventions, that it arises gradually, and acquires force by a slow progression, and by our repeated experience of the inconveniences of transgressing it." ([10], p. 490)*

Smith identified the origin of property in his proposition on justice, wherein actions that are intentionally hurtful to others provoke resentment and a desire to punish the action ([7], 1883, pp. 112, 114, 121). Hence, the origin was feelings of resentment, leading to the emergence of rules that naturally and rightly were part of the civil order of the community, long before their adoption by governments.

Smith doubted not the efficacy and efficiency of these rules, but in contrast with Hume, understood that this undoubted external achievement failed to explain why we follow them.

> *"In every part of the universe we observe means adjusted with the nicest artifice to the ends which they are intended to produce...But in these, and in all such objects, we still distinguish the efficient from the final cause...When by natural principles we are led to advance those ends, which a refined and enlightened reason would recommend to us, we are very apt to impute to that reason, as to their efficient cause, the sentiments and actions by which we advance those ends." ([7], 1853, pp. 126–127*

Hume's rational reconstruction is an important feature of human inquiry and understanding, but it is distinct from the origins of our actions. Utility theory redefined agent action in terms of its outcome, which was assumed to be both the origin and purpose of action. Rationality, thus, was a phenomenon that began with the individual and ended with the sum across what individuals did.

## 5. Conclusion

Unlike the neoclassical economists, who floundered in accounting for market price discovery, Adam Smith and the other classical economists sought understanding of market processes from the perspective and experience of the actors. Inadvertently, experimentalists, educated in the new tradition, were intellectually unprepared for the results of the first laboratory experiments wherein naïve subjects, informed only of their own private reservation values, easily discovered efficient clearing prices that were no part of their intention.

## Acknowledgements

This is a shortened and refocused version of: Smith, V. L., & Inoua, S. M. (2019). Cournot marked the turn from classical to neoclassical thinking. ESI Working Paper 19-14. Retrieved from https://digitalcommons.chapman.edu/esi_working_papers/272/

## Author details

Vernon L. Smith[1*] and Sabiou M. Inoua[2]

1 Chapman University, Orange, California, USA

2 Independent Researcher, Niger

*Address all correspondence to: vlomaxsmith@gmail.com

## References

[1] Alexander S. Beauty and Other Forms of Value. Collected Works of Samuel Alexander, Volume 4. London: Macmillan and Co.; 1933

[2] Inoua S, Smith V. The Classical Theory of Supply and Demand. ESI Working Paper 20-11. Economic Science Institute, Chapman University; 2020

[3] Inoua S, Smith V. Classical economics: Lost and found. The Independent Review. 2020;**25**(1):79-90

[4] Inoua S, Smith V. Neoclassical supply and demand, experiments, and the classical theory of price formation. History of Political Economy. 2021;**54**(1):37-73

[5] Inoua S, Smith V. Economics of Markets. Cham, Switzerland: Palgrave Macmillan; 2022

[6] Inoua S, Smith V. Adam Smith's theory of value: A reappraisal of classical price discovery. The Adam Smith Review (London: Routledge). 2024;**14**:55-80

[7] Smith A. The Theory of Moral Sentiments. Oxford: Oxford University Press; 1759 1976. Or with subtitle, An Essay Towards an Analysis of the Principles by Which Men Naturally Judge Concerning the Conduct and Character, First of Their neighbors, and Afterwards of Themselves, in the Dugald Stewart edition. London: Henry G. Bohn, 1853. Available from: https://oll.libertyfund.org/titles/smith-the-theory-of-moral-sentiments-and-on-the-origins-of-languages-stewart-ed

[8] Smith VL, Wilson BJ. Humanomics: Moral Sentiments and the Wealth of Nations for the Twenty-First Century. Cambridge: Cambridge University Press; 2019

[9] Smith A. An Inquiry into the Nature and Causes of the Wealth of Nations, Volumes 1 and 2, edited by Edwin Cannon. London: Methuen; 1776, 1904. Available from: https://oll.libertyfund.org/titles/smith-an-inquiry-into-the-nature-and-causes-of-the-wealth-of-nations-cannan-ed-in-2-vols

[10] Hume D. In: Norton DF, Norton MJ, editors. A Treatise of Human Nature. New York, NY: Oxford University Press; 1740, 2000